THE
# HONDA
STORY

# THE
# HONDA
## STORY

ROAD AND RACING MOTORCYCLES FROM 1948 TO THE PRESENT DAY

IAN FALLOON

First published in 2005

A catalogue record for this book is
available from the British Library

ISBN 1 85960 966 X

Library of Congress catalog card no. 2004113000

Published by Haynes Publishing, Sparkford, Yeovil,
Somerset, BA22 7JJ, UK

Tel: 01963 442030 Fax: 01963 440001
Int. tel: +44 1963 442030 Int. fax: +44 1963 440001
E-mail: sales@haynes.co.uk
Web site: www.haynes.co.uk

Haynes North America, Inc.,
861 Lawrence Drive, Newbury Park,
California 91320, USA

Page build by G&M Designs Limited,
Raunds, Northamptonshire
Printed and bound in England by
J. H. Haynes & Co. Ltd, Sparkford

# CONTENTS

# FOREWORD
## by Mick Doohan
500cc World Champion 1994–95–96–97–98;
winner 54 Grand Prix races

When I think of Honda and its motorcycles the main things that stand out are a commitment to performance and technology over many years. This culture within the company is one of the main reasons why Honda has been such a big influence in racing, as a motorcycle manufacturer and as an industry leader.

I've been involved with Honda Racing Corporation since 1989, first as a factory rider for 11 seasons until retiring in 1999, and since 2000 as General Manager of Racing of HRC. In that 15-year period Honda has been the dominant manufacturer in 500cc Grand Prix and MotoGP racing, with 10 World Championship titles, compared to Yamaha with three and Suzuki two. Statistics don't always tell the whole story, but in this instance Honda's sheer weight of results reflects a very successful period in its Grand Prix racing history.

As far as racing is concerned Honda has been more consistent than the other manufacturers in producing the best rider-motorcycle-tyre package. The company committed the resources needed to win at World Championship level, and coped best with changing regulations and all the other challenges and problems that occur in racing. People at HRC such as Oguma-san, Shinozaki-san, Ikenoya-san, and Kanazawa-san, have been driving forces in Honda's results.

Technically, Honda had two particularly good motorcycles over the past 15 years, first with the NSR500 two-stroke and then with the RC211V four-stroke machine. The company has always prided itself on being technically innovative, which helps with racing and also fast-tracks development for the motorcycles it sells in the marketplace. Honda introduced the 'Big-Bang' close-firing order engine to 500cc Grand Prix racing in 1992, which made the NSR500 easier to get on the power from low revs, and then the other manufacturers followed with their own versions. We had some problems with the NSR500 in early 1993, but Honda quickly turned things around and apart from that, it was consistently competitive. During the middle and late 1990s the suspension and chassis were refined each season to stay ahead of the opposition. The switch to unleaded fuel in 1998 made the 500s less powerful under acceleration, and again Honda adapted best. In fact, Honda riders filled the first five positions in the championship that year.

Honda prepared thoroughly for the introduction of the MotoGP category four-stroke bikes in 2002, which was a big technical challenge for all the manufacturers. The hard work undertaken by Honda was rewarded with Valentino Rossi, Alex Barros, and Tohru Ukawa winning 14 of the 16 races in 2002, and dominating the new Yamaha, Suzuki, Aprilia, and Kawasaki four-stroke machines. Another reason for Honda's success is the relationship between the racing teams and the HRC Research & Development (R&D) department in Japan. When I started in 500s the teams and riders sometimes found that technical improvements which might have looked impressive on a 'test bench' in Japan didn't always translate to quicker lap times. For example, extra engine power won't get you around a race-track any faster if you can't use it, or it tears the tyres up. You've got to find a balance between technology and performance, and Honda now has a good system. No-one can predict what will happen in the future, but Honda is as committed as ever to maintaining its position as a force in racing and the leader in the marketplace.

# INTRODUCTION AND ACKNOWLEDGEMENTS

As a motorcycle enthusiast for more years than I care to remember, I have always been fascinated by Honda motorcycles. When I first started riding motorcycles Hondas were different. Anyone could afford them, and although they were consumer items, everything worked and they lasted forever. Those early Hondas may not have stirred the soul, but there was a certain mass-produced chic about them. And even the most grudging cynic had to acknowledge that Honda's Grand Prix racers of the 1960s were remarkable. This is a company that has dominated motorcycling for more than 40 years, and has shaped the direction of motorcycle development, on and off the track. Driven by the will to succeed, Soichiro Honda was unique in the motorcycle industry. Always searching for a different path, Honda possessed a vision and philosophy that continues to characterise the company.

Writing a complete history of the world's largest and most successful motorcycle manufacturer was always going to be a daunting prospect. Because of the vast number of motorcycle road and racing models produced since 1948, I have concentrated on those I believe are significant. Most are the larger capacity motorcycles available in Europe and the USA, but also included is the occasional scooter, small capacity motorcycle, or dual-purpose model deemed important. Omitted is the myriad of Japanese market versions, show models, and ATVs. The emphasis is on the Honda motorcycles that have garnered an enthusiastic following over the years: the Hawk, Super Hawk and CB750 of the 1960s, the Gold Wing and CBX of the 1970s, and the VFR, CBRs and FireBlade of the 1980s and '90s. But it isn't only a story of success. Honda's history is characterised by an ability to accept failure, and persevere in the face of adversity, and their history is littered with disastrous models. As racing has also

been integral to Honda's success, I have included as thorough documentation of all the racing machines as possible. This has been a fascinating project and I have learnt a lot. I hope you enjoy it.

As with all books of this type, I couldn't have done it alone. The most thanks go to my wife Miriam, and sons Ben and Tim, without whose support I couldn't devote so much energy to research, photography and writing. Photographs are also one of the most essential components, and I would like to thank Mick Woollett and Alan Cathcart for allowing access to their unparalleled collections of racing photographs. As always, several magazines have been supportive in providing photos from their archives, particularly Ken Wootton, editor of *Australian Motorcycle News*; Jeremy Bowdler, editor of *Two Wheels;* David Edwards, editor-in-chief of *Cycle World,* and Greg Leech, editor of *Motorcycle Trader.* Thanks guys, I really appreciate your support. Others that came through with photos, or provided motorcycles for photography, were Mac McDiarmid, Peter Herbert, Roy Kidney, Hans Smid, and Heinz Tschinkel. As always, the editorial team at Haynes has been fantastic. Without the professionalism of Mark Hughes, Steve Rendle, Flora Myer, and Christine Smith this book wouldn't have been possible.

When it came to asking someone to write the foreword to this book I could think of no more fitting person than Mick Doohan. Honda has always been about racing, and with five consecutive 500cc World Championships Mick has been their greatest champion. Thanks Mick, and also to Mick's PR man Mike Porter for organising it.

Ian Falloon
Spring 2005

In 1963, the CB72 was one of
the most advanced motorcycles
available, and it took years for
other manufacturers to catch up.
*Author*

# 1 A DREAM FULFILLED

When Soichiro Honda was born, in November 1906, Japan was in the midst of an industrial revolution. Only a few decades earlier, under the Tokugawa Shogunate, Japan was feudal, but the Meiji Restoration of 1868, followed by the creation of a constitutional monarchy in 1889, saw a new state with the emperor in absolute power. This change was more than political. Emperor Meiji issued an imperial mandate to introduce Western civilisation, extending beyond merely adopting Western technological advances such as railways and electricity, to diet and clothing. This far-reaching cultural revolution was designed to eliminate much of the traditional Japanese culture. In the late 19th century, while Western imperialist forces invaded many other Asian countries, Japan remained independent and was able to initiate a massive industrial development programme. It was this environment, as the country was moving from agrarian society to an industrial one, which shaped Soichiro Honda.

Although Japan suffered an economic hiccup following the Russian-Japanese war of 1904–05, by 1910, the country was riding on the back of worldwide economic expansion. Japan (as an ally of Britain) benefited greatly from the First World War, and the post-war period that Soichiro Honda experienced as a child was extremely prosperous. All this changed in September 1923 with the Great Kanto Earthquake. Tokyo was virtually destroyed, and thousands died. However, for Soichiro Honda, recently moved to Tokyo to become an apprentice automobile mechanic with the Art Shokai (Art Automobile Service Station), it was a godsend. Instead of having to carry the boss's child around on his back all day, a shortage of labour enabled Soichiro to receive a thorough technical training in the repair of automobiles. Yuzo Sakakibara, the owner of Art Shokai was also a racing enthusiast and encouraged Honda to build a racing car in his spare time. Soichiro fashioned a car around an ex-military 8-litre V8 Curtiss-Wright aircraft engine, building everything himself, and the 100hp racing car provided the young Honda with considerable racing success.

Following a financial crisis in 1927, the economic climate was still difficult in Japan, but Honda managed to set up a Hamamatsu branch office of Art Shokai. Despite the Wall Street Crash of 1929, and the subsequent government policy of currency revaluation

Below: Often, Soichiro Honda was to be seen working on the assembly line or in the R&D department. *Honda*

Below: Soichiro Honda astride the most important motorcycle he produced: the C100. *Honda*

# SOICHIRO HONDA

In the early 20th century, in the small village of Komyo in Shizuoka Prefecture, Gihei Honda operated a blacksmith shop where he repaired bicycles. The family was poor, and on 17 November 1906, Soichiro was born. As a child, and the eldest of nine children, Soichiro helped with his father's business. From an early age, Soichiro was interested in machinery, and his favourite pastime was when his grandfather would carry him on his back to watch the petrol motor of a nearby rice polishing mill in action. In 1914, while in the second grade, Soichiro saw an aeroplane for the first time. Honda subsequently terrorised the village on a bicycle outfitted with bamboo propellers as he impersonated the pilot, Niles Smith. Stubborn and independent, Honda couldn't adapt to the authoritarian education system and was a poor student at school.

Despite his poor formal education, Honda showed redoubtable willingness to learn soon after establishing his piston ring business. He chose piston rings to manufacture as they required only a small amount of raw material and could be sold for a good profit, but as a self-taught metal caster, his die-cast piston rings were brittle and unreliable. Until then, he had assumed education was worthless, but having to work harder and even pawn his

wife's belongings, Honda approached Professor Fujii at the Hamamatsu High School of Technology for advice. He discovered the piston rings didn't have enough silicon and Honda went back to school to learn the secrets of metal casting. Nine months later, he produced a satisfactory piston ring and as the war spread, Tokai Seiki prospered. A shortage of manpower led to Honda developing automatic machinery to produce piston rings, and eventually aircraft propellers. After the Second World War, Honda sold the rest of Tokai Seiki to Toyota (for a small fortune at the time), and announced he was going to have a year off. He bought a large drum of medical alcohol to produce whisky, and spent his time partying and playing the *shakuhachi* (a Japanese wind instrument). Because petrol was rationed, Honda also purchased a pine forest with the intention of producing turpentine oil as an alternative fuel. Unfortunately his exuberance in dynamiting the roots of pine trees led to a forest fire and the loss of his investment. Undeterred, in October 1946 Honda established the Honda Technical Research Institute. Initially the company comprised a wooden shack, old belt-driven lathe, a couple of desks and 12 men, but from these humble beginnings emerged the Honda Motor Company in 1948.

As the company expanded, Honda continued to maintain a close watch on what was happening on the factory floor. Famous

Below: As a young man, Soichiro Honda saw Japan become increasingly industrialised. He eschewed formal education and was already working on repairing cars by the age of 15. *Honda*

for his gregarious personality and quick temper, his style of education was to shout at workers, but they soon learned how to build motorcycles. A hands-on company director, Honda was often seen among the workers in the manufacturing and research departments, working on technical solutions and sorting out problems. His vision was to succeed through innovation, and he constantly thought of new ideas. His thoughts were generally outside the usual parameters, and he was considered strange because he always wore a gaudy red shirt under his business suit.

But without Honda's vision there would have been no Super Cub, CB750, Gold Wing, CBX, or the superb racing machines of the 1960s. Not only did Honda engage in competition at all levels, but he also invested heavily in automated manufacturing equipment, advertising and promotion. In October 1973, Soichiro Honda stepped down, saying: 'I attribute the company's success to dreams and youthfulness,' but retained the title of Supreme Adviser. He never had any wish in passing company ownership down through the family, and both he and Fujisawa prevented their sons joining the company. In 1977, Honda set up the Honda Foundation, an organisation encouraging the use of technology to benefit the environment. He spent his retirement travelling widely, and having fun. Soichiro Honda died on 5 August 1991, but his legacy has continued.

which saw unemployment spiral, Honda continued to build racing cars in his spare time. One of these almost led to his death in July 1936, at the All-Japan Speed Rally held near the Tama River on the outskirts of Tokyo. Honda prepared a car suited to the counter-clockwise circuit, with a supercharged Ford four-cylinder engine tilted to the left. It was fast and reliable, and Honda was leading the race at over 75mph (120km/h) when a slower car pulled out of the pits in front of him. Honda's car somersaulted three times and both he and his brother riding with him were thrown from the car and seriously injured. The accident prompted a change in direction for Honda, and in 1937, as Japan was embarking on war with China, he established a company, Tokai Seiki Heavy Industries, to manufacture piston rings. Honda soon supplied Toyota, which eventually secured 40 per cent of the company.

After the Second World War, Japan was in a state of turmoil and there was a serious food and transportation shortage. Honda saw an opportunity, recycling small war-surplus engines by attaching them to bicycles. He even sold a special blend of turpentine and petrol, then set about developing a proper motorcycle. In March 1947, a recent graduate of the Hamamatsu College of Technology, Kiyoshi Kawashima joined Honda's company. Kawashima would figure prominently in the history of Honda Motor, managing the racing team and eventually becoming President. As supplies of the military motor dwindled, like several other competing manufacturers, Honda turned to Tohatsu generator engines. Soon the supply from Tohatsu also dried up, so Honda decided to produce his own engine. The resulting 50cc two-stroke was heavily based on the Tohatsu design. The vertical cylinder sat under the top frame tube, with the fuel tank above. Initially this was an ex-army issue hot water bottle. Producing a modest 1hp at 5,000rpm, there was only a single speed with belt drive to the rear wheel. A long thin exhaust pipe ran from the front of the engine to a silencer near the rear wheel. Although it still resembled a bicycle with a clip-on engine, Honda called the machine the Model A, but it was nicknamed the chimney due to the fumes emanating from the turpentine-based fuel. Production of the Model A was modest, but Honda couldn't manufacture enough to satisfy demand.

Soon afterwards, Honda found a sturdier frame from Kitagawa, with small cable-operated drum brakes and front and rear suspension. The fork was a girder

Honda was a very successful car racer, and achieved many victories with this racing car which he had built himself around a Curtiss-Wright engine. *Honda*

type, pivoting on a joint beneath the steering head, while the saddle was sprung. In 1948, Honda enlarged the Model A engine to 98cc, turned it around, and bolted it to a three-wheeled delivery tricycle. It included a revised girder fork and Honda called this the Model B. Later that year, with the 98cc engine uprated to 3hp at 3,000rpm, the Model C appeared. This now had a Model B fork, but retained the Kitagawa chassis. All along, Honda was working towards creating a complete motorcycle, and the prototype appeared in August 1949, at around the same time Honda first met Takeo Fujisawa.

# THE FIRST MOTORCYCLE: THE DREAM TYPE D

Rather predictably titled the Model D, Honda hosted a celebratory party at the office of Honda Motor. Honda and his 20 employees drank home-brewed sake, and an inebriated employee exclaimed: 'It's like a dream.' Honda then christened the new motorcycle the Dream. Not only was it Honda's first complete motorcycle, it

was the first produced by a Japanese manufacturer after the Second World War. The Dream also looked like a real motorcycle, albeit a pre-war BMW, with a chunky pressed-steel frame formed from two triangular sections, enclosing the fuel tank. At the front was a telescopic fork, and the 98cc two-stroke engine (with a square 50 x 50mm bore and stroke) produced 3hp at 5,000rpm. A solid brass external flywheel housed the points and coils for the magneto ignition, and the carburettor faced forwards, with the exhaust to the rear. There was a two-speed gearbox, chain final drive, and a kick-start instead of pedals. One of the problems was the close-fitting front mudguard which was prone to clogging with mud in winter on the primitive roads of the time. At this stage, Honda also continued to supply engines to distributors to fit in Kitagawa frames.

The Dream went into production, but as the version with the Kitagawa frame proved more popular, many of Honda's distributors continued to sell both. Fujisawa was by now installed as managing director, but Kitagawa endeavoured to control the supply of engines by reducing frame production, leaving a surplus of Honda engines. This severely restricted Honda's cash flow and Fujisawa showed his business strength by

Below: The first Honda vehicle was the Model A, with a single-speed two-stroke motor.
*Honda*

Bottom: With the 98cc Model C motor installed in a Kitagawa chassis, Honda moved closer to producing their first motorcycle.
*Honda*

demanding an ultimatum from his distributors. They could either sell the Dream or buy engines for the Kitagawa frame, but not both. Although some distributors threatened him with knives, Fujisawa successfully reorganised the distribution network, losing some dealers but ending up with a more satisfactory solution of one dealer in each territory.

In March 1950, the company purchased a sewing machine factory in Tokyo and with a loan from the Japanese government converted this into a motorcycle plant. Full-scale production commenced soon after, but the Dream wasn't particularly successful. While stronger than other motorcycles, it was still a noisy two-stroke. Fujisawa convinced Honda the market preferred the sound and economy, of rival side-valve four-stroke designs. Honda was proud of learning from his mistakes, once claiming: 'Success can only be achieved through repeated failure and introspection.' Even though he held these side-valve designs in disdain, Honda was prepared to risk expensive retooling to follow a new path.

## THE FIRST FOUR-STROKE: THE DREAM TYPE E

In May 1951, Honda presented Fujisawa with the plan for a 146cc overhead valve four-stroke engine. At a time when only expensive imported cars featured overhead valves this was a radical solution for mass production. Drawn up by Kawashima, this engine was an unusual design, with two inlet valves and one exhaust. The camshaft was in the rear of the crankcase, and the motor produced 5.5hp. Kawashima himself tested the prototype two months later in the rain, to the top of the Hakone Mountains. Honda and Fujisawa followed behind in a Buick, but the car was left behind as the new Dream Type E comfortably climbed the summit in top gear at an average speed of 43mph (70km/h). The Type E was launched in October 1951, and soon replaced the Type D. Although the rigid pressed steel frame didn't provide exceptional handling, and the engine burned oil, the Type E was hugely successful. Eventually, the E acquired a three-speed gearbox and plunger rear suspension, and 32,000 were produced during 1953. The innovation of the Type E contributed substantially to the dominance of Honda as a motorcycle manufacturer, and ensured the demise of many of his competitors.

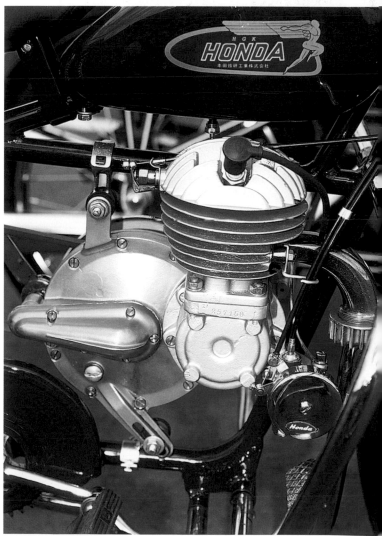

# MORE TRANSPORTATION FOR THE MASSES: THE CUB TYPE F

Sensing a continued demand for low-cost transportation, by March 1952 Honda completed a prototype for the Cub Type F, returning to the bicycle clip-on motor design. The 50cc two-stroke engine was similar to the earlier Type A, but the motor (uprated to 1.2hp) clipped alongside the back wheel. It was neatly executed, but the success of the Type F was primarily due to Fujisawa's astute marketing. Rather than using traditional motorcycle dealers, he sent letters to the 55,000 bicycle retailers and was swamped with 30,000 replies. The demand for the Cub was so strong it not only provided important cash flow, but allowed

Fujisawa to create separate dealer networks for different models. This innovative marketing strategy was decades ahead of its time.

The growth of the company during 1952 was staggering. In May, production of the Dream was moved from Tokyo to a new plant in Shirako, but to expand, Honda required more capital. With more than 200 motorcycle manufacturers vying for limited bank credit, Honda and Fujisawa found it difficult. By November 1952, Fujisawa somehow managed to raise 15 million yen, and this allowed the acquisition of further land (at Yamato, later known as Wako) and Hamamatsu (for the Aoi plant). In October, exports of the Dream began to the Philippines, and in November 1952 Soichiro visited the USA to purchase new machine tools (worth 450 million yen). During December 1952, 7,000 Cubs were produced, 70 per cent of the total Japanese output.

# TAKEO FUJISAWA

Born in November 1910, Takeo Fujisawa entered a comfortable environment in Tokyo where his father Hideshiro successfully operated an agency producing commercial slides for picture theatres. All was well with the Fujisawas until the huge earthquake of 1923 left the uninsured Hideshiro at the mercy of his creditors. Takeo's subsequent years were thus spent in poverty, and when he graduated from school in 1928, the depression was so severe he couldn't find work. Forced to support his ailing father and the entire family, in 1930 Takeo volunteered for the Imperial Army as a cadet. After one year, he left the army, intent on becoming a merchant, and in 1934 found a job with Mitsuwa Shokai, a small steel commission merchant company. Soon his talents as a salesman were obvious, and when the company's owner was called to the war in China Fujisawa took control, successfully boosting profits. In 1939, he set up his own company, the Japan Machine and Tool Research Institute, manufacturing cutting and grinding tools. It took three years to achieve satisfactory tool quality, but soon Fujiwara was able to sell tools to the military. Unlike other employers, Fujisawa also believed in paying his employees generously, and these higher wages ensured employee loyalty, and ultimately more profit for the company. Sensing that bombing could destroy Tokyo, in early 1945 he shifted his company to Fukushima in northern Japan.

At the end of the war, Fujisawa bided his time before returning to Tokyo. He saw the Japanese economy ruled by the black market, but a chance meeting during 1948 with an old friend, Hiroshi

Takeshima, led Fujisawa to Honda. Fujisawa already knew of Honda as a brilliant inventor, and Honda was looking for a backer so he could expand into proper motorcycle production. The two met in August 1949, and immediately agreed to work together. Fujisawa was to be the business force, and Honda the technological. It was an amazing partnership where both men shared the same goals, but set about attaining them by different routes. Fujisawa, well read and philosophical, complemented Honda, dominant and enthusiastic about technology. Fujisawa also retired in 1973, content to pursue his hobbies of theatre and classical music. He died in 1988.

Honda's first complete motorcycle was the Dream Model D of 1949. Still a two-stroke, this was not a great success. *Honda*

# THE FIRST REAL MOTORCYCLE: THE MODEL J (BENLY)

This economic buoyancy allowed Honda to move another step with the Model J, or Benly, during 1953. Meaning 'convenient' in Japanese, the Model J heralded a long line of Benly models and was quite obviously a copy of the German NSU. The three-speed 89cc pushrod overhead valve motor produced 3.8hp at 6,000rpm, and the chassis included a tidier pressed-steel frame with a telescopic fork, and unusual rear suspension with the engine and swingarm moving together around a central pivot. Unfortunately, the noisy tappets and gears made the Benly unpopular.

By early 1954, Honda also released their first scooter, the Juno, with a 200cc three-speed motor. Also patterned on European examples, this was the first scooter with glassfibre bodywork, and featured small wheels with the engine situated at the rear. Unfortunately, the Juno engine suffered from overheating under the bodywork and sales stalled. At the same time the engine capacity of the Dream Type E was increased to 225cc, this proving too much for the design that began life as 146cc. As if these difficulties weren't enough, a recession hit Japan following the end of the Korean War, coinciding with the growth of union power as the workers demanded higher wages. Honda's profits slumped from 514 million yen in 1953 to only 68 million yen in 1954. Fujisawa considered bankruptcy, but fortunately the union understood Honda's plight, as did the various component suppliers. Working around the clock the Type E, with a new Mikuni carburettor, was improved, and the Model JA Benly capacity increased to 140cc, with a more traditional twin-shock rear suspension set-up. With a 200 million yen loan from the Mitsubishi Bank the company managed to survive.

Although unremarkable basic transportation, the Type F two-stroke clip-on engine was extremely popular in 1950. *Honda*

## THE FIRST OVERHEAD CAMSHAFT: THE DREAM SA AND SB

During this turbulent period Honda not only managed to initiate a racing programme, but also sought to expand the range. For 1955, the single-cylinder JB Benly was reduced in capacity to 125cc, with only 7hp, but the most exciting development was the creation of the first mass-produced overhead camshaft motorcycles, the 250cc Dream SA and 350cc Dream SB. As always, Honda refused to be constrained by existing doctrine and to him an overhead camshaft was the only solution as revs increased. The overhead camshaft was driven by a chain on the right side of the vertical cylinder. Although the frame remained pressed steel, but with front downtubes and the bulky styling extending to deeper mudguards, a headlight nacelle and a fully enclosed drive chain, the Dream S hinted at things to come. Although now the leading Japanese motorcycle manufacturer, taking over from Tohatsu in September 1955, before the Dream could make an impact, Honda produced, arguably, his most significant model of all, the C100 Super Cub.

## THE C100 SUPER CUB

Despite worsening labour relations and lower sales, Honda and Fujisawa managed to see through 1955, and during 1956 Japan enjoyed an unprecedented economic boom, called the 'Jimmu Boom', after the first emperor of Japan. The JC57 Benly of 1956 had its power output boosted to 8hp, and it gained a leading link front fork and an enclosed drive chain. At the end

of 1956 Honda and Fujisawa went on a trip to West Germany and saw a huge market for mopeds and lightweight motorcycles. But they were particularly unimpressed by what they saw on offer and on his return Honda set about designing a unique lightweight motorcycle, the incredible Super Cub. At this time, 1957, the Japanese economy again entered recession, and industrial problems resurfaced. In March and April 1957 workers went on strike, and in May, Honda fired four union leaders. Eventually, these disturbances were resolved as the company became more profitable and could afford to pay higher bonuses.

For 1957, the JC58 Benly featured oil-damped bottom link suspension and produced 9.5hp and the 250cc twin-cylinder Dream C70 was introduced, but it was Fujisawa's economic acumen which saw Honda prosper. During the boom of 1956 Fujisawa managed to restrain costs and output, somehow anticipating the recession. When this hit, he immediately increased production and in the midst of the recession Honda captured 80 per cent of the Japanese motorcycle market. Sales in 1958 were nearly double those of only two years earlier, and profits trebled to 1,157 million yen – most of this was due to the C100 Super Cub.

Not only was the Super Cub cheap to manufacture, it was simple, economical, reliable, and provided some weather protection. Honda learnt from his mistake with the Juno, this time placing the pushrod overhead valve 49cc (40 x 39mm) motor in the more conventional location between the rider's legs. The engine made 4.5hp at 9,500rpm, and the low (8.5:1) compression ratio ensured easy starting with a kick-start. Lubrication was rudimentary, with a splash-fed crankshaft and gearbox, and ignition by a crank-mounted magneto. There was a three-speed gearbox and automatic centrifugal clutch, and while changing gear took some getting used to, it took the terror out of motorcycling. Everything was conveniently hidden away under plastic panels with leg shields. The frame was pressed steel, the wheels 17-inch, the brakes were drum (with a twin leading shoe on the front), and the suspension a leading link on the front and twin shock swingarm on the rear. While the 55kg C100 struggled to attain the claimed top speed of 43mph (70km/h), the C100 was so robust and reliable it completely changed the face of motorcycling. In August 1958, the first examples rolled off the production line, and the design has been one of the most enduring of all motorcycles. It has certainly been one of the most significant.

The early 1950s saw a proliferation of Honda manufacturing plants, including a new factory opened at Shirako in 1952. *Honda*

# OVERHEAD CAMSHAFT TWIN-CYLINDER DREAMS

## (C70, CA71, CE71, CA76, CS76 and CSA76 1957–60)

By 1957, Soichiro Honda was convinced that the only way to increase revs and reduce vibration, was through smaller capacity cylinders. September 1957 saw the first Honda twin, the C70 Dream, with a pressed-steel frame, leading link front suspension, single-shoe drum brakes, and 16-inch wheels. The 247cc overhead camshaft twin drew heavily on the NSU Rennmax that Honda remembered from the Isle of Man in 1954, and was quite innovative for a production model. Unit construction, with horizontally split crankcases, the traditional 360° pressed-up crankshaft ran in four ball main bearings. There was a gear primary drive, an unusual crankshaft-mounted clutch and four-speed gearbox. A central chain drove the overhead camshaft, and with a single carburettor, the square (54 x 54mm) twin produced 18hp at 7,400rpm. Lubrication was dry sump, with a separate oil tank. The C70 weighed 160kg, around 20kg less than the Type E single. For 1959 the C70 became the C71 (with electric start), and was joined by a larger, 305cc (60 x 54mm), CA76, the 'A' designation indicating America. With a small Amal M22mm carburettor, the power was 21hp at 7,200rpm. Also specifically for America in 1959 was the rare CE71 Dream Sport 250, of which only 390 were produced. This featured a new fuel tank, and early examples had 18-inch wheels, with later versions, 16-inch.

Also produced specifically for America were the CA76 and CSA76 Dream Sport 300 of 1960. An increased compression ratio saw the power increased to 20hp. They had upswept pipes, one on each side, with a chrome fuel tank with rubber knee pads. The two models differed only through the handlebars, the CSA76 receiving a high chrome type instead of the pressed-steel painted ones. Although capable of 85mph (137km/h), the Dream Sport 300 also suffered through having a single carburettor. While many sniggered that they had no torque and didn't handle, these early twins already typified Honda's engineering approach. They didn't leak oil, were beautifully engineered and finished, and had electrical systems that were reliable.

# SOICHIRO GOES TO THE ISLE OF MAN

Despite the considerable difficulties facing the company during 1954, Soichiro Honda remained optimistic. While concentrating on technical development, Honda separated himself from the industrial and financial problems. Always looking ahead, Honda believed the only way to achieve superiority in the crowded Japanese motorcycle market was by proving himself on the race track.

In February 1954, Honda entered an international race to celebrate the 400th anniversary of São Paulo, Brazil. It was a very inauspicious racing beginning, with Mikio Omura finishing a lowly 13th on a two-speed Model E 125. Undeterred, only one month later Honda declared that his company would participate in the prestigious Isle of Man Tourist Trophy, then the most important race in the world. In complete anonymity Honda travelled to the Isle of Man to observe and absorb, but came in for a nasty surprise.

The European machines were astonishingly fast, and there was still considerable anti-Japanese feeling in Britain in the wake of the Second World War. Honda was particularly in awe of the 125cc NSU Rennmax that revved beyond 11,000rpm, and produced 18hp when his racing Dream produced only ten. Dismayed, but not deterred, Honda persevered with his dream of contesting the Isle of Man. In 1958, a Honda team returned, but with high-quality cameras to photograph everything possible in preparation for the assault in 1959.

No other motorcycle has symbolised Honda's success like the C100 Super Cub. Robust and reliable, the C100 changed the public perception of motorcycling. *Honda*

# BENLY TWINS

## (C92, CS92, CB92, CB92R and C95 1958–66)

While the C100 put the world on two wheels, the C92 Benly showed Honda was serious about performance. This took the idea of smaller, higher revving cylinders further than the C70 Dream, the 1958 C92 twin-cylinder 125cc Benly (44 x 41mm) producing 11.5hp at the then amazing 9,500rpm. The Benly was essentially a smaller version of the C70, and for 1959 received an electric start and a dual seat (still single seat on some Japanese models) to become the C92 (CA92 in America). Alongside this was the CS92 sport, with high exhausts system. The most interesting variant was the CB92 Benly Super Sport 125 (B indicating sporting),

also released in 1959. Honda's first serious attempt at a sporting motorcycle, the CB92, was used by Honda's riders as a practice bike at the Isle of Man that year. The wet-sump engine retained the 360° crankshaft, but the camshaft was driven from the left end of the crank, and the clutch was on the transmission mainshaft. Still with a single carburettor (18mm) and a compression ratio of 10:1, the power was 15hp at 10,500rpm. There was a four-speed gearbox, but the chassis wasn't so innovative, retaining the leading link front fork. The wheels were 18-inch, with an 8-inch magnesium double leading shoe front brake. Setting the CB92 apart were the alloy fuel tank, side covers, and front mudguard, and a small headlight-mounted windscreen. This amazing little machine weighed 110kg, with a claimed top speed of 81mph (130km/h).

Seeking to capitalise on their racing success, Honda also offered an accessory racing kit which included engine parts, megaphone exhaust and a 13,000rpm

Bottom: One of Honda's most successful models in America was the CT90 trail. With an eight-speed transmission, this rugged little machine pre-empted the rise of the ATV. *Motorcycle Trader collection*

Below: Another variation on the moped was the interesting P50 of 1967–68. The 50cc engine and centrifugal clutch was built into the rear wheel assembly. *Honda*

# SUPER CUB SPIN OFFS

So successful was the Super Cub that more than 30 million have been sold since 1958, it still remains in production, and has been Britain's best-selling 50–100cc commuter for the last 15 years. Amazingly robust and competent, there have also been a large number of Super Cub variations over the last 45 years. An essential ingredient in the American Honda line-up, for 1960 the Super Cub (C102) gained an electric start and was joined by a 5hp C110 Super Sports Cub, with a normal motorcycle fuel tank and a manual clutch. For 1961, there was a C100T Trail 50, without leg shields but with a huge rear sprocket and knobby tyres. The year 1962 brought a name change, to C100 (CA100) Honda 50, along with the electric start C102 (CA102) Honda 50, C110 (CA110) Sport 50, and C111 (with a low exhaust pipe). The Sport 50 also gained a four-speed transmission, and there was even a factory racing kit available that included a racing piston, valve springs and megaphone exhaust.

The overhead valve engine grew to 54cc with the C105T Trail 55 of 1962–65, and was enlarged further to 87cc for 1963 with the C200 Honda 90 (later C200 Touring 90). This was more of a motorcycle than step-through, with a pressed steel backbone frame. The 49 x 46mm overhead valve engine produced 6.5hp at 8,000rpm. The same motor ended up in the CT200 Trail 90 for 1964, lasting until 1966. Also from 1964 was a new 89.6cc (50 x 45mm) overhead camshaft motor. This powered the S90 Super 90

motorcycle (now with a telescopic front fork), followed by the CM91 Honda 90 step-through, CT90 Trail 90 (with eight-speed dual range transmission), and the CL90 Scrambler. Further small overhead camshaft singles followed, including the CS65 Sport of 1965, and the C70M Honda 70 step-through in 1970.

Many of these, like the CT90 Trail that lasted until 1979, had long production runs. The CT90 gained a telescopic fork for 1969, and was enlarged to 110cc with the CT 110 Trail 110 for 1980. Production continued until 1986, a nearly 20-year run for the same model. Although extremely rugged and reliable as 90cc, the little horizontal overhead camshaft single was stretched to the limit at 110cc and cooling was marginal. In 1970, a new 100cc engine with a vertical cylinder, replaced the 110 for all applications except the CT110 Trail. The 70cc overhead camshaft motor lived on in the C70 Passport step-through, still virtually identical to the original C100 Super Cub, the CL70 Scrambler, CT70 Trail, SL70 Motosport, XL70, and XR70. These models remained in production until 1998.

The 50cc overhead camshaft motor also powered the P50 Little Honda of 1967–68, with the engine and transmission built into the rear wheel. The engine was placed in the middle of the frame with the PC50 of 1969. For 1968 the 50cc engine also went in the Z50 Mini Trail 50, this lasting until 1999. The sheer proliferation of small-capacity models descended from the humble Super Cub is almost mind boggling. Over half a million Super Cubs were sold every year from 1960, peaking at 900,000 in 1963. Many other variants sold in their thousands, some are still in production, and it has been the profits from the sales of millions of these small-capacity motorcycles that have allowed Honda to develop their dominating racers. When the 100 millionth Honda rolled out of the Kumamoto factory in 1997, it was a Super Cub.

With the 1958 C92 Benly, Honda showed they were serious about performance, and prepared to mass-produce high-specification engines. *Honda*

tachometer. They then included these components in the CB92R Benly Super Sport Racer 125 for 1961. This produced 16hp at 10,500rpm, with a top speed of 87mph (140km/h). Although it may seem unremarkable today, this speed was astonishing for a 125 in 1961, and more comparable to some 350cc, or even 500cc machines. They were uncomfortable to ride though, with a stiffly sprung leading link fork and narrow powerband. Lasting through 1962, the CB92, more than any other production model, established Honda as a leading manufacturer of sporting motorcycles. They were undoubtedly superior to other machines available at that time, but they weren't perfect, and holed pistons could occur if run too hard without checking the spark plugs regularly.

Alongside the beautiful CB92 was the mundane 154cc C95 (CA95) Benly Touring 150. Looking almost identical to the C92 Benly Touring, the 150 produced 16.5hp at 10,500rpm, for a top speed of 84mph (135km/h). In America, the CA95 replaced the CA92 for 1960, and although it was not particularly successful, continued until 1966. Although the CB92 Benly finished in 1962, the 125cc twin made a comeback in 1967 with the CL125A Scrambler and the SS125A Super Sport. The engine design was similar to the CB92, with a left side camshaft chain, but the single carburettor was now a constant vacuum type. There was also a dual carburettor version. The pressed-steel frame was similar to the S90 and these unremarkable 125s disappeared during 1969.

# HAWKS, DREAMS AND SCRAMBLERS

## *(C72, CB72, CL72, C77, CB77, CL77 and CSA77 1960–67)*

While the dry-sump 250cc C70 and 305cc CA76 twins were greeted with amiable interest when first displayed in Europe and America, the release of the next-generation wet-sump twins in 1960 (as 1961 models) completely changed the public perception of Honda motorcycles. The C72 and C77 Dream may have looked similar to the earlier version, but the CB72 Hawk and CB77 Super Hawk lost the ungainly angular styling of the Dream and were real sporting motorcycles. Even those who dismissed the CB92 Benly as high revving and uncomfortable couldn't ignore the CB72 and CB77. The CB77 was capable of around 99mph (160km/h), the short-stroke motor redlined at 9,500rpm. The 159kg CB77 (and the 153kg CB72) also handled surprisingly well, and the engines were quite smooth. To the chagrin of British motorcycle enthusiasts, a well-ridden CB77 could humiliate most British 500cc twins, and run harder all day long, than many 650s.

As with the dry-sump models, the 250 and 305 versions were very similar, but the CB72 Hawk and CB77 Super Hawk differed markedly from the CA72 and CA77 Dream. All engines were now wet sump, but while the Dream retained the earlier 360° crankshaft, apart from some early examples, the sporting CB models featured a 180° crank. The primary drive was still by single-row chain, but the clutch was moved to the transmission shaft. The compression ratio was 10:1 for the CB72 and 9.5:1 for the CB77, and there were dual carburettors (PW 26mm on the CB77 and PW 22mm on the CB72). The combustion chamber featured a cast-iron skull, with the valve seats cut in. The power of the CB77 was 28.5hp at 9,000rpm, with the CB72 making 24hp. All Dreams and Hawks had an electric start and 12-volt electrics. The single-carburettor C72 Dream (CA72 for America) produced 20hp at 8,400rpm, while the larger C77 (CA77) produced 24hp at 8,000rpm. The carburettor was a VM22 or PW22H on the C77, and VM24 or PW24H on the C77.

Although the 143kg C72 and C77 Dream (and high-piped CSA77 Dream Sport) retained the pressed-steel frame, limp leading link front suspension, and 16-inch

wheels, the CB72 and CB77 featured an updated chassis. The single-loop tubular steel frame incorporated the engine as a stressed member, and there was a telescopic front fork, albeit an under damped one with skinny 33mm fork legs. Very early examples had a single leading shoe front brake, with a double leading shoe rear, but during 1961 all brakes were 8in double leading shoe. The 18-inch wheels were shod with narrow 2.75in and 3.00in tyres. With its abbreviated mudguards, simplified headlight and instrument layout that included a tachometer, the CB72 and CB77 were far more purposeful than the chunky Dream.

The release of the CB72/77 coincided with racing success at the Isle of Man and Honda was keen to promote their production models through racing. While they had CR71/76 production racers approved by the AMA in 1960, Honda wanted to see more than a handful of bikes racing, so they offered YB race kits to upgrade the CB72/77 into road racers. This comprehensive kit included clip-on handlebars, rear-set footpegs, racing seat, alloy wheel rims, racing camshafts and Keihin CR racing carburettors. These race-kitted CB72/77s were incredibly popular, and so successful that many an aspiring road racer began his career on one.

As the CB72/77 was so advanced, development was minimal during the 1960s. Most of Honda's R&D engineers were involved in developing racing motorcycles and cars, so there were only minor updates to the CB72/77 through until 1967. Early examples had sand-cast crankcases, with a hump at the rear for the engine breather which was later deleted. Although the CB72/77 was considerably more reliable than other

American Honda began with
this humble office in Los Angeles
in 1959. *Honda*

# YOU MEET THE NICEST PEOPLE ON A HONDA

Honda and Fujisawa took a huge gamble with the C100 Super Cub. Anticipating big demand, Honda Motor began the construction of a large factory in Suzuka City, Mie Prefecture, to mass-produce the Super Cub. For many observers, investing 10 billion yen when their paid up capital was only 1.4 billion appeared reckless. Honda had previously only sold 3,000 motorcycles a month and this new plant was designed to produce 30,000 motorcycles a month. Another initiative was the design of the plant layout which was left to the employees, so they could feel intrinsically involved. When the factory was completed during 1960 it was the largest motorcycle plant in the world. From every perspective the C100 Super Cub was an ambitious undertaking. But the big question facing Fujisawa was how to sell such a large number of motorcycles?

Fujisawa knew that Honda needed to create overseas subsidiaries, and while others (including Kihachiro Kawashima) favoured expansion in Asia and Europe, Fujisawa saw America as an untapped market. Motorcycle sales in America at that time were only around 50,000 a year, and while all the other distributors believed this would not grow, Fujisawa disagreed. After some difficulty in persuading the Japanese government to allow the investment of foreign capital, American Honda Motor Company Inc. was officially opened in June 1959, at 4077 West Pico Boulevard, in Los Angeles. Headed by Kawashima, initial sales were slow, as Honda was faced with the poor image of motorcycling in America.

Always unorthodox, Honda approached the Gray advertising agency in Los Angeles and established an inspired advertising campaign for the Super Cub. The 'Nicest People' advertising appeared in the leading mainstream magazines including *Life, Saturday Evening Post,* and *Playboy,* as well as on television. Dealers for the Super Cub were established in sporting stores and hobby shops and American sales rose from around 8,000 in 1959 and 1960, to 17,000 in 1961, 35,000 in 1962, and 90,000 in 1963 (following the release of the 'Nicest People' advertisement). In only three years Honda controlled 60 per cent of the American motorcycle market. But it was more than advertising that saw Honda succeed in America. Honda needed to overcome the image that Japanese products were cheap, flimsy imitations that broke down. He ensured his motorcycles were reliable, and continued running, turning the folk-lore about Japanese products upside down.

The success of American Honda soon saw Honda subsidiaries in Europe and Asia. A subsidiary was established in Germany in 1961, Belgium in 1962, and France in 1964, but it wasn't until 1965 that Honda UK was established in London. By 1964 there were also Honda offices in Bangkok, followed by the Philippines and Malaysia.

One of the most inspired promotional campaigns of all was the 'Nicest People' advertisement. This resulted in Honda trebling sales in a year. *Honda*

Left: The C77 Dream of 1961–69 continued with the leading link front fork, and some also had a solo seat like this 1961 example. *Author*

Below left: This 1965 CB77 Super Hawk has some YB factory racing parts, including the seat. *Author*

Below: More popular than the CB77 in America, the CL77 Scrambler featured a different frame and upswept exhaust system. *Author*

motorcycles of the day, there were problems with the two-part camshaft, kick-start, and sometimes the centrifugal clutch of the electric start. During its production run there were numerous updates to internal components, including crankshaft, main bearings, lubrication, clutch, transmission, cam chain tensioner, valves, and spark plugs. The 1961 models also had 10mm spark plugs with 12mm plugs from 1962, while during 1964, the compression ratio was lowered to 9.5:1 (CB72) and 8.5:1 (CB77). The power claim was reduced to 22hp for the CB72 and 26.5hp for the CB77. As with the motor, Honda pursued a system of continual development with the chassis. CBs had aluminium mudguards for 1961, later becoming steel, and a different frame. Until early 1965 the speedometer and tachometer needles rotated in opposite directions, and there were flat handlebars until 1966. Also from

1966 were alloy fork legs with external springs under covers, and a change in steering geometry.

Alongside the Dream and Hawk was the CL72 Scrambler from 1962. As Honda's first serious dual-purpose design, in many ways the Scrambler was even more significant than the CB72/77. Offered as a 250 only until 1965, they were also more popular in America than the Hawks and Dreams. Most Scramblers had the 180° twin-carburettor motor of the CB72, but without an electric start, while some were fitted with the 360° Dream engine (still with twin carburettors), but with only one set of points and a single dual-lead ignition coil. Early CL72s also had a higher compression ratio (9.5:1), with an 8.5:1 compression ratio during 1964. When the CL77 was released in 1965 it had the lower compression pistons. As with the CB72/77 there were a large number of

Another successful variation of the single overhead camshaft parallel twin was the Rebel. This is a 1994 CA250TS. *Australian Motorcycle News*

engine updates during the production run.

The chassis for the CL72 Scrambler was completely different to the other twins, with a single downtube tubular-steel frame, splitting into a cradle under the engine. An unfortunate downside to this additional frame rigidity was increased vibration, and the Scramblers suffered with many components fracturing. The raked out steel telescopic fork included gaiters and the original high exhaust pipes on the left didn't include a muffler. With 19-inch wheels front and rear, fitted with unremarkable universal tyres, the CL72/77 until 1966 was also fitted with weak, 6in single leading shoe brakes front and rear. Although not very effective, they did assist in keeping the weight down to only 153kg. During 1966, the front fork was upgraded with alloy sliders, along with vastly improved 8in double leading shoe brakes front and rear. The front brake looked similar to that of the CB77 but included the internals of the CB450K0 front brake.

While the final CB72/77 and CL72/77 looked virtually identical to the first models, more cosmetic changes were in store for the CA72/77 Dream. The square styling was inherited from the CA71/76, and they retained the leading link front fork, single leading

shoe brakes, and 16-inch wheels (now with whitewall tyres). For 1963 there was a new fuel tank, and narrower band whitewall tyres. All along the Dream retained a single 22mm carburettor and a lower (8.2:1) compression ratio, and the CA77, with 23hp at 7,500rpm was capable of around 87mph (140km/h). One short-lived model was the CSA77 Dream Sport with the same bodywork and high exhaust pipes as the CSA76. This lasted only from 1960 until 1963.

# BABY SUPER HAWKS

## (160s, 175s, 200s and Rebels)

The 161cc CB160 Sport appeared during 1964, filling the small-capacity void left after the demise of the CB92 Benly Super Sport. Soon joined by a touring CA160 and Scrambler CL160, these featured new motors, with the cam chain running between the cylinders like the CB72/77. In other respects the four-speed 160 motor differed from the CB72/77. There were two pairs of straight-cut primary gears, staggered to reduce noise, the cylinder head featured normal

With the CB450, Honda not only moved into a larger displacement category, they also produced the most technologically advanced mass-produced motorcycle available. *Honda*

shrunk valve seats, and there was a 360° crankshaft like the C72/77 Dream. The CB 160 and CL160 50 x 41mm twins, with an 8.5:1 compression ratio and two 20mm carburettors, produced 16.5hp at 10,000rpm. The CB160 included an electric start, which was initially absent on the CL160 Scrambler but featured on the CL160D from 1967. Braking was by 7in drums, with a double leading shoe on the front, and the wheels 18-inch. All 160s were intentionally styled to mimic their larger brothers, and the CA160 included a single carburettor, leading link front fork, and 16-inch whitewall tyres.

Despite weighing 127kg, and only barely freeway legal in America, with a top speed of 75mph (120km/h), the 160s were very popular. They were still full-sized motorcycles, if somewhat underpowered. In 1967, the 160 was updated to 175cc, with a five-speed gearbox in the CB175 and CL175. The single carburettor CA175 Touring retained the four-speed transmission, and finally gained a telescopic front fork. These 175 twins were produced until 1973, their styling mimicking the larger CB350 and CL350 from 1969. This year also saw the engine cylinders raised from inclined to nearly vertical. An SL175 Motosport, with a high front mudguard and low exhaust, was

available from 1970, but lasted only until 1972.

For 1974, the CB175 evolved into the graceless CB200, the 198cc twin (55.5 x 41mm) including a 20mm Keihin carburettor. This was a particularly uninspiring model, *Cycle* magazine comparing it to the Porsche 914. 'Like the 914, it is relatively expensive, has great brakes, and just dreadful rear shocks.' There was also a similar CL200 Scrambler, this lasting only one year while the CB200 became the CB200T from 1975 until 1976. After a year the overhead camshaft twin was resurrected with the 1978–80 CM185 Twinstar, a mini-custom with chopper-style handlebars, and the CM200 Twinstar from 1980–82. The motor then grew to 234cc (53 x 53mm) with the CM250C Custom and later CMX250C and CA250TS Rebel. This was another very successful model for Honda, the

# WHAT THE PRESS SAID ABOUT THE EARLY HONDAS

In their December 1958 issue, *Cycle* magazine tested a C76 Dream, finding 'the electric starter and directional lights will not appeal much to the purist rider who will consider them as car-like features.' Early imports of Honda motorcycles into Britain were initially handled by Maico GB, following an advertisement in *Motor Cycling* magazine in September 1959, seeking a distributor. After 1961, Hondas were supplied to Britain through Honda Motor GmbH in Germany, but Hondas were not cheap motorcycles. A CB72 cost £298 14s in 1962, more than many 500s. *Motor Cycle News* tested the £214 2s 2d CB92 Benly Super Sport in October 1962, and were seduced by 'a champagne-like exhilaration,' and brakes that 'worked with remarkable force.'

Testers were also similarly impressed with the CB72 and CB77. While looking to find faults, *The Motor Cycle* in July 1965 was

impressed with 'the excellent detail finish, and quality you would expect on much more expensive machinery,' but were less impressed with the handling and revvy nature of the motor. American reports were generally more sympathetic, and *Cycle World*, in May 1962, found 'the road behaviour every bit the equal of its speed potential.' The CB77 also appeared in the 1964 Elvis Presley movie *Roustabout*, his CB77 fitted with braced CL77 handlebars and crash bars.

Until the advent of the CB450, the British press and manufacturers were largely unperturbed by the rise of Honda, and even with the release of the CB450 they remained smug. *Motorcycle Mechanics* put a stock CB450 up against a Triumph Tiger 500 with blueprinted engine and full café racing equipment, concluding: 'If you have a well-tuned British 500 parallel twin then you need have no fear.' They also criticised the suspension, with 'both front and rear units alarmingly soft, giving the impression of riding a giant elastic band.' Honda also earned the ire of British enthusiasts by launching an advertisement depicting a Vincent V-twin and the CB450 with the heading 'Who will win the CC vs RPM war?', and slogan 'the one that's reliable.'

The 1972 CB450K5 was styled similarly to the CB750, and came with a front disc brake for most export markets. *Motorcycle Trader collection*

Honda tried to get as much life as possible out of the CB450 by making it the CB500T in 1975. *Motorcycle Trader collection*

chopper-style Rebel becoming one of the best selling individual models in America at one stage. For 1991, the venerable 234cc motor powered the entry-level CB250T (Nighthawk) in America. Thrifty and reliable, the CB250 remains in production, virtually unchanged except for cast alloy wheels. Not a bad effort for a design that originated in the 1960s, but indicative of Honda's production strategy of not updating models unless it is really necessary.

# THE BLACK BOMBER: CB450 AND CB500

By 1965, Honda was the world's largest motorcycle manufacturer, and dominated Grand Prix road racing. Spy pictures taken in October 1964 showed a new large-capacity twin in the final development stages, so the announcement of the CB450 in March 1965 wasn't unexpected. As with the CB77, Honda chose an untraditional capacity, and in an era where all large capacity motorcycles featured engines with pushrod operated overhead valves, the CB450 was exceptionally advanced. Many sceptics didn't even believe it was a bone fide production model. The CB450 may have been conservatively styled, but it signified Honda's intention to dominate motorcycle production in all displacement classes.

As with all Japanese motorcycles of this period, and even into the 1980s, the motor dominated the CB450. This all alloy unit, with horizontally split crankcases, was the first mass-produced double overhead camshaft motorcycle engine. The crankshaft was supported by four roller bearings, and while the export version featured a 180° crankshaft with two sets of ignition points, examples for the Japanese market had a 360° crankshaft. Primary drive was by straight-cut gears, to a wet multiplate clutch and four-speed gearbox with very odd ratios. The bore and stroke were 70 x 57.8mm, providing a displacement of 444cc, and the compression ratio a mild 8.5:1.

A double overhead camshaft cylinder set the CB450 apart, with the twin camshafts driven by an extremely long (128-link as opposed to the CB77's 94-link) chain.

The camshafts were supported in bearings in the cylinder head end-plates, rather than by four ball bearings as in the CB77. Valve sizes were 35mm and 31mm, with the valves set at a quite unfashionable wide included angle of 80° in the cylinder head with a cast-iron skull, as on the CB77. The most unusual aspect of the design was the use of torsion bars instead of coil valve springs. These torsion bars twisted under a load acting perpendicular to the rod's axis, and speculation that their service life would be short proved unfounded. Valve clearances were accomplished by a clever system of eccentric shafts. Another innovation, initially greeted with scepticism, was the use of automotive-style 36mm Keihin constant vacuum carburettors. With 43hp at 8,700rpm, the 'Black Bomber' could run to 106mph (170km/h), more than equal to most British 500s.

While the motor was a technological tour de force, the chassis was lacklustre. The double downtube cradle frame was new for Honda, but the front fork and 200mm double leading shoe front brake were patterned on the CB77. The rod-operated rear brake was now a single leading shoe, and the soggy rear shock absorbers copies of the CB77. While the tyre sizes were increased to 3.25 and 3.50 x 18-inch, the overweight, 187kg CB450 taxed the chassis to the limit.

Although the CB450 was greeted with awe, and received incredible publicity for its amazing technology, it wasn't warmly received. The finish was exemplary, it didn't leak or use oil, the 12-volt electrics were reliable as was the convenient electric start, but the functional CB450 lacked style and grace. The handling was limp, the Japanese Dunlop tyres incredibly slippery, the seat seemed made of cast-iron, and it was considered ugly. Early bikes suffered oil pump and carburetion problems, but generally the CB450 was extremely reliable. In the first year sales fell far short of expectations, but it wasn't until 1968 that an updated model appeared.

In an effort to improve the CB450's appeal in America, the CB450K1 was restyled, with a smaller fuel tank, separate speedometer and tachometer, and chrome mudguards. The motor now incorporated a five-speed transmission and included a new crankshaft, oil pump

# RACING CB450S

While Honda was busy developing their 500cc four-cylinder RC181 racer in Grand Prix racing, in an attempt to boost stagnating sales of the CB450 in the USA, zealous enthusiasts were also campaigning the CB450. Bob Hansen, employed by Honda's parts subsidiary in Wisconsin, was noted for the preparation of immaculate Matchless G50s, and persuaded Honda to produce some special CR450s for AMA racing during 1967. These CR450s featured cast magnesium cylinder heads, 9.2:1 pistons, racing cams, and 35mm Keihin racing carburettors. Other special components included a cast primary drive cover with fittings for the twin oil coolers, long tapered megaphone like the works racers, and a strengthened frame and swingarm. The front brake was an 8in four-leading shoe, and the bodywork aluminium. Four CR450s were at Daytona, the 142kg racer capable of around 137mph (220km/h), but the machines didn't live up to expectations. The next year, a privately entered CB450 won the 100-mile Amateur race at Daytona. Bill Lyons rode a Precision Machining CB450, his carefully prepared machine featuring 71mm 10.4:1 pistons and 35mm Keihin carburettors. It weighed 161kg, and was capable of 134mph (215km/h).

In Europe, Bill Penny gave Honda their first Production Race win at the Isle of Man in 1969, winning the 500cc class at an average speed of 88.18mph (141.88km/h). John Williams repeated this in 1971, with Penny second, both their racers based on the CB450K1 with a drum front brake. Williams's speed this year over the four laps was an impressive 91.04mph (146.48km/h), nearly 3mph (5km/h) faster than Bill Smith's victory in the same event two years later, on a new CB500 four.

and clutch. The valve sizes increased to 37mm and 32mm, the compression ratio went up to 9:1, and with smaller, 32mm CV carburettors, the power was 45hp at 9,000rpm. New was a set of De Carbon-type rear shock absorbers, but they offered little improvement. Alongside the CB450 was also a CL450 Scrambler, with a high exhaust system on the left.

A CB450K1 had the distinction of being the 10 millionth Honda to roll off the production line. The CB450K2 of 1969 was styled similarly to the new CB750, and for 1970 it received a 19-inch front wheel, and for some markets (notably the UK and USA) the 750's front disc brake. The weight went down to 179kg, and the CB450 continued until the K7 of 1974 with only cosmetic updates, and a slight reduction in power (to 41hp at 9,000rpm). So did the CL450 Scrambler (this always retaining the front drum brake),

but for 1975 and '76 the motor grew to 498cc with the CB500T. There was a longer (64.8 mm) stroke, new crankshaft with ball instead of roller bearings, a lower (8.5:1) compression ratio, but the weight went up to 193kg. The CB500T was also slower than the 450, with a top speed of 95mph (153km/h).

Despite its innovation, Honda completely missed the mark with the CB450. It may have been enough to scare the British motorcycle industry in 1965, but it was always slow and overweight. Later developments did little to increase the 450's appeal, and the final CB500T was a particularly uninspiring model. Despite advertising claiming the CB500T a 'Neo-Classic Twin for Mature Motorcyclists' no-one really wanted it, especially when the alternative was the CB500 four.

# TWINS FOR EVERYONE

## (CB250, CB350, CL350 and SL350 Motosport 1968–73)

Although the CB72/77, and CL72/77, began their life as extremely advanced motorcycles, they were outdated by the late 1960s. A four-speed transmission was now inadequate, and the CB72/77s were quite complicated and expensive motorcycles to manufacture. The new middleweight twin, the CB250/350 and CL350, released in 1968 and lasting until 1973, represented a change in direction from the enthusiast-orientated Hawk and Super Hawk. Glittering with polish and chrome, they were hugely successful, and in America, the 350s were the biggest selling 'real' motorcycles throughout this period. During 1971, 140,400 350cc twins were sold in America, accounting for over 20 per cent of Honda's sales. These weren't enthusiast's motorcycles, but were the only four-stroke 350 twins in a market dominated by two-strokes; they were reliable, extremely well detailed, and easy to use.

There was a good reason for the success of the new twins. After the disaster of the CB450, Honda's engineers opted for a more conservative approach, with a single overhead camshaft, careful balancing of the four main bearing (one ball and three rollers) 180° crankshaft, and rubber mounting the cylinder head to the frame. The engine unit was substantial, weighing 57kg, further damping vibration. Unlike the Hawk and Super Hawk, the camshaft rode in aluminium end-caps

Although uninspiring, the CB350 was the most popular real motorcycle in America in the early 1970s. This is the 1970 example. *Author*

rather than ball bearings. The redesigned, sand-cast cylinder head was in two pieces and included 34mm intake and 28mm exhaust valves. The oil pump was a plunger type with a wear-prone eccentric drive machined in the back of the outer clutch basket. There was a five-speed gearbox, a staggered double-pair geared primary drive, and displacement of the 350 went up to 325cc (64 x 50.6mm). The 250 was identical but for 56mm pistons. With a pair of 36mm rubber diaphragm CV Keihin carburettors, the CB350 produced 36hp at 10,500rpm. The CL350 Scrambler, with 33mm carburettors, made 33hp at 9,500rpm. An ignition advance unit and points mounted on the end of the camshaft contributed to easier maintenance, so did the rockers on eccentric spindles like earlier twins. Although there were some initial problems with solenoids burning, generator failure, camshafts and the hydraulic cam chain tensioner, hundreds of thousands of owners were more than happy with the reliability of the CB/CL350.

The double-cradle frame was basically a scaled down version of the CB450, and the suspension included very marginal gas-filled De Carbon style shock absorbers. The brakes were also quite weak, a double leading shoe at the front and single leading shoe at the rear. While the CB250/350 was never going to set any new performance or handling records, and there was still a vibration at high speed, it did set a new standard for production quality and attention to detail. When *Cycle* magazine tested the CB350 in May 1968 they concluded: 'It's the best Honda we've ever seen. Does that mean it's the best motorcycle ever built? Only time can provide the answer, but we would venture a lightly qualified, yes.'

There were only detail updates for the next few years. The CB350 fuel tank lost the rubber knee pads for 1970, and each year the front fork was improved. The final version was the disc-braked CB350G of 1973. The CL350 Scrambler, with high rise exhaust on the left, was sold alongside the CB350 in America, but didn't receive a disc brake. From 1969 there was also the SL350 Motosport, with high front mudguard, and low exhaust pipes. Based on the CL350, the SL350 emerged as a more serious dirt bike following Honda's

A breakthrough model for Honda was the dual-purpose XL250 Motosport of 1972. This featured Honda's first production four-valve engine. *Honda*

victory in the 1968 Baja 1000 race with a modified CL350. An improved SL350 K1 Motosport appeared for 1970, with a new frame and suspension, and without an electric start. The weight was down but it was still a compromise. By the early 1970s motorcycles were already moving towards specialisation. Modified street bikes were less suited to dirt duties, but that didn't stop the success of the CB350.

# LARGER SINGLES

## (100s, 125s, 175s, 250s, and 350s from 1970)

The new near-vertical cylinder 100cc overhead camshaft single-cylinder motor of 1970 was destined to grow further and power a wide range of road and off-road motorcycles. These 99cc (50.5 x 49.5mm) and 122cc (56 x 49.5mm) singles had a one-piece cylinder head, and five-speed gearbox, and were produced in the usual CB, CL and SL versions from 1970. In 1974, the XL100 and XL125 replaced the SL100 and SL125, and these successful little dual-purpose machines lasted (with annual updates) until 1985. The CB125 was also long running, receiving a cable-operated front disc brake in 1974. In 1976, the capacity was increased to 124cc, and there was a two-piece cylinder head, the

CB125 continuing until 1985.

Always prepared to tread new ground, Honda was very aggressive in its marketing approach during the early 1970s. Every year the range of machines expanded, and as in the past, they were prepared to create new categories. Because they sold millions of small-capacity machines Honda had the resources to develop new models, and take bold marketing risks. The growth of dual-purpose and off-road motorcycles in America prompted the release of the XL250 Motosport, Honda's first purpose-built off-road motorcycle, and the only four-stroke dual-purpose machine available at that time. While concentrating on road and racing machines, the XL250 deserves consideration because it was a technical breakthrough.

Central to the XL250 was Hondas' first production four-valve motor. Designed specifically for an off-road motorcycle, the 74 x 57.8mm motor was very compact, with a chain-driven single-overhead camshaft, and an angled intake port for the rubber-mounted 28mm Keihin slide carburettor. Other standard Honda features for the time were the built-up crankshaft, geared primary drive and five-speed transmission. Ignition was by flywheel magneto, the engine side covers were magnesium, and the power was 22hp at 8,000rpm.

Complementing this engine designed specifically for off-road use was a chassis with a single-cradle frame, Ceriani-type front fork, and a 21-inch front wheel, with an 18-inch rear. The 127kg XL250 Motosport was still not a really serious off-road motorcycle, but it was far more successful in this genre than the CL350 twin. The XL250 had a dual seat in 1974 and for 1976 it received a new straight-port cylinder head, frame and exhaust system. There were further updates for 1978, the XL250S receiving a 23-inch front wheel. It lasted until 1982 when the XL250R, with Pro-Link rear suspension replaced it. From 1984, the XL250R had a radial valve (RFVC) cylinder head and six-speed gearbox, it finishing in 1987.

The XL250S soon spawned the smaller XL175 (based on the XL125), and the larger XL350. The XL175 first appeared in 1973, lasting until 1978, when the XL185 replaced it, finishing in 1983. The XL350 single replaced the SL350 Motosport in 1974, the 79 x 71mm four-valve engine featuring a 32mm Keihin carburettor and producing 30hp. While the engine was impressive, the weight went up to 137kg. A revised XL350 appeared in 1976, with a new straight-through intake manifold, a new frame, and a longer and

The CB360 replaced the CB350 in 1974, this even more mundane motorcycle doing little to enhance Honda's performance profile. *Motorcycle Trader collection*

stronger swingarm. The weight went up to 142kg, too much for a dirt bike, and the XL350 was dropped in 1978. The XL350 made a brief return in 1984 and 1985, with Pro-Link rear suspension, but increasing specialisation killed the XL Hondas. It may have been compromised, but the XL250 remains a breakthrough model for Honda.

# MORE UNEXCITING TWINS

## (CB250, CB360, CJ360 and CL360 1974–77)

By 1973, the best-selling CB250/350 was into its K4 series, and a replacement was nigh. This duly appeared for 1974, and although it looked similar was quite a different design. The overhead camshaft motor was new, with no interchangeable parts, and the camshaft supported by three bearings in a one-piece cylinder head with valve adjustment by the more usual screw and locknut. There was a six-speed gearbox, and the additional displacement of the 356cc CB360 obtained with 67mm pistons. Other detail updates included ball bearings for the outer mains, and a trochoidal oil pump with a pressure-fed transmission lubrication. The roller cam chain tensioner made way for a slipper type.

Carburetion was by twin 30mm CV Keihins, and the power for the CB360 was 31hp at 9,000rpm. The similar CB250, with 28mm carburettors, produced 27hp at 10,000rpm.

Complementing this new engine was a tubular steel frame, rather than the CB350 pressed-backbone type. This lowered the seat by 25mm, and improved access to the motor, but wasn't as rigid. The swingarm was also longer, increasing the wheelbase to 1,345mm. Most CB360s came with a single front disc, while the CB250 had the twin leading shoe drum. The new CBs were improved over their predecessors in many ways, but the larger motor still vibrated, and the performance from the 162kg twins was uninspiring. The CL360 Scrambler was offered for 1974–75, and a five-speed CJ360 became available in 1976. This budget model had a two-into-one exhaust system, no electric start, and no centre-stand, and was so unpopular it finished in 1977.

Although sold into 1977, these twins marked the end of the Honda and Fujisawa era. Not only was Honda successfully expanding into car and truck manufacture, their motorcycle dream now lay with four-cylinder machines. In October 1973, Kiyoshi Kawashima assumed the presidency and his collective leadership system of management would see gross turnover treble by the end of the decade.

The 250cc RC161 made its debut at the Isle of Man in 1960 in the hands of Tom Phillis and Bob Brown. This is Phillis, who retired with gearbox problems while fourth. *Mick Woollett*

# 2 HONDA ENTERS, HONDA WINS:

## RACING IN THE SIXTIES

Honda arrogantly released a formal statement on 20 March 1954, announcing his intention to compete at the Isle of Man the following year. But despite his dejection on his return from the Isle of Man a few months later, he was still determined to initiate a racing programme. Always willing to learn, as he wasn't allowed to purchase a complete motorcycle at that time, he procured many racing motorcycle components from Europe. Honda knew he couldn't return to the Isle of Man in 1955 as he originally envisaged, but in the meantime had his engineers work on the flywheels of the Type E to safely raise the revs to 10,000rpm for domestic racing.

Honda had already entered Japanese motorcycle events such as the 2,700km Sapporo to Kagashima endurance race in 1953, and continued to race modified Benlys and Dreams during 1955. In July 1955, the 250 Dreams dominated the third Fuji volcano climb, and in November, in the First All-Japan Motorcycle Endurance Road Race at Asama, Honda won both the 350cc and 500cc classes, but lost the 125 and 250. In 1956, Honda managed to purchase a 125 Mondial single-cylinder racer and carefully analysed it. This made twice the power of his Benly but was constructed of far superior quality metals than were available in Japan at that time. At the second All-Japan Race, in October 1957, Honda again lost the 125 and 250 classes, while winning the 350. These defeats prompted a change in direction for Honda who said: 'We should never imitate foreigners, and must win the Isle of Man Tourist Trophy with our own technology, however hard it is to develop.' It was a prophetic statement.

During 1957, Honda created an R&D Centre at the Shirako Plant, and instructed two young engineers, Tadashi Kume and Kimio Shimmura, to design a racing engine. Honda believed that more power could be generated through research into combustion, something no-one else was engaged in at that time, and knew he had to increase the revs to raise the power. Thus was born the philosophy of smaller pistons and shorter strokes that would see Honda's eventual racing domination.

The first Honda racer to appear in Europe was the twin-cylinder 125cc RC141. The two-valves per cylinder RC141 had a side-mounted spark plug. *Mick Woollett*

# THE 125cc TWIN-CYLINDER RC141 AND RC142 (1959)

The result of Kume and Shimmura's work was the 125cc RC141. A technically impressive effort, the 44 x 41mm twin featured double overhead camshafts driven by a shaft and bevel gears on the left with spur gears for the separate camshafts. A magneto was driven from the right end of the inlet camshaft. Lubrication was wet sump, but a scavenge pump to return the oil to the crankcase. The vertical cylinders required sheet metal ducts to provide additional cooling. With two valves per cylinder and a 10.5:1 compression ratio, the power was unremarkable, around 18hp at 13,000rpm, and a six-speed gearbox helped tame the narrow powerband. The chassis was also inferior. Racing in Japan during the 1950s was on unpaved tracks, and the RC141, with its cumbersome leading-link front fork, was set up for the dirt tracks like Asama rather than tarmac racing. When Honda took their RC141s to the Isle of Man in 1959 they even had knobby tyres as they weren't able to test the machines prior to freighting to the island in May. After substituting the knobby tyres for a set of Avons, still with an unfashionable larger diameter wheel on the front than the back, at high revs there were problems with the RC141 valve train. Already looking at ways to reduce valve train inertia, Honda immediately flew in sets of four-valve cylinder heads from Japan for four of the five works machines. With spark plugs in the centre of the cylinder head, and deflector plates to cool them, the power went up to 18.5hp at 14,000rpm. At this time, four-valves per cylinder were considered an anachronism by the European manufacturers constrained by tradition. Although paired valves had been unsuccessful in the past, Honda was on an independent route. The four-valves per cylinder RC142 provided Honda with an impressive Isle of Man debut, but the 87kg racer was still underpowered and lacked handling finesse.

# THE 250cc FOUR-CYLINDER RC160 (1959)

While the RC142 was technically interesting, it wasn't really ground breaking. Then for the Asama race in August 1959 Honda produced a remarkable machine, their first four-cylinder racer, the 250cc RC160. Basically two RC142 engines side by side, the cylinder head layout was similar to the RC142, with double overhead camshafts driven by a shaft and bevel gears, and four valves per cylinder. With special Keihin carburettors the power was 35hp, the chassis retained the leading link fork, and the 134kg RC160 was good enough to provide Sadao Shimakazi with victory in the prestigious Asama race. The RC160 would never win in Europe, but its success provided the impetus for further multi-cylinder development.

Below: With its leading link front suspension set up for dirt track racing, the RC142 didn't handle well at the Isle of Man. *Mick Woollett*

Bottom: Honda's first four-cylinder racer was the ungainly RC160 of 1959. This machine won the Asama race that year, but wasn't competed in Europe. *Honda*

# THE 125CC TWIN-CYLINDER RC143 (1960)

For the Isle of Man of 1960 Honda produced an updated 125cc twin, the RC143. Although this still retained a vertical shaft and bevel gears on the left to drive the double overhead camshafts, the cylinders were inclined forward 35° to improve cooling. Battery and coil ignition replaced the magneto, with contact breakers behind the cylinders, and there were new Keihin flat-slide carburettors. More powerful than before, the 44 x 41mm RC143 motor produced 22hp at 14,000rpm.

The open-cradle loop spine frame was similar to the RC142, but strengthened, and while initial versions retained the leading link front fork, by the Isle of Man they had a telescopic front fork. There was a new style of fairing and the weight went up to 93kg. Australian Tom Phillis lined up alongside Taniguchi, Giichi Suzuki, Tanaka, Moto Kitano, and Shimakazi. Although still not satisfied with the handling Phillis qualified second

fastest, spark plug problems seeing him finish tenth in the race. The RC143 still wasn't fast enough to beat the MVs, with Taniguchi the strongest in sixth. This year Honda contested all five European Grands Prix, but injuries from a crash on the 250 at Assen saw Phillis's Rhodesian friend Jim Redman take over his 125. Redman stunned everyone with a strong fourth, and

Teisuke Tanaka was a last-minute replacement for the 1959 TT, and finished eighth on the two-valve RC141. *Mick Woollett*

# 1959: THE FIRST ISLE OF MAN FORAY

In 1959, World Championship motorcycle racing was largely an amateurish pursuit, and the professionalism of the Honda Team at the Isle of Man created a sensation. With a thoroughness that would later be synonymous with Honda, manager Kawashima and his team arrived with their own cook, dried fish, dried seaweed, rice, overalls with logos, and set up at the Nursery Hotel in Onchan. Heading the riders was 30-year-old General Sales Manager of American Honda, Bill Hunt, a winner at the 1958 Asama race. Hunt travelled to the island a few months prior to the event, sending back films and maps. It was in 1959 that the last 125 race was held on the shorter (17.365km) Clypse circuit, and Hunt was aided by four Japanese riders from the Honda Speed Club. They were Naomi Taniguchi, Junzo and Giichi Suzuki, and Teisuke Tanaka, replacing Kunihiko Akiyama who was killed in a road accident a few days before the team left for the Isle of Man. As his riders had not previously raced on tarmac, Honda always aimed to win the team prize. Although Hunt was disappointingly slow, crashing out on the second lap, and none of the RC142s could stay in touch with Tarquinio Provini's MV, Taniguchi provided Honda with their first World Championship points with sixth place, albeit more than seven minutes in arrears. With the other Hondas filling seventh, eighth and eleventh places (Tanaka on the two-valve RC141), Honda won the 125cc manufacturers' award at their first attempt. But Honda knew there were lessons to be learnt, and one was that he needed foreign riders to win. The Japanese riders were unaccustomed to riding at high speeds and lacked the experience to improve technical aspects of the machinery. When Honda returned in 1960 he had new machines, and foreign riders.

for the first time proved the Honda was able to run with the MVs.

# THE 250cc FOUR-CYLINDER RC161 (1960)

As well as the RC143, Honda fielded a team of four-cylinder RC161 250s during 1960. Like the early RC160, this was essentially two 44 x 41mm 125cc twins side-by-side, the RC161 based on the RC143 with forward-canted cylinders but now with a set of central spur gears to drive the double overhead camshafts. There was also a six-speed gearbox, and this engine was the blueprint for all the Honda racers that would become so dominant during the 1960s. Each inlet port included a knife-edge dividing wall someway upstream of the valve heads, and the weight of the twin 18mm inlet valves was only 12 grams. The total reciprocating weight of the valve, spring, and followers was only 20 grams, allowing the engine to rev safely to 17,000rpm. To provide internal oil cooling, a large-finned sump attached underneath the engine, and the cylinders and crankcase were die-cast in one piece to stop oil leaks. A cast-iron skull in the cylinder head eliminated the problem of loosening valve seat inserts, and as with the RC143, there were new downdraft flat-slide Keihin carburettors without metering needles and with remote float bowls. Ignition also reverted to battery and coil to assist push starting. The power was still 35hp at 12,000rpm, but this rose to 40hp during the season.

The open cradle frame was still based on that of the RC160, and although the front fork was now telescopic, it was a fairly flimsy unit and the chassis wasn't yet up to harnessing the power. For the Isle of Man Lightweight TT another Australian, Bob Brown, was drafted alongside Phillis. Brown gave Honda their best result to date, finishing fourth. A new chassis appeared for Assen, using the engine as a stressed member, and John Hartle was scheduled to ride the

Below: John Hartle tested the RC161 in practice at Assen in 1960, but didn't ride in the race because of a conflict in oil company contracts. There was a revised frame and the carburettors were steeply downdraft. *Mick Woollett*

Below: Bob McIntyre gave the RC161 its first victory in Europe, at an International race at Aintree in England in September 1960. Standing alongside him in this photograph are Jim Redman and Pym Fleming. *Mick Woollett*

RC161. However, his Mobil contract conflicted with Honda's Castrol contract and Redman rode instead. When Brown died following an accident at Solitude a month later, Redman again took over. At the Ulster Grand Prix, Phillis and Redman finished second and third, with Redman second at the final GP at Monza, to finish fourth in the World Championship. The RC161 was improving with every race, but there were too many intrinsic problems. The new chassis, and a combination of friction and hydraulic steering dampers, did little to quell steering oscillation under acceleration, while the front fork lost its oil, and damping periodically. As the engine was mounted very high to provide acceptable ground clearance the frame and tank were uncomfortably humped over it. On top of the handling woes, the ignition often failed at high rpm, while the chrome-plated exhaust system cracked.

The RC161 may have been beset with problems, but it was only a minor impediment to Honda's advancement. This was only the calm before a storm of unparalleled ferocity.

# THE 125cc TWIN-CYLINDER RC144 (1961)

The withdrawal of MV, Benelli, Morini, and NSU from the 125 class at the start of the 1961 season didn't deter Honda from continuing development of the RC143, and the 1961 RC144 was considerably improved. Again with magneto ignition, and retaining the bevel drive to the camshafts, there were new dimensions (42 x 45mm). The longer stroke engine was slightly less powerful than before (21hp). The frame

Below: Tom Phillis on the RC144 at the Isle of Man in 1961. He finished third, behind Hailwood and Taveri, but won the 125cc World Championship. *Mick Woollett*

Bottom: Phillis's 2RC143 at the Sachsenring. This still had bevel-drive overhead camshafts, and sidedraft carburettors. *Mick Woollett*

Tom Phillis was also a competent mechanic and helped Honda improve their early racers. Here, he is with the RC144 at the 1961 Belgian Grand Prix where he came second. *Mick Woollett*

was now a dual loop type, inspired by the Norton 'Featherbed', but without the lower cradle, and still retaining the engine as a stressed member. The handling was superior to the RC143, and riders were now queuing up for the Hondas. Kawashima showed he appreciated loyalty by offering the RC144 to Phillis and Redman, over Swiss champion Luigi Taveri. Taveri was offered a year-old RC143, but did get to ride the RC144 at the Isle of Man. But it was Phillis who rewarded Honda with their first Grand Prix victory, at the opening round at Barcelona.

For the Isle of Man Ultra Lightweight TT, the great racer Mike Hailwood rode Taveri's RC143 to victory ahead of the RC144s of Taveri, Phillis, Redman and Shimakazi. Initially denied a Honda, Hailwood's father Stan secured the year-old machine through some clever negotiation. The TT massacre of the European opposition was Honda's finest to date, the dream of 1954 finally becoming a reality.

While brilliant at the Isle of Man, throughout the rest of the 1961 Grand Prix season the RC144 struggled to match the speed of the two-stroke MZ of Ernst Degner. This prompted the creation of the 2RC143 mid-season, with the more powerful RC143 motor in the more stable RC144 chassis. This was a successful match, and Honda won the championship, and all but three 125 GPs that year.

## THE 250cc FOUR-CYLINDER RC162 (1961)

Although Degner gave Honda a run for their money in the 125cc World Championship, it was a completely different story in the 250cc category. After losing the first Grand Prix at Barcelona to Hocking's MV Agusta, the new RC162 was totally dominant. The RC162 was considerably updated over the RC161, with only 10 per cent of the earlier model's parts retained in the design. The 16-valve four-cylinder engine now included dry sump lubrication (without the finned sump), with the oil carried in a tank underneath the seat. To take the kink out of the chassis, the cylinders were slightly more upright (30°), reducing the carburettor downdraft angle. The Keihin carburettors had integral float chambers and round throttle slides, and were mounted on rubber manifolds to insulate them from vibration. To cure high rpm ignition failure, ignition was by double-ended coils. With black-painted exhaust pipes that no longer

## HONDA'S FIRST WORLD CHAMPION: TOM PHILLIS

One of many Australians who travelled to Europe during the 1950s to contest the motorcycle World Championships, Phillis was so impressed by Honda's 1959 effort, that he approached Honda independently regarding a ride for 1960. As no-one else was queuing for rides at that stage, the 26-year-old Phillis became Honda's first gaijin pro, or foreign rider. His technical knowledge helped Honda improve the machines so much for 1961 that Phillis won six GPs that year, including the 125cc World Championship, Honda's first. For 1962 Phillis was due to compete in 50, 125, and 250 classes, but took over Redman's RC171 for the Isle of Man Junior TT. He died on it at a crash at Laurel Bank, only two days after finishing third in the Lightweight TT. This was an era when riders accepted the risks and diced with death. Only a few weeks after Phillis died, Bob McIntyre was killed at Oulton Park in a non-championship event. Gary Hocking, stunned into retirement from motorcycle racing by Phillis's death, was then killed in a racing car accident at the end of the year. It was a very grim year for motorcycle racing in 1962.

The RC162 was considerably updated over the RC161, with the dry-sump motor mounted lower in the frame. The pit facilities were primitive at the Isle of Man. *Mick Woollett*

cracked, the power was up to 42hp at 14,000rpm, later climbing to around 45hp. The chassis also followed the style of the later RC160 and RC144, with a double-loop upper cradle, but the lower dry-sump engine was placed lower in the frame. A new smooth fairing wrapped the underneath of the engine, while a new internal spring front fork and Redman's preferred Girling rear shock absorbers improved the handling.

In 1961, Honda was determined to win the World Championship, not only providing RC162s to Phillis, Redman and Kunimitsu Takahashi, but also leasing them to Bob McIntyre and Mike Hailwood. Takahashi was the first Japanese rider to win a World Championship Grand Prix when he won the 250 race at Hockenheim, but it was Hailwood who stole the glory that year. After starting the season on a year-old RC161, by the Isle of Man his father Stan had negotiated a new RC162. Hailwood was almost upstaged by McIntyre, in one of the finest rides in TT history. McIntyre set an astonishing lap for a 250 of 99.58mph (160.258km/h). This overheated the oil

from the dry sump oil tank, which blew out all over the rear tyre before the engine seized. Hailwood then went on to win the 250 TT, ahead of Phillis and Redman, with RC162s filling out the first five places. A privateer ahead of all the factory bikes, Hailwood won the 1961 250cc World Championship. The RC162 was so dominant that it occupied every podium spot after Hockenheim. Honda had already achieved what they intended, and it was time to look beyond 125s and 250s.

# THE 50cc SINGLE-CYLINDER RC111 (1962)

A new 50 cc World Championship was established for 1962, and for this Honda produced the RC111. Virtually a shrunken half of the RC145, the 40 x 39mm single included double overhead camshafts driven by spur gears, and with four valves, produced 9.5hp at 14,000rpm. Initially the gearbox was six-speed, and

Bob McIntyre astride the RC162 at the Isle of Man in 1961. This was one of the most astonishing rides in TT history, when McIntyre lapped at almost 100mph (62km/h). With McIntyre are Reg Armstrong, Pym Fleming, and journalist Vic Willoughby. *Mick Woollett*

with tiny 2.00 x 18-inch tyres, the RC111 weighed 60kg, and was capable of around 87mph (140km/h).

The 49cc four-stroke couldn't match the eight-speed two-stroke Suzuki and Kreidler opposition, and at the opening Grand Prix in Barcelona Taveri could only manage third. For the next Grand Prix in France only a week later the RC111 also had an eight-speed transmission, and by the Isle of Man there was a nine-speed gearbox. Here, Taveri and new recruit, Irishman Tommy Robb, finished second and third. Although still outpaced, the hard-riding Taveri managed one victory, in Finland, towards the end of the season. This humiliation in the World Championship prompted Honda's engineers to pursue the smaller cylinder, high rpm route even further, with the amazing twin-cylinder (two-valves per cylinder) RC112. This was revealed at a non-championship race at the new Suzuka circuit at the end of 1962, but the 50cc twin wasn't to be seen in Europe until 1964.

# THE 125cc TWIN-CYLINDER RC145 (1962)

Despite the improvement of the two-stroke MZs and Suzukis during 1962, there was little competition for the Hondas in the 125 class. The updated twin, the RC145, had square engine dimensions of 44 x 44mm, and the double overhead camshafts driven by a train of spur gears on the left. The power was increased to 24hp at 14,000rpm. Prior to the beginning of the season it was planned for Takahashi to win the 125cc World Championship, and while he won the first two GPs, a heavy crash on the Isle of Man ended his title aspirations. Taveri then had the factory's blessing to win the championship, which he did convincingly with six GP victories. At the Isle of Man, Hondas again filled the first five places in the 125 Ultra Lightweight TT, and the RC145s won every GP they contested.

# THE FOUR-CYLINDER 250cc RC163 AND 350cc RC170 (1962)

As the 250 competition primarily consisted of the single-cylinder Morini, Aermacchi, Moto Guzzi, and two-stroke Bultaco and MZ, Honda reasoned little

development was required to maintain the 250cc four's dominance. Updates for the RC163 for 1962 saw the motor producing 46hp at 14,000rpm, but with this increase came decreased reliability, as the engine often suffered an elusive misfire. To cure overheating problems the oil capacity was increased. The chassis was also stronger, and the overall weight slightly higher at 128kg. New for the TT this year were four-leading shoe double drum brakes, and after Redman won the first two GPs it was expected he would also win the all-important 250cc TT. But the misfiring RC163 failed to match the speed of the 1961 RC162, and while McIntyre scorched into the lead, lapping at 99.06mph (159.39km/h), his ignition failed on the second lap. Derek Minter, on an RC163 borrowed and entered by the British importer Hondis, then led Redman and Phillis home, disobeying orders not to beat the factory entries. With his crankshaft broken, Minter wasn't even aware he was in the lead, but as far as the factory was concerned he had blotted his copybook, and never again rode for Honda.

The 1963 50cc CR110 production racer was a replica of the factory RC111, and featured double overhead camshafts driven by a train of gears on the right. *Peter Herbert*

Only a few 125cc CR93s were produced. This 1962 example has a single leading shoe front brake. *Peter Herbert*

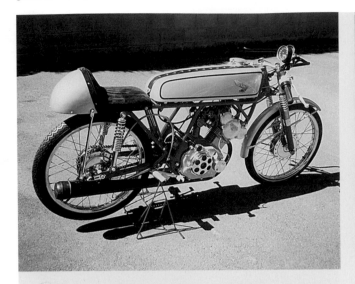

# PRODUCTION RACERS: CR110 AND CR93

Buoyed by the 1961 success, early in 1962, Honda proudly published a booklet describing all their racing machines in detail. They also released two production racers, the single-cylinder 50cc CR110, and twin-cylinder 125cc CR93. The CR110 was available as a racer or with full road equipment, including high exhaust and muffler, lights and speedometer. Powering the CR110 was a single-cylinder (40 x 39mm) motor based on the RC111, with double overhead camshafts driven by spur gears, and four valves. The chassis was also similar to the racing RC111. The power for the five-speed road version was 7hp at 12,700rpm, and the top speed was 161mph (100km/h). The racing version was eight-speed, with 8hp, and capable of over 200mph (125km/h).

In addition to the jewel-like CR110, was the equally magnificent CR93, also available in racing (for Europe) or road trim (primarily for Japan). The road version had higher handlebars and a front fork with enclosed springs. Powering the CR93 was a 44 x 41mm twin, derived from the factory RC145, with a 180° crankshaft and double overhead camshafts driven by spur gears from the left. There were two 18mm inlet valves and two 17mm exhaust valves per cylinder, a pair of 22mm Keihin carburettors, and a claimed 21hp at 10,500rpm. The loop frame was also derived from the RC145 and most 1962 versions had a single leading shoe front brake. Examples in 1963 had the more usual double leading shoe front brake, but very few of these machines were produced (around 220), with reputedly 43 sold in Britain. Both the CR110 and CR93 were beautifully crafted machines, but they were more suited to club, rather than international, racing.

As pre-arranged, Redman went on to win the 250cc World Championship, only losing three races, but he was often pushed hard by team-mates McIntyre, Robb, Tanaka, and Taveri. Mike Hailwood, this year riding for MV Agusta in the larger classes, also pressured Redman at the Sachsenring on an MZ, while Provini, on the amazing Morini single pressed Redman hard at Monza. After the dominance of 1961, there were already signs that Honda wasn't going to have it all its own way in the future.

For 1962, Honda decided to contest the 350cc World Championship, boring the RC163 to 285cc (47 x 41mm) to create the RC 170. The power went up to 49hp at 14,000rpm and as the MV 350s were showing

their age, Honda was confident their RC170 was superior. It was arranged before the season for McIntyre to win the title, with Redman in support. The season didn't start well for the RC170 at the Isle of Man. Phillis was killed; McIntyre retired, and at the next round, Hailwood on the MV also pushed Redman to the limit. Honda responded with a 339cc engine (49 x 45mm) at Ulster, and this was fast enough to provide Redman with a World Championship double.

Things started to go awry for Honda during 1963. Flushed with success, the ambitious Soichiro decided to become involved in Formula 1 car racing. He diverted many engineers from motorcycle development and scaled down the motorcycle racing effort. Following

Below: Three 250cc RC163s, with three 125cc RC145s behind, at Monza in 1962. Although little changed from the previous year they completely dominated their respective championships. *Mick Woollett*

the humiliation of the RC111 during 1962, Honda withdrew from the 50cc World Championship, racing the RC112 twin only in Japan. There were small developments to the 125cc RC145 twin, but these were not enough to cope with the vastly improved Suzuki rotary valve two-stroke twin of New Zealander Hugh Anderson. After Taveri won the opening GP at Barcelona, Anderson completely dominated the championship, prompting Honda to bring out the 125cc RC146 four at the final round at Suzuka.

# THE FOUR-CYLINDER 250cc RC164 AND 350cc RC171 (1963)

With resources stretched to the limit, and only five mechanics (headed by Michihiko Aika) servicing 15

factory RC and 29 CR production racers, 1963 was the toughest yet for Honda. The new RC164 was slightly lighter (125kg) but little changed from the RC163. Now team manager as well as rider, Redman suffered humiliating defeats at Barcelona, Hockenheim, and Monza when Provini rode the amazing 35hp 250cc Morini single to victory. Redman did win the Isle of Man Lightweight TT, but third-place finisher Bill Smith rode a CR72 production racer. The 250cc championship went down to the final race at Suzuka, Redman narrowly winning from Fumio Ito on the Yamaha two-stroke twin. Redman won his second 250 title, but it was a close call. Also little changed for 1963 was the 350cc RC171. The power of the 339cc four was 52hp at 12,000rpm, and this was just enough to see off Hailwood on the old MV, and John Hartle on the even older Gilera. Redman won five GPs to score another World Championship double, proving an enlarged 250 was still a better formula for a 350 than a downsized 500 (like the MV and Gilera).

Although heavy and unreliable, the CR72 production racer was a beautifully crafted machine. This is Bill Smith's CR72 at the Isle of Man in 1963, where it took third place in the 250cc TT. *Mick Woollett*

Below: Jim Redman was Honda's most successful rider of the 1960s, winning six World Championships. *Mick Woollett*

# MORE PRODUCTION RACERS: CR72 AND CR77

With only a few works RC bikes available, during 1962 and '63 Honda produced limited numbers of production racing versions of the CB72 and CB77 twins. These were primarily provided to Honda team riders to race in non-international events, and at the season end were sold to privateers. While sharing the dimensions of the production CB twins (54 x 54mm and 60 x 54mm), these motors were technological marvels. There were double overhead camshafts running in four ball bearings, driven by a central set of spur gears, and four valves (23.6mm inlet and 22mm exhaust) per cylinder. The 180° crankshaft ran in two ball and two roller bearings, and primary drive by straight-cut gears to a six-speed gearbox. The multiplate clutch was dry, ignition was by magneto, and with twin Keihin 29mm smoothbore carburettors, the power for the CR72 was 40hp at 12,000rpm. While this was admirable, the sand-cast engine cases contributed to a very heavy, 60kg motor (2kg heavier than the RC163 four). Also, the high rpm stretched the limits of piston speed in the early 1960s and the CR72/77 earned a reputation for fragility. As the chassis of the CR72/77 was unremarkable, with the single-loop type frame of the pre-1961 factory racers, these were also not particularly good handling machines. Always rare, although they never achieved any notable success, today, the CR72/77 is prized.

# HONDA STALWART: JIM REDMAN

Born in London in 1931, Jim Redman was Honda's most successful rider of the 1960s. When his father committed suicide and his mother died of a brain haemorrhage after the Second World War, Redman was called up for military service. He immediately fled to Rhodesia with his younger brother and sister, later opening a motorcycle shop and racing a Triumph. As with many 'colonials', Redman was attracted to racing in Europe, heading there in 1958. Redman initially struggled at GP level, and was rejected by MZ for a factory ride in 1960. His big break came when he substituted for Phillis on the RC143 at Assen in 1960, and he didn't look back. By 1962, he was Honda's leading rider, and for 1963, team manager.

Toughened by life experiences, and always the consummate businessman, Redman was perfectly suited to the demands of racing in the 1960s. Unlike others, he was able to continue winning even when his colleagues were killed, and all his 45 Grand Prix victories were on a Honda. Hired for steadiness rather than brilliance, Redman was always Honda's most loyal rider, never complaining about the machines in public. He was particularly successful at the Isle of Man, winning the Lightweight and Junior TTs three years in succession. Although chosen ahead of Hailwood to take the 500 title in 1966, this was not to be and injuries following a crash at Spa prompted a premature retirement. In an era when many of the top riders died in racing accidents, Redman was a survivor, and has continued as a Honda ambassador many years after his racing retirement.

Honda's first 350cc racer was the 1962 RC170. Basically a larger 250, Redman rode it to victory in the 350cc World Championship. *Mick Woollett*

# THE 50cc TWIN-CYLINDER RC113 AND RC114 (1963–64)

Recognising the two-stroke's BMEP (brake mean effective pressure) superiority, and shaken by their annihilation in the 1962 50cc World Championship, Honda sought to gain power through more revs. This led to even shorter strokes and smaller cylinders, and some extraordinary motorcycles. Heading this new formula was the twin-cylinder 50cc RC113. This nine-speed 33 x 29mm twin, with four tiny valves (13mm and 12mm) per cylinder, a central 10mm spark plug, and a 180° crankshaft, initially produced 10hp at 17,500rpm. The double overhead camshafts were driven by a set of spur gears on the right, and this engine would become the test bed for Honda's

four-stroke development. The magic figure of 200hp per litre was astounding for 1963, and over the next few years Honda's engineer, Shoichiro Irimajiri, managed to increase this figure by 40 per cent. The tiny RC113 weighed 50kg, and was capable of around 84mph (135km/h). The front brake was a friction-saving bicycle type, with a caliper gripping the wheel rim, and thin aluminium discs were clipped to the spokes to smooth out the eddies. The tyres were a tiny 2.00 and 2.25 x 18-inch, and the first appearance of the RC113 was at Suzuka for the final GP of 1963. Here, Taveri vindicated Honda's philosophy, soundly beating the Suzukis. The diminutive Ralph Bryans was chosen to ride the updated RC114 in the 1964 50cc World Championship, and after a slow start began to put pressure on Anderson's Suzuki at the Isle of Man. He then won three races in a row, but an engine failure in Finland allowed Anderson to take the title.

Now team manager as well as leading rider, Jim Redman again won the 250cc and 350cc World Championships in 1963. Here he is on his way to victory in the 350cc Dutch TT at Assen. *Mick Woollett*

# THE FOUR-CYLINDER 125cc RC146 AND 2RC146 (1963–65)

Also appearing at Suzuka at the end of 1963 was the first 125cc four-cylinder, the RC146. The seven-speed 35 x 32mm four produced 27hp at 17,000rpm (later 28hp at 18,000rpm with the 2RC146), and weighed only 87kg (10kg less than the twin). While Redman's Suzuka debut was inauspicious, he was beaten by Frank Perris on a Suzuki, the RC146 was one of Honda's most reliable and balanced racing machines. A long, narrow sump, with fins projecting through the fairing, provided an improvement over the 250cc RC164's dry sump. During 1964, Suzuki sacrificed their air-cooled two-stroke twin's reliability in a search to match the 2RC146, and with five victories, Taveri rode away with the title. Heading a Honda 2RC146 clean sweep at the Isle of Man, Taveri set an amazing new 125cc lap record of 93.53mph (150.49km/h), winning from

Redman by only three seconds. Following Taveri's success of 1964, Honda decided the 2RC146 was still sufficient to win in 1965. Along with Formula 1 cars, their 15 R&D engineers were stretched to the limit developing the 50cc RC115 and six-cylinder RC165, so they left the 125 alone. This allowed Suzuki and Yamaha to adapt water-cooling to their two-stroke twins, and with newfound reliability, Taveri was swamped. Not only did he fail to finish several races due to chronic misfiring, his best result was second at the TT. Honda withdrew from the 125 championship mid-season, allowing Irimajiri time to create his next masterpiece, the five-cylinder 125cc RC148.

# THE FOUR-CYLINDER 250cc 2RC164 (1964) AND 350cc RC172 (1964)

While concentrating on developing the new 50cc and 125cc RC113 and RC146, the four-cylinder 250 and

Below: One of Honda's most efficient racing machines was the four-cylinder 125cc 2RC146. Taveri won the 1964 125cc World Championship on this machine. *Mick Woollett*

Bottom: While he had little trouble winning the 1964 title, Taveri struggled during 1965. His best result that year was, as seen here, second in the 125cc TT at the Isle of Man. *Mick Woollett*

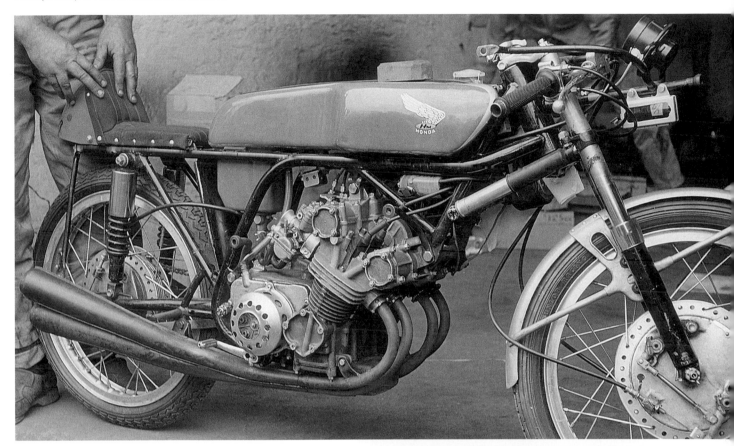

350 racers were evolutionary. The 2RC164 250 was now at the peak of development, producing 48hp, but the two-strokes were on the rise. The rotary-valve two-stroke Yamaha RD56 produced 55hp, and Suzuki had a new 54hp water-cooled square-four that looked promising on paper, if not in reality. Yamaha also secured the services of a world-class rider in Phil Read and the battle for the 1964 250cc World Championship between Redman and Read was one of the hardest fought of all. Ultimately, the Yamaha survived seizures and fouled plugs to deprive Redman of his third 250 title. This prompted the release of a new weapon towards the end of 1964, the six-cylinder RC165.

Redman had a much easier time in the 350cc Championship. The RC172 was now a full 350cc (50 x 44.5mm), and produced 53hp at 13,000rpm. Not only was the RC172 a paragon of reliability, it was extremely fast. Redman was timed at almost 149mph (240km/h) at the Isle of Man, and won all eight rounds of the 1964 350cc World Championship.

The RC172 was an evolutionary development of the earlier 250cc and 350cc fours but still with a dry sump. Redman easily rode to victory in the 1964 350cc World Championship. *Mick Woollett*

Right: Redman taking the 250cc six out for its first practice session at Monza, at the end of 1964. *Mick Woollett*

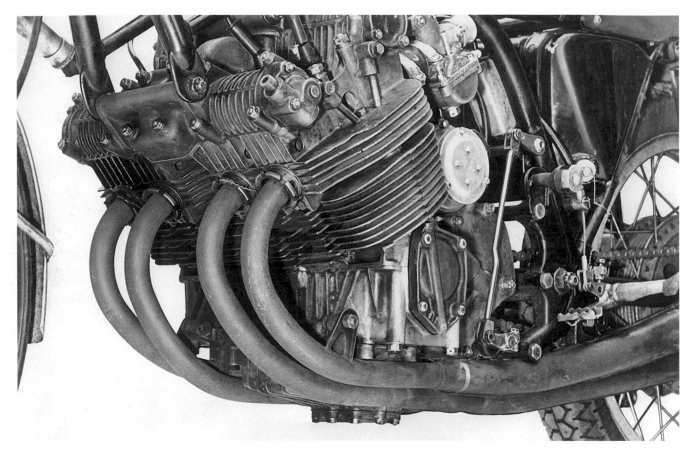

# THE 250cc SIX-CYLINDER RC165 AND 2RC165 (1964–5)

Although rumours had been rife for some months, when the 250cc six was unveiled at Monza in September 1964 it created a sensation. The six sounded like nothing else, and was blisteringly fast. Redman and chief mechanic Aika managed to get the RC165 to the Italian Grand Prix, flying it as hand luggage disguised under a blanket. To maintain its secrecy it was registered for the race as the 3RC164, with only four exhaust pipes fitted, the other two installed just prior to practice. Although early testing in Japan showed the handling to be woeful, Redman hoped its impressive speed would psychologically unbalance Read. He was right; Read was initially devastated, but in the race the RC165 overheated, causing the carburettors to vapour-lock, and Redman finished third. For the final 1964 GP at Suzuka the RC165 was fitted with oil coolers, the

wheelbase lengthened 90mm, and Redman provided its first victory.

Continuing a philosophy of smaller cylinders and higher revs that was so successful on the 50cc twin, engineer Irimajiri managed to create a six-cylinder engine with four-valves per cylinder that, at 35.6mm, was no wider than a four. With a bore and stroke of 39 x 34.5mm, the six followed the usual RC layout of a central train of spur gears driving double overhead camshafts and four valves per cylinder. The valves were set at a quite wide included angle of 75°, the advantages of a shallower combustion chamber not yet appreciated. The roller bearing crankshaft had no flywheels, so it stalled easily below 14,000rpm, and could break. The compression ratio of 12:1 was higher than usual for Honda racers, NGK supplied special 8mm spark plugs, and ignition was by magneto with three sets of contact breakers and the usual double-ended coils. Carburetion was by six magnesium Keihin round or flat-slide carburettors, ranging in size from 17mm to 22mm. The bank of carburettors was pre-set up on a bench, allowing easy installation at the track.

Lubrication was by a long narrow wet sump, similar to the 125cc RC146. The attention to detail and quest to reduce internal mass was staggering, with three different types of 70mm con-rod, the ones in the centre receiving larger big-end bearings where the load was higher. Ignition was by a gear-driven magneto, with three sets of points and three, two-spark coils. According to Irimajiri, the power of the six-speed RC165 was 52hp at 14,500rpm.

From the outset, the RC165 chassis was barely up to the task. Irimajiri admitted: 'In the late Sixties we didn't understand chassis rigidity.' The frame was similar to the RC164, with the engine as a stressed member, the front fork included welded steel sliders and the handling was poor. Braking was by a 220mm front, and a 200mm rear twin-leading shoe drum brakes.

While theoretically the 2RC165 should have had the better of the Yamaha twin during 1965, this was not to be. Now with a seven-speed gearbox (with many titanium components), Formula 1 commitments led to indifferent machine preparation and several gearbox

failures. With Redman alone contesting the 250 and 350 titles, he found it too much. Injuries and handling difficulties meant Redman didn't make the start line for six GPs and despite four victories, including another Isle of Man TT, the title was as good as lost by mid-season. Honda then signed Mike Hailwood to ride the six. Hailwood loudly criticised the handling of the RC165, throwing the Japanese-made shock absorbers in a nearby lake after the first practice session. With Girlings fitted, Hailwood contemptuously ran away from the field on it in the final 1965 250 GP at Suzuka.

## THE TWIN-CYLINDER 50cc RC115 (1965) AND RC116 (1966)

Irimajiri's diligence in developing the RC114 paid off with the RC115 for 1965. With a shorter stroke (34 x 27.8mm), the power of the nine-speed 50 was now 12.8hp at 21,000rpm. In the hands of Bryans and

At the 1965 French Grand Prix journalist Mick Woollett took this first photograph of the 2RC165 without its fairing. This prompted a heated exchange between Redman and Woollett, but the photo was taken from outside the fence. *Mick Woollett*

Redman on the 2RC165, on his way to victory at Assen in 1965, but he couldn't win the World Championship. *Mick Woollett*

Taveri it was finally enough to see off the Suzukis, and only beaten once, with Bryans taking the championship. For 1966, the RC116 had a larger bore and even shorter stroke (35.5 x 25.14mm), and the power was an extraordinary 14hp at 21,500rpm. Still slightly superior to the Suzuki, and with three wins between them, Taveri or Bryans looked set to win the 50cc World Championship. That was until Honda boycotted the final event in Japan because it was moved from their track at Suzuka to Fisco, handing the championship to the Suzuki of Hans-Georg Anscheidt. With Honda deciding to concentrate on the larger capacity classes after 1966, there was no more official Honda entry in the 50cc World Championship.

# SHOICHIRO IRIMAJIRI

Born on 3 January 1940, Shoichiro Irimajiri graduated from Tokyo University with a degree in aeronautical engineering in March 1963. One month later he joined Honda's R&D department. 'Actually I wanted to design aircraft, but at that stage this was still prohibited because of the defeat in World War 2,' remembers Irimajiri. Along with blueprints for the 125cc RC146 four-cylinder, his initial project was to extract more power from the 50cc RC113 twin. 'I worked every day changing cam timing, valve size, megaphone, and con-rod length to increase the power to 11.8hp at 21,000rpm for the first race at Suzuka at the end of 1963.' The quest to reduce friction saw a reduction in the number of piston rings to only one, 'even changing a crankshaft seal resulted in 0.5 per cent less friction.' After experimenting with, and discarding desmodromic valve actuation, Irimajiri worked at increasing the revs through improved materials. The lessons learnt from the 50 were then applied to the five-cylinder 125cc RC147, and the 250cc six. Irimajiri was attracted to the six because it had perfect primary balance, and began work on the design in February 1964, with a bike completed by June.

After designing the six Irimajiri was assigned to the V12 1.5-litre RA271 Formula 1 car engine, and when Honda withdrew from GP racing, was involved with car projects until 1975. With the establishment of a new motorcycle research centre at Asaka, Irimajiri then headed the CBX1000 project, and was then involved in the disastrous NR500 racer. He became a director in 1979, and from 1984 to 1988 he was Executive Vice-President at Honda's Marysville, Ohio Plant. Heart problems saw him leave Honda in 1992, when he took up kiko, a Chinese breathing method. Irimajiri joined electronic games company Sega in 1993, and was President from 1998 until his resignation in 2000.

Below: Redman's final World Championship was the 1965 350cc title. The 2RC172 was evolutionary, but still fast and reliable. This is Redman heading to victory at the Dutch TT. *Mick Woollett*

Bottom: Ralph Bryans was perfectly suited to the tiny twin-cylinder RC115, and provided Honda with their only 50cc World Championship, in 1965. Here he is at Assen en route to victory. *Mick Woollett*

One of the most astounding racing Hondas was the 1966 125cc five-cylinder RC149, providing Taveri with another World Championship. The high exhaust is for the central cylinder. *Mick Woollett*

# THE FOUR-CYLINDER 350cc 2RC172 (1965)

While the 250cc four was beaten, and the 250 six suffered teething troubles, the venerable 350cc four continued to reign supreme during 1965. Continual evolution resulted in the improved 2RC172, but there was more opposition this year. MV Agusta finally realised that a downsized 500 was never going to beat Honda's scaled-up 250, and also that two-valves per cylinder had had their day. They produced a 350 12-valve triple for Mike Hailwood and new recruit Giacomo Agostini. While a formidable opponent, the MV 3 in its early developmental period was still no match for Redman and the 2RC172. Redman won the 350cc title, his sixth and last.

# THE FIVE-CYLINDER 125cc RC148 (1965) AND RC149 (1966)

Going into the 1966 season Honda was tired of humiliation by the two-strokes in the 125 class, and they unveiled another Irimajiri masterpiece at the Japanese GP at the end of 1965. The success of the 50cc twin-cylinder RC115 led Irimajiri to multiply this two and a half times, creating the five-cylinder RC148. With the same 34 x 27.5mm dimensions as the 50cc twin, and sharing similar architecture, the power of the eight-speed five was 32hp at 19,500rpm. The camshaft drive was between the second and third cylinders, with the centre exhaust pipe sweeping over the clutch and under the seat. Lubrication was dry sump, with a pair of oil coolers. Bryans and Taveri rode the 'five' at Suzuka, where it was clearly the fastest until Taveri lost power, to finish second.

Ralph Bryans was also a qualified mechanic, and is seen here working on a CR72 production racer at Silverstone in 1965. In the van are Taveri (in leathers), and Suzuki champion Anscheidt. *Mick Woollett*

Below: Mike Hailwood was never satisfied with the handling of the Hondas, experimenting with alternative frames and brakes. Here, he is at Brands Hatch in March 1967 testing a Lyster double front disc brake on a 350cc four-cylinder RC173. *Mick Woollett*

# SMALL BORE CHAMPIONS: LUIGI TAVERI AND RALPH BRYANS

Like Tom Phillis, Luigi Taveri was one of the first foreign riders to recognise Honda's potential. Born near Zurich in 1949, Taveri was already a veteran by the time he approached Honda during 1961, and with all the factory rides taken it wasn't until 1962 that he received priority equipment. Taveri then gave Honda their second 125cc World Championship, repeating this biannually as Honda responded to the two-stroke challenge with the four-cylinder RC146 and five-cylinder RC149. Taveri retired at the end of 1966.

Ulsterman Ralph Bryans was signed by Honda to ride the little RC114 50cc twin for 1964, rewarding Honda with their only title in this class in 1965. He probably would also have won the 1966 title if he had raced in the final round, and was a valuable backup rider to Taveri in the 125 class. Bryans also provided a strong backup to Hailwood during 1967, and was one of only three riders to win on the six. Bryans continued to campaign the 125 five during 1968 in non-championship events, and his last ride was on a factory CB750 at Daytona in 1970.

# THE GREATEST OF ALL: MIKE HAILWOOD

Hailed by many as the greatest rider of all time, Stanley Michael Bailey Hailwood was only a works Honda rider for two years, but has become known for his legendary riding of the six and unruly RC181 500cc four. Born on 2 April 1940, the young Mike was strongly supported by his wealthy father Stan who owned a chain of motorcycle shops. In the early days of his career Mike suffered criticism through having a millionaire father who provided the best equipment and tuners. However, he quickly overcame this and established himself as a racer of extraordinary talent, with the ability to ride any capacity of motorcycle. He won all four British titles (125, 250, 350 and 500) in 1959 and 1960, and in 1961 was the first rider to win three TTs in a week. He was also Honda's first 250cc World Champion that year. When hired by Honda, Hailwood had just won four consecutive 500cc World Championships on the MV Agusta and really had nothing more to prove.

Paid £50,000 by Honda not to contest the 1968 World Championship, Hailwood rode the RC181 at some non-championship events, before turning his hand to car racing. Here he was also successful, winning the 1972 European Formula 2 Championship. Hailwood made a spectacular TT comeback when he won the 1978 TT F1 race on a Ducati, returning to take the Senior TT on a Suzuki RG500 in 1979. After years of dicing with death on powerful, ill-handling motorcycles with inadequate tyres, Mike Hailwood was tragically killed in a road accident near his home on 22 March 1981.

The 500cc RC181 at its second outing, the 1966 Dutch TT, which Redman won. *Mick Woollett*

For the 1966 World Championship the five-cylinder 125 became the RC149, now with the RC116 dimensions of 35.5 x 25.14mm, and 34hp at 20,000rpm. A first for a racing Honda was the glassfibre fuel tank with translucent fuel level gauge. Taveri was perfectly suited to the RC149, rising to the challenge of the new water-cooled Yamaha twin of Bill Ivy. Taveri won five GPs to Ivy's three to take the World Championship, but this was the swansong for the 'five', and the 38-year-old Taveri. At the end of 1966, their most successful racing season yet, Honda announced they would concentrate only on the larger classes for 1967.

# THE SIX-CYLINDER 250cc RC166 AND FOUR-CYLINDER 350cc RC173 (1966)

For 1966, Honda decided to contest every World Championship, aiming to repeat the domination of 1961. They needed another leading rider to share the burden with Redman, Taveri, and Bryans, and procured Mike Hailwood. Hailwood was undoubtedly the most brilliant rider of the era, but by the end of 1965 was beginning to tire of MV's preference for their new Italian star, Agostini. So Hailwood signed for Honda for 1966, concentrating on the 250 and 350 titles. Thus began two magical years with Hailwood on the Honda six; possibly the best rider of all time, on one of the most charismatic racing motorcycles of all time.

After the disappointment of 1965, the 250 was completely redesigned for the following year, with the RC166. There were new cylinders, and to improve cooling the cylinder head, had additional fins and cut-outs. The sump had extra alloy fins welded on to it with oil coolers fitted in the fairing. The RC166 was now pumping out 56.8hp at 17,500rpm. Hailwood requested improved handling, and the RC166 frame was built of stronger tubing (35mm at the steering head) with additional gussets under the fuel tank. The two-piece tubular steel swingarm included additional box-section steel bracing. There was also a new front fork, and the rider moved forward to take advantage of the improved grip provided by the new Dunlop triangular-shaped racing tyres.

The combination of Hailwood's talent and the improved RC166 overwhelmed Read and the Yamaha twin. Yamaha provided Read with the ill-tempered and difficult handling water-cooled V-four, but the speed and reliability of the RC166 was faultless. Hailwood won all ten races he entered, absolutely blitzing the championship. It was a similar scenario in the 350cc Championship, with Hailwood riding another evolutionary 350 four, the RC173. Now producing 70hp at 14,000rpm, and capable of more than 150mph (240km/h), the RC173 was still good enough to keep Agostini's MV 3 at bay. With six wins, Hailwood took his second World Championship that year. However, there were already signs that the days of the four were numbered. Narrower and lighter, the MV 3 handled better, and despite a power deficit, was close to matching the RC173. For 1967 Hailwood would have a six.

# THE FOUR-CYLINDER 500cc RC181 (1966)

For their assault on the 1966 500cc World Championship, Honda produced the RC181. In many respects this was a conventional Honda four-cylinder racer, and a continuation of the double overhead camshaft four-valve per cylinder formula initiated back in 1960 with the 250cc RC161. Unlike the later 250s and 350s, lubrication was wet-sump, with twin oil radiators in the fairing. The six-speed 57 x 48mm four displaced 489.94cc, and with four flat-slide Keihin carburettors produced 85hp at 12,000rpm.

Honda preferred Redman to retire from racing to concentrate on running the team, but Redman had different ideas, wanting to add the 500 title to his list of six World Championships. Having been enticed by

For 1967, the 250 six received bigger pistons and a shorter stroke, but reliability suffered as Hailwood attempted to match the speed of the V4 Yamahas. *Mick Woollett*

the prospect of a competitive 500, Hailwood was unhappy with the arrangement, and ultimately Redman's decision to ride the RC181 in preference to Hailwood cost Honda the championship. Redman made a strong start, winning on the RC181's debut at Hockenheim, but Hailwood didn't ride the 500 as Redman requisitioned his machine after his own engine failed. Redman's victory prompted MV to create a larger 350 triple, the 420, for Agostini at the Dutch GP, but again Redman triumphed. Hailwood crashed out while leading, after his gearbox stuck in neutral.

After Redman retired following a crash in the Belgian GP, Hailwood was left to try to win the 500cc Championship, as well as the 250 and 350. He was cruising in the smaller classes, but was already too far behind Agostini in the 500. Hailwood also found the rear weight bias of the powerful RC181 uncomfortable, and the handling frightening. This still didn't stop Hailwood winning the Senior TT and

setting a fastest lap of 107.07mph (172.27km/h). The RC181 was also the first motorcycle to break the 150mph (240km/h) barrier, flying through the Highlander speed trap at 151.30mph (243.44km/h). He went to the final GP at Monza, needing a win to take the championship, but the RC181 broke a valve, allowing Agostini to take his first World Championship.

## THE SIX-CYLINDER 250cc RC167 (1967)

The 1966 racing season had been Hondas' most successful ever, winning the manufacturers' title in every category, but their increased involvement in Formula 1 car racing was stretching resources to the limit. For 1967, the motorcycle programme was rationalised, with only two riders (Hailwood and

Bryans) competing in three categories. All the expectations were on Hailwood, but it was too much too expect even his genius to win three classes.

Honda provided Hailwood with a new 250 six, the RC167, with a bigger bore and shorter stroke (41 x 31.5mm) and the power increased to 60hp at 18,000rpm. There was an updated chassis, and Hailwood started the year with an emphatic victory at Barcelona. Then difficulties began, his RC167 retiring after two laps at Hockenheim, while gearbox troubles in France slowed him down after comfortably leading. Hailwood then went to the TT, where he rode the RC167 to his tenth TT victory, at 103.07mph (165.84km/h), following this with a victory at Assen. At Spa, the V4 Yamahas of Bill Ivy and Read found speed and reliability to completely overwhelm Hailwood's Honda. Obviously revving the motor harder than ever, Hailwood's engine blew at the Sachsenring, he lost again at Brno, but managed to beat the Yamahas in the wet in Finland. A victory at Ulster saw Hailwood regain the points lead, but his engine failed again at Monza. Hailwood won in Canada, and Read and Hailwood went head-to-head in the final round in Japan with equal points. Neither finished, and there was some initial confusion as to who was World Champion. Hailwood was declared champion because he had five race wins to Read's four.

# THE SIX-CYLINDER 297cc RC174 (1967)

Hailwood started the year on the older 350 four, experimenting with a Colin Lyster double front disc brake at Brands Hatch in March, but for the World Championship had a 297cc six. This was a 250 six, enlarged as much as possible to 297cc (41 x 37.5mm). There were two 17mm intake and two 14.5mm exhaust valves per cylinder, and with six 24mm round-slide Keihin carburettors the power was 65hp at 17,000rpm. While this wasn't quite as much as the four-cylinder RC173, the RC174 weighed only 118kg (compared to the RC173's 144kg) and was a considerably better balanced machine. Apart from generally running the larger RC181 front brake, the RC174 was visually similar to the RC167. The RC174 was always Hailwood's favourite, and he started the season by absolutely crucifying Agostini at Hockenheim, winning by nearly a minute. Hailwood

then went to the Isle of Man, winning the Junior TT at 104.68mph (168.43km/h), with an absolute lap record of 107.73mph (173.34km/h). Whereas the 250 six was problematic, the 297 was invincible. Further victories at Assen, Sachsenring and Brno saw Hailwood clinch the World Championship with three rounds to go.

Below: Chief mechanic Aika and Hailwood discuss the RC174 at its European debut at Hockenheim in 1967. Hailwood won the race. *Mick Woollett*

Hailwood at the start of the 1967 Senior TT. Widely regarded as the greatest ever, he went on to win, setting a lap record that would last nine years. *Mick Woollett*

## THE FOUR-CYLINDER 500cc RC181 (1967)

Hailwood had an updated RC181 for 1967, the engine bored slightly to 57.56mm to displace 499cc. The power was still quoted at 85hp, but Honda admitted they had managed 93hp on occasion. The power output was rather academic, as it was more than enough for the chassis. After initially agreeing for Hailwood to test an alternative Lyster-built frame for the RC181, Honda insisted on a factory frame for the GPs. By the opening round at Hockenheim he had the third new frame, but it was the motor that failed. The crankshaft broke while he was well ahead of Agostini.

The next 500 GP was the Isle of Man, widely claimed as the best TT race ever. Agostini and Hailwood battled only seconds apart, Hailwood struggling with a loose twistgrip, until Agostini's chain broke. Hailwood then won in record time, setting a lap of 108.77mph (175.01km/h) that would last for nine years.

Hailwood then won the 500 GP at Assen, but MV produced a larger triple (489cc) at Spa, leaving the RC181 in its wake. It was then Honda's turn to respond, and for the East German GP the RC181 had a lighter engine, with magnesium crankcases, a new frame, and a lighter front fork with alloy sliders. Despite these updates, the gearbox failed and Agostini won again. Honda's mechanics worked frantically over the next week, improving the RC181 so that Hailwood won at Brno. Although Hailwood crashed at Imatra, a win at Ulster kept his championship hopes alive. This was dashed when the gearbox failed at Monza, again while Hailwood was in a commanding lead. Hailwood won the final race in Canada, but with an equal number of wins, Agostini took the title because he had three second places to Hailwood's two. Hailwood had come extremely close to winning all three World Championships, and if his RC181 had been more reliable would probably have done so.

There were rumours that Honda planned some outrageously exotic machines for 1968, such as a three-cylinder 50, and a 125cc six. However, the change in FIM regulations limiting the number of cylinders and stipulating six-speed gearboxes prompted Honda to withdraw from GP racing altogether. Hailwood and

Below: Development of the RC181 throughout the 1967 season saw Hailwood still in contention for the 500cc World Championship, and at Ulster he won easily. *Mick Woollett*

Bottom: Although forbidden to ride the RC181 in the World Championship during 1968, Hailwood rode at some Italian events. Here, he is heading for victory at Cesenatico in April, on the RC181 with a Reynolds frame. *Mick Woollett*

Bryans were summoned to Japan in February 1968, and both were provided with machines, along with mechanic Nobby Clark, to race in non-championship meetings. Hailwood had already raced with an alternative Italian frame and Ceriani fork, winning at Rimini during 1967. For 1968 he tried a Ken Sprayson Reynolds frame, and Rickman fork with Lockheed front disc brake, and was reasonably successful in Italian and British events. Bryans also campaigned the 125-five during 1968, and provided the 250-four with one last victory, at the 1970 North-West 200 in Northern Ireland. He borrowed the eight-year-old RC163 from Luigi Taveri and won at 101.95mph (164.04km/h).

Honda's retirement coincided with the end of one of the golden eras of Grand Prix racing. In the space of nine years Honda had changed motorcycle racing, and emerged as the world leader in motorcycle technology. They had sold millions of motorcycles and were a household name. But they still hadn't added the 500cc rider's World Championship to their collection, and Honda would return. In the meantime, their emphasis was on expanding the production range, with another milestone motorcycle, the CB750 four.

The CB750 was dominated by
the single overhead camshaft
four-cylinder motor. *Greg Leech*

# 3 A NEW ORDER:

## THE AIR-COOLED FOUR-CYLINDER

Four cylinders have always been a magical configuration in motorcycling. The Henderson and Indian fours were exotic and expensive, while fours were invincible in Grand Prix's premier 500cc class. But by the mid-1960s, a four remained a dream for most people. The Ariel square-four finished by 1958, and the only production motorcycles with four cylinder engines were the hugely expensive, and virtually unobtainable. These were the enormous Munch Mammoth, and the hideously ugly 600cc MV Agusta. With the release of the CB750 everything changed. The CB750 provided performance, refinement, civility, and reliability previously unheard of in a mass-produced machine. While the C100 successfully changed the public perception of motorcycling, the CB750 created a new motorcycle order. Affordable and effective, the CB750 effectively killed the British motorcycle industry. It eventually forced other Japanese manufacturers to abandon two-strokes, twins, and triples. Later CB750 fours were more refined, but none matched the impact of the original, seminal, CB750.

## THE CB750 (1969–78)

The beginnings of the CB750 go back to early 1968. Honda was about to withdraw from Grand Prix racing, and with their flagship CB450 struggling in the marketplace, Soichiro Honda had an idea to produce a 'King of Motorcycles'. Speculation at the time expected the new engine to be based on the existing twin-cylinder N360 car, but a trip to Japan in February 1968 by Bob Hansen and some managers from American Honda changed this. Hansen (Eastern Region Manager and team manager of the CR450s at Daytona in 1967) mentioned to Soichiro Honda that they should develop a four-cylinder machine. Hansen's recommendation forced Honda to reassess the project, and over the next six months the head of R&D, Yoshiro Harada, and stylist Einosuke Miyachi produced a prototype CB750. The first public showing was at the Tokyo Show in October 1968, and by June 1969 the first examples were available in the USA.

The CB750 four-cylinder engine incorporated many departures from usual Honda practice. Undersquare dimensions (61 x 63mm) were chosen to minimise engine width, and the crankshaft was a forged one-piece

Below: Powerful, reliable and
easy to live with, the CB750,
released in 1969, changed
motorcycling for ever. *Honda*

type with five plain main bearings and relatively small (36mm) journals. Unlike the CB250/350 twins the primary drive was by dual endless chains driven from the centre of the crank, to a multiplate clutch and indirect five-speed gearbox. Gone were the CB450 double overhead camshafts and torsion bar valve springs, with a single overhead camshaft driven by a single-row chain in the centre of the motor, and normal coil valve springs. The one-piece cylinder head featured two valves per cylinder (32mm intake and 28mm exhaust), with an included valve angle of 60°. Honda's usual cast-iron combustion chamber skulls were absent, and like the cylinder head, the cylinder block was a single casting, with removable liners. The four cast-alloy pistons provided a compression ratio of 9:1, and carburetion was by four 28mm round-slide Keihin carburettors with four individual cables. Another departure from the Honda norm was an automotive type high-pressure twin-rotor trochoidal oil pump mounted under the gearbox mainshaft, with dry sump lubrication and a frame-mounted oil tank. Ignition was by points and coil, with two sets of points positioned on the right end of the crankshaft, while an automotive-style three-phase 210-watt alternator sat on the other end. The 12-volt system included a contact point type regulator while an electric start motor behind the left cylinders completed the electrical specification, ensuring a new generation of riders was able to experience 750cc motorcycling. No longer was there a natural selection of riders due to their ability to kick-start the motorcycle, and the electrical system was so reliable that the CB750 could be ridden across country without fear of failure. The power output of the 736cc four was a moderate 67hp at 8,000rpm, but this was still more than the 58hp of the rival BSA and Triumph triple.

The heavy (78kg) four-cylinder motor was the focal point of the CB750, and as was usual for Japanese motorcycles of this period, the chassis wasn't as impressive. The 218kg dry weight and reasonable power taxed the double cradle mild steel frame and Showa suspension if ridden to the limit. The front fork featured alloy legs and rubber gaiters, but the 35mm fork tubes were weak, and the steering head bearings were still the ball type. The swingarm was a two-piece welded stamping rather than the usual tubular steel, and the rear shock absorbers may have been of a De Carbon type, but their only adjustment was a three-way spring pre-load. They looked better than they worked though, being fully chrome-plated with upper spring covers. The 19-inch front and 18-inch rear wheels were normal for large capacity motorcycles of the period, but the Japanese-made 3.25 x 19 and 4.00 x 18-inch Dunlop or Bridgestone tyres were particularly unsatisfactory.

The most interesting chassis component was undoubtedly the front brake, claimed to be the world's first hydraulic disc brake on a production motorcycle. Although the pre-production CB750 included a CB450 double leading shoe drum brake, the earliest show examples had a disc. In the interest of maintaining a clean look, Honda fitted a 300mm stainless-steel front disc instead of the superior, but rusting cast-iron type. They also installed a finned Tokico single floating piston caliper, again inferior to the twin opposed piston type, and one that unfortunately required periodic adjustment. The underlying impression of the chassis design was one where function was secondary to form, and in this respect the CB750 still left something to be desired.

Where the CB750 really scored was in its looks and finish. From the distinctive four chrome-plated mufflers to the rather brutish 16-litre fuel tank, the CB750 was imposing, and one of the more attractive Japanese offerings. It may have been heavy, long, high and wide, but the CB750 was the perfect motorcycle for America where razor-sharp handling was considered less important than reliability and load-carrying capacity.

The earliest production models included a number of differences to later examples, and like the CB72/77 there were some initial problems. Many of these were quite serious, and in the first year Honda released 100 pages of technical and bulletin updates. The newly formed Four Owners Club in America even wrote to Congress and the Governor of California (then Ronald Reagan) complaining of the problem. There were continual

Even after five years in production, the CB750 was Honda's best-selling model in America so the 1975 K5 version, seen here, was little changed. *Author*

modifications, and amongst the most noticeable were updated crankcases. Until number 1007414 the engine cases were roughly finished die-cast, which looked sand cast. This was because Honda didn't anticipate demand to be so strong and were not fully geared for full-scale mass production. Many early crankcases were also smashed when the drive chain broke, and the five-cable throttle set-up could lead to the throttle sticking open. A large number of early CB750s were produced (53,399), and despite their problems have become the most sought after of the genre.

After a small number of interim CB750K0 models, with linkage carburettors, the considerably revised CB750K1 replaced the CB750 in September 1970. There were further improvements to the engine sprocket and chain lubrication, and the carburettors included a dual cable push-pull throttle set-up. Cosmetic updates saw smaller side covers (without slots), and a different seat, and the air cleaner box was now only available in black, and not colour matched as before. The range of colours was expanded and production increased to 77,000 before it was replaced

by the CB750K2 in March 1972. It took a seasoned expert to tell the difference between the CB750K1 and K2, but visually there were chrome-plated headlight brackets and a new instrument panel with four warning lights, borrowed from the CB500. A quieter exhaust system was undoubtedly responsible for a drop in performance, but Honda was on a roll, and production still totalled 63,500.

Although not released in the UK, the 1973 CB750K3 received new fuel tank stripes and a number of engine modifications to reduce oil consumption and noise. The performance was further diminished, but the suspension was redesigned (with conventional five-way adjustable rear shock absorbers), and a small mudguard was fitted to the front brake disc. There were only small updates to the 1974 CB750K4, and apart from colours it was visually similar to the K3. By now the Kawasaki 903cc Z1 had usurped the CB750 as the supreme production roadster, but this still didn't stop Honda selling 60,000 CB750K4s to become the top-selling motorcycle in the USA in 1974. All along it received little updates, and while not the fastest

Superbike, the myriad of refinements and attention to detail ensured its popularity. For 1975, the CB750K5 was little changed, but was usurped by the GL1000 Gold Wing as the range leader.

By late 1974, the CB750 was six years old, and Honda figured it needed an update to ensure continued sales. They responded with the more sporting CB750F, initially primarily for America, but the CB750F was a confused model. The exhaust system was a four-into-one, and the engine included a new cylinder head, higher compression (9.2:1) pistons, and new camshafts. The primary drive ratio was higher, and new fourth and fifth gears provided a closer ratio gearbox. The frame

## HOW THE PRESS FOUND THE CB750

As the CB750 was primarily intended for the US market, the press there received test machines as soon as they were available. And they were unanimous in their praise, *Cycle World* in August 1969 describing the CB750 as the finest production road machine available. Rival magazine *Cycle* expressed the CB750 as something that 'handles like a road racer, is comfortable, and has fantastic brakes.' These magazines backed up their opinions with comprehensive performance data, with *Cycle World* achieving a standing quarter mile in 13.38 seconds at 100.11mph (161.08km/h). This was an impressive figure in 1969.

The CB750 was slower to arrive in Britain, and the first comprehensive test was in *Motor Cycle* in April 1970. They achieved a top speed of 121mph (194.69km/h). As the CB750 was updated, the power dwindled, despite power and speed claims remaining unchanged. When *Motor Cycle* tested a CB750K2 in October 1974 the mean top speed was only 114.57mph (184.34km/h).

Refinement was the term most testers used to describe the CB750K3, with *Cycle* impressed by the short neoprene sleeve added to the carburettor return spring to stop the two float bowl vent hoses chaffing. They still found the ride and handling inferior to the CB500 four. *Cycle* found the CB750F to be the best handling Japanese Superbike, although they were not impressed with the right-side cornering clearance. With the CB750F1, Honda restored the performance of the earlier models, and *Motor Cycle* achieved a mean top speed of 122.34mph (196.85km/h). Their CB750F2 was the fastest of all, managing a mean 124.65mph (200.56km/h). By 1977 *Bike* magazine was still impressed with the CB750K7, saying: 'The CB750 hasn't really, aged, it's simply matured.'

featured revised steering geometry and a longer wheelbase, and a rather unnecessary rear disc brake. Not only larger than the front (300mm), this was more powerful than the front as it featured a dual opposed piston brake caliper. Along with strange styling, updates included a recessed fuel cap and combined ignition and fork lock, the weight was somehow more than the CB750K5, at 227kg. Although the engine performance was increased, the high handlebars and strange styling did little to provide a sporting image, and sales were slow in America. Not long after the release of the CB750F in the USA, the virtually identical CB750F1 became available in other parts of the world, as a 1976 model. While it was initially intended to replace the CB750K-series with the F-series, customer feedback saw the return of the CB750 with the K6 in 1976. This was also mainly a European model, and while it retained the K5 motor, updates included a stronger, F1-type swingarm (although it was shorter).

The 1976 Model Year also saw the CB750 evolve into the ill-fated CB750A automatic (Hondamatic). This was another case of market misjudgement, but the CB750A included many unique features. The engine was detuned, with a lower compression ratio (8.6:1), softer camshaft, and 24mm carburettors, while the lubrication was wet sump, with a corresponding increase in oil capacity. This provided the space for a larger, 20Ah, battery. The alternator was uprated to 290 watts, and with a four-into-one exhaust system, the power was 47hp at 7,500rpm. There was a Hy-Vo chain primary drive and this went straight to a torque-converter, the same as fitted to the N600 car. The transmission was two-speed, with manual selection of low and high gears. The foot lever operated a hydraulic valve, which directed pressure to the appropriate clutch. It worked reasonably efficiently, but the acceleration was unremarkable for a 750. In order to justify the high price ($2,194 when released in the USA), Honda equipped the CB750A with many high-quality features, including the DID aluminium wheel rims from the early Gold Wing. The rear wheel was also a 17-inch. While designed to appeal to inexperienced riders, most found the size, and hefty 262kg, intimidating.

The CB750 soldiered on into 1977, facing increasing competition from the new double overhead camshaft Suzuki and Kawasaki. Slow acceptance of the CB750F1 saw the considerably updated CB750F2 introduced, and at the same time, the CB750K7 was significantly

The sporting CB750F was introduced in 1975, but didn't prove as popular as the standard CB750. *Mick Woollett*

revised. The sluggish CB750A was largely unchanged, but for a four-into-two exhaust system. With the CB750F2 the venerable overhead camshaft four finally moved into the late 1970s, the black-painted engine tweaked to produce 73hp at 9,300rpm. Along with larger ports, and 34mm and 31mm valves, there were revised valve angles and a hotter camshaft. While the compression ratio dropped back to 9:1, all the engine internals were beefed up (including RCB-type con-rods), and the Keihin carburettors included an accelerator pump. Still with the four-into-one exhaust, the result was a more frenetic engine that was less pleasant to live with. The rest of the CB750F2 was another triumph of styling over function. With its black accentuation and dubious Comstar wheels (with steel spokes riveted to alloy rims), it was only the slightly improved suspension and dual 275mm front discs (with new Nissin calipers) that redeemed it. The CB750F lasted one more year, only in America, as the virtually unchanged 1978 CB750F3. This year too the CB750A Hondamatic received the Comstar wheels, but in both

these guises the CB750 was now past its use by date.

More successful were the final versions of the K-series, the CB750K7 and K8. These were deliberately distanced from the performance CB750F, the K7 receiving many of the CB750F engine updates, along with the higher 9.2:1 compression ratio. The styling was updated, with the larger (19-litre) fuel tank of the CB750A, new seat, and a neater looking exhaust system. The rear wheel was also 17-inch like the Automatic, but with steel rims. Despite being in the twilight of its life, Honda continued to update the K7, and there were a considerable number of engine and gearbox modifications during its production run. As an all-purpose touring motorcycle the CB750K7 had nothing to prove and provided an exceptional balance between looks, comfort and function. America received a slightly revised CB750K8 for 1978, with a two-tiered contoured seat and a few more engine updates. The rest of the world soldiered on with stock of the earlier excellent K7, but the four-valve double overhead camshaft era was about to begin.

Below: Veteran racer Dick
Mann rode a special CB750R
to victory in the 1970
Daytona 200-mile race. *Mick
Woollett*

# RACING THE CB750

Almost as soon as it was released the CB750 was raced, and considering it was a production road motorcycle, it achieved some surprising racing results. At Suzuka, in Japan in August 1969, Sumiya and Hishiki won a ten-hour endurance race for production machines, and Honda then asked British racers Tommy Robb and Bill Smith to race at the revived Bol d'Or at Montlhéry in September. Robb and Smith were not permitted to race under the French regulations, and young local riders Michel Rougerie and Daniel Urdich provided the CB750 with an astonishing victory. Averaging 72mph (116km/h) over 24 hours on the factory-prepared 72hp racer, they provided the CB750 with such a sales boost in France and Germany that Honda now looked seriously at the Daytona 200 the following March.

Daytona was the most important race in America, and Honda produced very special CB750Rs (also known as the CR750) to take on the Triumphs, BSAs, two-stroke Suzukis and Yamahas. The engine included magnesium crankcases and carburettors, and the usual high-performance camshafts, higher compression pistons, larger valves, and close-ratio gearbox. The frame was a lighter chrome molybdenum type, with a lower steering head, and the 155kg machines bristled with light-weight titanium and magnesium. As Honda decided to coordinate the race effort through Honda Britain, the four machines were flown to the UK in January 1970 for testing at Oulton Park. After choosing Smith, Robb, Ralph Bryans and Steve Murray to ride at Daytona, team manager Yoshio Nakamura decided it would be politic to include an American rider. Bob Hansen was asked to recruit a rider, selecting past champion Dick Mann, who at 36 years old, was considered by many past his prime. The four CB750Rs had power ranging from 90.2hp to 96.2hp, and Mann was given the least powerful.

In practice, Bryans was timed at 164mph (264km/h), but he crashed and his machine burst into flames, the burning magnesium providing a spectacular display. Mann qualified fourth, but already there were signs of cam chain tensioner failure. With a new cam chain, he fronted the start line, and in a race of attrition both the other Hondas retired with cam chain failures. Mann went on to win, his machine getting rougher as the cam chain stretched. Eventually, he gave Honda a historic victory, winning by ten seconds over Gene Romero's Triumph, and setting a new race record of 102.69 mph (165.23km/h). The CB750 had truly arrived, and Honda made the most of this victory in their advertising.

Although Honda subsequently offered a limited number of racing kits, a rumoured five kits at $10,000, after Daytona they abdicated from racing in the USA. At Daytona in 1971 and 1972,

Gary Fisher was the most prominent Honda rider. On a Yoshimura machine, Fisher led the race both years, prompting a factory return in 1973. Bryan Hindle and Clive Knight won the Australian Six-Hour production race in 1972, and 1972 saw the creation of Formula 750 for production-based racers. Honda provided machines for Smith and John Williams for the Imola 200, but they weren't very successful, finishing seventh and 12th. Smith did win the 750 race at that year's Southern 100, nicknaming the machine *Smoking Bertha* because it burnt so much oil.

At Daytona in 1973, the factory team was again managed by Nakamura, with three bikes ridden by Morio Sumiya, Steve McLaughlin and Roger Reiman. Now with a four-into-one exhaust, the 100hp CB750 racers were overwhelmed by the TZ350 Yamahas, and the best finish was Sumiya's sixth. In European endurance racing the CB750 provided the mainstay of the grids in the early 1970s. Most significant were the Japauto Hondas, featuring 950cc motors and aftermarket frames, a Dresda in 1972, and a PEM in 1973. Georges Godier and Alain Genoud won the 1972 European Endurance Championship, but after 1973, the Kawasaki Z1 became the favoured endurance racing engine. This prompted the creation of the superb RCB750 endurance racer for 1976. A modified CB750F2 (810cc) in a 1976 RCB chassis provided Phil Read with a contentious victory in the first TT F1 at the Isle of Man, the same machine later winning the F1 race at Silverstone in the hands of Ron Haslam. For the 1978 TT F1 race Read had a 969cc version, producing around 95hp, but retired when an oil cooler unit split.

Below: Although based on the production CB750, the CB750R was a full factory racer that was bristling with special components. *Mick Woollett*

Bottom left: Honda returned to Daytona in 1973 with factory 750s. These machines had different cylinder heads and engine covers. *Mick Woollett*

Bottom right: Moriro Sumiya finished in sixth place on this factory CB750 in the 1973 Daytona 200. *Mick Woollett*

Below: The CB500 was a new design, with vertical cylinders and a higher specific output. *Honda*

The first CB750 was a visceral motorcycle that gradually became sanitised over its lifespan. Although the later examples were improved in nearly every respect, something was lost in the evolution. So influential was the CB750 that the transverse-mounted in-line four-cylinder has become a template for the large-capacity motorcycle. More importantly, the CB750's function was so superior to earlier motorcycles that it revolutionised the industry. Production may have numbered more than half a million over nine years, but the CB750 is the classic motorcycle of its era.

# THE CB500, CB550 AND CB650 (1971–82)

The incredible success of the CB750 led to the release of a range of smaller four-cylinder machines, headed by the CB500 in 1971. If the CB750 four was Honda's entry into the world of Superbikes, the CB500 four of 1971 was their way of saying 'we can do anything'. Almost ostentatious in its complexity, when most other 500s at the time were two-strokes, the arrival of the CB500 redefined this once-popular displacement category. Not only was the CB500 a technological tour de force, it was one of best balanced motorcycles available.

Although seen as a scaled-down 750, the CB500 motor was a new design, 11kg lighter, and arguably superior. Unlike the CB750, the motor was wet sump, with vertical cylinders and oversquare dimensions of 56 x 50.6mm, and a Hy-Vo chain primary drive. Carburetion was handled by four slide-type 22mm Keihins, and with the usual chain-driven single

overhead camshaft and with two valves per cylinder, the CB500 delivered an impressive 50hp at 9,000rpm. At the time, 100hp per litre was a magical mark and the CB500 four set a new benchmark for production four-strokes. Supremely smooth, the only downside of this high power output was a noticeable lack of torque at lower engine speeds, and judicious use of the five-speed gearbox was required to maintain rapid progress.

With a scaled-down version of the CB750 frame, and with a swingarm the same length, the CB500's handling was superior. Despite weighing a considerable 185kg, the 500 could corner like the best British bikes of the day. A single, front 267mm disc brake ensured adequate stopping, but the most appealing feature of the CB500 was its compactness, especially compared with the large CB750. There were only a few updates to the CB500 over the next couple of years. The transmission ratios were revised for the 1973 CB500K2, but more significant developments occurred with the CB550 for 1974 when 58.5mm pistons provided 544cc and there was a higher primary drive ratio, with a redesigned shifting mechanism. New carburettors provided improved fuel consumption, but otherwise the CB550 was similar to the CB500. It was still a well-balanced, good handling machine, *Cycle World* describing the handling as 'positively inspired for a 458-pound pleasure cushion aimed at a conservative clientele.' While the CB550 replaced the CB500 in America, in Europe, the CB500 remained available, sharing the cosmetic updates of the large US-spec version.

For 1975, the café racer CB550F Super Sport appeared. With a four-into-one exhaust system this didn't capture the market the way the standard machine did. While it looked a high-performance machine, the Super Sport was an honest, but boring motorcycle. The CB550F finished in 1977, and the CB550K this year received new mufflers and a smaller fuel tank. The final year for the CB550K (and European CB500) was 1978, and with the release of the CX500 twin, the four grew to 627cc with the CB650 for 1979. With a bore and stroke of 59.8 x 55.8mm, the CB650 was the final single overhead camshaft two-valve four. Carburetion was by four 26mm Keihins, and the cam chain was now a Hy-Vo. There was electronic ignition and a four-into-two exhaust system, and the power went up to 63hp. The USA received a different version to Europe, the chunky styling including reverse-spoke black accentuated

In 1974, the CB500 grew to 550cc, and were well-balanced motorcycles, continuing until 1978 with few changes. This is the 1976 version. *Author*

Comstar wheels, the rear a 17-inch. The weight climbed to 195kg but the CB650 was the fastest middleweight of its day, *Cycle* magazine punting it through the standing quarter mile in 12.993 seconds at 102.38mph (164.73km/h). Wire-spoked wheels replaced the Comstars for 1980 and there was a twin piston front brake caliper for 1982, but otherwise the CB650 was little changed. From 1980–81 there was also a CB650C Custom, with four mufflers and Comstar wheels, the rear a 16-inch. It was an inauspicious way for the venerable single overhead camshaft motor to bow out.

# THE CB350F AND CB400F

When Honda released the CB350F in 1972 most people asked why? Easily the heaviest, most complex, and most expensive machine in its class it offered no more than the best-selling CB350K. But the CB350K was another corporate statement by Honda continuing

where the CB500 left off. The single overhead camshaft four-cylinder motor was similar in layout to the CB500, but with 47 x 50mm dimensions to displace 347cc. With a 9.3:1 compression ratio, four 20mm Keihin carburettors and a four-muffler exhaust the five-speed CB350F produced a very moderate 32hp. Smooth and sophisticated, the little engine had to work hard to power the 170kg CB350F. Excruciatingly slow, it became the CB350F1 for 1974. It was never sold in the UK, but didn't gain any market acceptance anywhere else.

For 1975, Honda replaced the CB350F1 with the CB400F Super Sport, one of the most charismatic of all Honda motorcycles. The four-cylinder motor was enlarged to 408cc (399cc for Japan), with 51mm pistons, and a new cylinder head included larger valves. The compression ratio went up to 9.4:1 and updated crankcases contained a six-speed gearbox. The power went up to 37hp at 8,500rpm; still not enough to make it competitive with the sporting 350 two-strokes, but enough to provide lively performance.

While the motor was improved over the sluggish

Below: Russ Collins's triple CB750-engined dragster was the quickest motorcycle in the world in 1975. *Mick Woollett*

Bottom: After the destruction of the 12-cylinder drag bike, Collins built this supercharged twin CB750-engined dragster. *Mick Woollett*

# DRAG RACING THE CB750

The strength of the CB750 motor encouraged Californian Russ Collins to build a triple-engined drag bike in 1973. This was a 386kg, 3,288cc 12-cylinder fuel injected top fuel dragster which produced around 500hp. Although plagued by driveline breakages, at Ontario Raceway in California in 1975 Collins's Honda was the first motorcycle to break the eight-second barrier for the quarter mile, with a 7.861-second run at 178.92mph (287.88km/h). The triple was reduced to rubble following a spectacular 170mph (273km/h) cartwheel crash at Akron, Ohio in June 1976, but a battered Collins emerged for 1977 with a twin-engined, supercharged, fuel-injected CB750-based dragster. Nicknamed the *Sorceror*, this managed a record 7.55-second pass, at 199.55mph (321.08km/h).

The centrepiece of the CB350 was the beautiful four-cylinder 347cc overhead camshaft engine. *Mick Woollett*

Overweight, and underpowered, the CB350 wasn't a recipe for success. *Two Wheels*

CB350F, the style of the CB400F was quite radical for a Japanese motorcycle. With a low flat handlebar and rear set footpegs, the riding position was semi-sporting. The tasteful, clean and understated styling, subdued paint, studded seat and distinctive four-into-one exhaust accentuated the café racer style. The skinny front fork was no longer the fully enclosed type, but the general chassis specifications were unremarkable. With 18-inch wheels and a single 260mm front disc, the 170kg CB400F handled surprisingly well. The press loved it. 'The CB400F is a marvel: it handles remarkably well, stops with authority, snaps through the gears precisely, and motors along smartly. Even a card-carrying Anglophile would have to agree that the CB400F has real character,' said *Cycle* magazine.

A bright red CB400F, bought new in 1976, was the author's first Honda, and while it impressed with smoothness to 10,000rpm, the rear shock absorbers were found wanting. But the short, 1,372mm wheelbase and quick steering provided exceptional agility on tight roads. Ground clearance was a problem on the right, but the CB400F was fun to ride. Thoughtful touches abounded on the CB400F. There was a guard on the brake lever to prevent the rider's foot being sandwiched between the engine and the lever, and there were Heim joint connectors on the gearshift linkage. Two-up riding was discouraged because the passenger footpegs were mounted on the swingarm, and there was considerable drive line lash. While generally very reliable, the cam chain tensioner design could have been better.

Apart from black side covers there were few changes for 1976, but the café-styled CB400F didn't sell too well in America. In an effort to redress declining sales there, the CB400F was updated for 1977 with higher handlebars and forward-mounted footpegs. There were new colours and a flip-up cover for the fuel filler. Apparently, some 1975 models' caps popped open in crashes and Honda wanted to avoid any liability. European CB400Fs continued much as before, with new colours of maroon or yellow and the passenger footpegs mounted on a subframe. The CB400F only sold well in England, Germany and France, and it was rumoured that Honda lost more than they made on the little four because it cost as much to build as a CB750. During 1978, the CB400F was replaced by the twin-cylinder CB400T, and while this unremarkable model has faded into oblivion, the CB400F hasn't been forgotten. Over 16,000 were sold in Britain and 39,760

Few Japanese motorcycles have stood the test of time as well as the first CB400F. Stylish and functional, they were characterised by the subtle styling. *Mick Woollett*

in the USA. The CB400F was the first Japanese factory café racer. It may not be rare, but it is a motorcycle worthy of 'classic' status.

## DOUBLE OVERHEAD CAMSHAFTS AND FOUR-VALVES

Double overhead camshafts and four-valve cylinder heads were features that provided Honda with World Championships during the 1960s, but it wasn't until 1979 that these made their way to a new range of street bikes. At the top of the line-up was the incredible six-cylinder CBX (covered in Chapter 4), and new double overhead camshaft four-cylinder 750s and 900s replaced the single overhead camshaft CB750. While America received the sporting CB750F, for Europe and

elsewhere there was the CB900F. Additionally there was the touring CB750K.

## THE CB750, CB900 AND CB1100 (1979–83)

By 1979, the RCB Endurance racers had proved their dominance and to capitalise on this success Honda released a new range of 750cc and 900cc fours. The CB900FZ was also titled the Bol d'Or, but there was very little in common between the CB750-based RCB and the new engines. They represented a change in direction from the previous evolutionary theme. In addition to double overhead camshafts and four valves per cylinder, the primary drive was by Hy-Vo chain to a jackshaft that included the clutch and spring-loaded damper. The alternator was on the right end of the five-bearing forged crankshaft, with electronic ignition on

There were new colours, higher handlebars and revised passenger footpegs for the final CB400F, but the essential character remained. *Author*

Right: The CB750KZ, with a double overhead camshaft 16-valve engine, replaced the venerable classic CB750 for 1979. While efficient motorcycles, they lacked the charisma of the original four. *Mick Woollett*

the left. There were two cam chains, with a Hy-Vo chain connecting the crank with the exhaust camshaft, and a shorter chain driving the intake camshaft from the exhaust. Valve clearance adjustment was shim on top of the cam follower. The cylinder head design was similar to the CBX1000, with a relatively wide 63° included valve angle. Valve sizes were 25mm inlet and 22mm exhaust for the 750, with 26mm and 22.5mm for the 900. The CB750F and K had square dimensions (62 x 62mm), and with a bank of 30mm Keihin CV carburettors produced 79hp (77hp for the K) at 9,000rpm. The F included a four-into-two exhaust system, while the K retained four mufflers. The 902cc CB900FZ (64.5 x 69mm) featured a lower compression ratio (8.8:1), four 32mm Keihin CV carburettors, and an oil cooler fitted to the front frame downtubes. The output was 95hp at 9,000rpm.

There was also little exceptional about the chassis, the double-cradle steel frame including removable right-side frame rails, but with more gusseting around the steering head than earlier 750s. The F models also featured frames built of thicker tubing, but all included

nylon swingarm bushes. The front fork had only 35mm tubes, the rear shocks were adjustable FVQ (on the CB900FZ), there were twin 280mm front discs, and the wheels 19 and 18-inch aluminium Comstars. The US CB750K included wire-spoked wheels (19 and 17-inch), a single front disc, and drum rear brake. There was also a CB750K Limited Edition to celebrate the tenth anniversary of the CB750, with different paint, and black Comstar wheels. While not especially light, the CB900FZ weighed 233kg and the CB750K 236kg, the performance of the new fours was impressive. *Motor Cycle* achieved a top speed of 128.4mph (206.6km/h) for the CB900FZ, and 127.64mph (205.37km/h) for the CB750KZ, and they received a very favourable press reaction, *Bike* magazine stating the CB900FZ 'did most things excellently.' If there was any flaw in the character of the CB750F, KZ and CB900FZ it was that they were a little bland. Without the individual personality of their predecessor, these were almost the perfect 'Universal Japanese Motorcycle', a description coined by *Cycle* magazine in 1976 for the ubiquitous Japanese across-the-frame-

four. Although blighted by the perennial Honda cam chain problem, these were steady, undistinguished motorcycles that improved gradually every year.

Updates for 1980 saw welcome needle roller swingarm bearings, an air-assisted front fork, and two Custom models, the CB750C and CB900C. Along with a stepped seat and highlighted Comstar wheels, the CB900C took the European CB900FA engine, added a driveshaft and two-speed secondary transmission, and resulted in a long and heavy (255kg) touring motorcycle. For 1981, a CB750FA became available alongside the CB900FB in Europe, both sharing larger diameter forks (37mm), and dual-piston calipers (from the CB1100R). Other updates on the CB900FB (there were 31 differences) included a welcome stronger cam chain tensioner, and different valves. The CB900F was also sold in the USA this year, differing from European examples with its rubber-mounted engine, air-assisted 39mm fork, strengthened frame and a wider rear Comstar wheel. Outside America there was also the CB900F2B, with a 16-piece ABS three-quarter fairing and leg shields. This also housed a clock and voltmeter.

Evolutionary development resulted in the European-spec CB900FC and F2C (with a fairing) for 1982. Included was the rubber-mounted motor from the US CB900F, while the 39mm front fork with TRAC (torque-reactive-anti-dive) and 18-inch 'Boomerang' style Comstar wheels came from the CB1100RC. Also from the 1100R were shock absorbers with piggyback reservoirs, but the weight went up to 242kg for the CB900FC, and a massive 253kg for the CB900F2C. The final CB900 was the FD of 1983, with different-style wheels, a black-painted engine, a grab rail, and new paintwork. Also for 1983, the engine grew to 973cc (67 x 69mm) with the CB1000C, and 1,062cc with the CB1100F.

Of all the series-production CB750-1100 fours of this era, the CB1100F was the most developed, and probably the finest. The engine came from the European CB1100R, although with slightly less compression (9.7:1), and this was rubber-mounted in the frame (unlike the 1100R). Much of the running gear (39mm fork with TRAC and piggyback shocks), came from the 1100R, but the CB1100F included new

Top left: An improved CB750FA was available in Europe from 1981, but time was running out for the 750 four and it was about to be replaced by a new V-four. *Mick Woollett*

Top right: The emphasis moved from sporting to touring in 1982, the CB900F2 including a comprehensive fairing. *Australian Motorcycle News*

Bottom: Only offered for one year, the 1983 CB1100F represented the end of the era for the large displacement air-cooled sporting inline four-cylinder. *Cycle World*

CB750SC of 1982, taking the existing CB750 engine and placing it in a new chassis. Stylistic considerations saw the Comstar wheels replaced by 18 and 16-inch cast alloy wheels, with the front fork including TRAC. The CB750SC lasted only two years, and in 1983 another new-design four-cylinder motor appeared in a range of smaller Nighthawks, specifically for the USA. Now in 650cc as well as 550cc, developments included a straight-cut gear primary drive, the generator mounted behind the cylinders, and hydraulic valve lash adjustment. The CB650SC (60 x 58mm) included four-valve combustion chambers with 23mm and 19.5mm valves set at a shallow included angle of 38°, a six-speed gearbox, and shaft final drive. There were four 32mm Keihin carburettors and the power was an impressive 75hp at 9,500rpm. With 19 and 16-inch cast wheels, and weighing a moderate 195kg, the 650 Nighthawk set new standards of performance in its class, and was

Below: Even the four-cylinder CBX400F and CBX550F were unconventional, with enclosed disc brakes. *Mick Woollett*

Bottom: Virtually identical to the CB650 Nighthawk, the CBX650E was virtually maintenance free. *Author*

One of the finest sporting motorcycles of the early 1980s was the limited-edition CB1100R. Intended primarily for production racing in Australia and South Africa, this is the 1980 CB1100RB in its Australian guise, without a fairing. *Australian Motorcycle News*

# RACER FOR THE ROAD: THE CB1100R

During 1980, Honda created the limited-production CB1100RB, specifically for production racing in Australia and South Africa, but also available in Europe. Based on the CB900FZ, the black-painted motor displaced 1,062cc (70 x 69mm), and with hotter camshafts, a 10:1 compression ratio and four 33mm Keihin CV carburettors, produced 115hp at 9,000rpm. To cope with this higher output, the primary chain was wider, and the clutch and some transmission parts stronger.

For a racing machine the CB1100RB was massive. The red-painted frame was a stronger version of the CB900FZ, without the removable lower section, and the wheels 19 and 18-inch Comstars. The CB1100RB was also the first production Honda with twin-piston brake calipers, and nitrogen-charged piggyback shock absorbers. Dry weight was a considerable 235kg, and the wheelbase a stretched-out 1,490mm. The CB1100RB came with a frame-mounted half fairing and solo seat, but fairings were outlawed under Australian production regulations and so these versions were naked. It may have been large, but the CB1100RB was the fastest motorcycle available in 1981, capable of more than 150mph (240km/h). An extremely competent chassis provided slow steering, and exceptional, European-style, stability.

A slightly revised CB1100RC was available for 1982, with wider-rimmed new-style gold Comstar wheels, an 18-inch on the front, four-way adjustable TRAC on the front 39mm fork, and vented front disc brakes. The steering head angle was altered to quicken the steering, there was a full fairing with a rectangular headlight and carbon-fibre under cowl, and a standard dual seat. The weight was also reduced slightly, to 233kg. The final CB1100R was the 1983 D, almost identical to the C but for slightly different colours and a rectangular-section steel swingarm. The claimed power was now 120hp at 9,000rpm. By 1983, the CB1100RD may have been a dinosaur, but the CB1100Rs remain some of the most appealing of all production Hondas. As there would be no more air-cooled racers, these wonderful motorcycles represented the end of an era.

virtually maintenance free. The short-lived CB550SC (1983 only) styling was more radical, and the engine was virtually identical to the 650 except for a shorter stroke of 50.6mm. Almost identical to the CB650 Nighthawk was the European CBX650E, lasting until 1987 in some markets. The domestic market also received a CBR400, with a 55 x 42mm 16-valve air-cooled 58hp four-cylinder engine. The chassis included all the state-of-the-art components expected by the fashion-conscious domestic market, including a rectangular-section alloy frame and racing Comstar wheels.

In response to the lukewarm reception and questionable reliability of the VF750F V-four, a new sporting CBX750F, based on the CBX650E, was

Below: The end of the line for
sporting air-cooled fours was the
excellent CBX750F of 1984.
*Author*

produced for Europe for 1984. The engine cases and crankshaft were more substantial than the 650, and the valves were larger (25mm and 22.5mm). Still with hydraulic valves, the 67 x 53mm four was the final high-performance air-cooled 750. There were four Keihin 34mm carburettors (with dummy velocity stacks), and it produced an impressive 91hp at 9,500rpm. The chassis included a 39mm fork with TRAC, Pro-Link rear suspension, and 16 and 18-inch Comstar wheels. Designed to tackle the new Kawasaki GPz750 and Suzuki GSX750ES, the 193kg CBX750F was arguably superior to the VF750F, and was joined by the fully faired CBX750FII in 1986. The CBX750F was available in some European countries until 1989.

Between 1984 and 1986 the predominant Nighthawk in the USA was the CB700SC, the image changing from cruiser to performance special. The motor was identical to the European CBX750F, but with a shorter stroke of 49.4mm to displace 696cc. This was to circumvent the US tariff that imposed an additional surcharge over 750cc. The six-speed CB700SC included 31mm carburettors, 25 and 22.5mm valves with hydraulic adjusters, and produced 80hp. The frame was new, including a box-section backbone, and utilising the two

front frame downtubes as oil lines to the oil cooler. There was a shaft final drive instead of the CBX750F's chain, and dual rear shock absorbers. Rolling on 16-inch cast wheels front and rear, the CBX was chunky, and very effective. Fast and easy to live with, the CB700SC Nighthawk was proof there was life left in the air-cooled four. Unfortunately, Honda thought otherwise, and it was discontinued after 1986.

The CB750 Nighthawk was resurrected for 1991, based on the chain-drive European CBX750F. There were smaller, 24mm and 20.5mm, valves, milder cams, and a quartet of 34mm CV carburettors. Now a bargain-basement motorcycle, with cost-cutting evident everywhere, the five-speed CB750 Nighthawk was *Motorcyclist* magazine's 1991 Motorcycle of the Year. This was because it provided an exceptional combination of features, power and handling, all for less than $4,000. Following a year's sabbatical, the CB750 Nighthawk reappeared for 1995, lasting through 2003 virtually unchanged before quietly disappearing. Throughout this time it remained listed for some European markets as the CB750. After nearly 35 years, the era of the air-cooled Honda four was over, but the legacy remained.

The 1975 GL1000 Gold Wing
was a groundbreaking design,
and changed the face of touring
motorcycles. *Mick Woollett*

# 4 MORE KINGS OF MOTORCYCLES

While the success of the CB750 ensured the dominance of the across-the-frame-four-cylinder with chain final drive, not all companies were committed to this layout. The early 1970s was an era of experimentation in motorcycle layouts, from the triples of Triumph, Kawasaki, Laverda, and Suzuki, to the twins of Moto Guzzi, Ducati, and BMW. Engine layouts had become corporate statements, and it was within this climate of diversity that Soichiro Honda expressed the desire for a new flagship; the largest, fastest, and finest grand touring motorcycle ever, 'The King of Motorcycles'. Even then, the notion of a large-capacity liquid-cooled flat-four shaft-drive motorcycle was a radical one

In the autumn of 1972 a group of engineers headed by Shoichiro Irimajiri began work on a project code-named the M1, with a 1,470cc horizontal six-cylinder engine. After discarding this design, a flat-four was agreed as a more practical solution. Toshio Nozue took over as project leader, and the 'King of Motorcycles' became the 'Gold Wing', after the company emblem. The Gold Wing pioneered a number of firsts for a Japanese motorcycle. It was the first with shaft-drive, the first with triple disc brakes, and the first four-stroke with water-cooling.

The new engine needed to be larger than the Kawasaki Z1, and more powerful than the Harley-Davidson FLH-1200, and the eventual size was 999cc (72 x 61.4mm). There was a single overhead camshaft on each cylinder bank, driven by toothed rubber belts. Although relatively new to motorcycles at that time, toothed belts were already widely used in cars, and the Gold Wing's were identical to those on the Honda Civic.

The cylinder head design was not unlike the CB750, with two (37mm and 32mm) valves per cylinder. The two-piece camshafts were supported in aluminium bearings, the cylinders and crankcase halves were cast together, and the forged crankshaft was supported by three plain main bearings. Primary drive was by a Hy-Vo chain, with the gearbox mainshaft parallel and underneath the crankshaft. The wet multiplate clutch and gearbox could almost have come from the CB750, including identical ratios, although few parts were interchangeable. Nozue was particularly proud of his engineering tour-de-force,

Left: For 1976, there was a Limited Edition GL1000 for America. Included were gold-anodised wheel rims. *Roy Kidney*

The final 1,000cc Gold Wing was this 1979 GL1000. *Honda*

the 300-watt alternator and counterbalance shaft, driven by a straight-cut gear behind the primary drive, rotating in an opposite direction to the crankshaft cancelling any torque reaction. This feature alone opened the Gold Wing to a whole new world of touring motorcyclists previously deterred by torque reaction as inherent in the BMW boxer.

Carburetion was by four Keihin 32mm constant vacuum carburettors, and to maintain a low centre of gravity the fuel tank was underneath the seat, between the frame tubes. A fuel pump driven from the rear of the right camshaft provided fuel pressure. The compression ratio was a mild 9.2:1, and the power from the first Gold Wing was a moderate 80hp at 7,500rpm. More than anything else, the quietness of the motor set the Gold Wing apart from other motorcycles.

There was little that was revolutionary about the Gold Wing chassis, but some features were innovative for a touring motorcycle. Instead of a conventional fuel tank, the tank was a storage compartment, containing tools and the electrical components. The brakes were by discs all round, the rear stainless-steel disc 295mm, with a dual opposed piston brake caliper. The front brakes were smaller (273mm) stainless-steel twin discs, with single floating piston brake calipers. Also reflecting the quality of the Gold Wing were the wire-spoked wheels with lightweight DID aluminium rims. These wheels were not quite strong enough for the power and weight, particularly the rear 17-inch wheel. The 4.50H 17A Bridgestone rear tyre was specially developed for the Gold Wing, but the front was a conventional 19-inch.

The front fork had larger (37mm) fork legs than the CB750, and the limp rear shock absorbers were adjustable only for spring preload. The frame was a conventional tubular steel duplex full cradle type, and the Gold Wing rewrote the rules regarding acceptable size and weight in a mainstream motorcycle. The 265kg was cleverly disguised by the flat-four engine layout that provided a low centre of gravity. The GL1000K0 was released at the Cologne Show in October 1974, but the first-year sales of only 5,000 GL1000s were well under the forecast 60,000. While testers in America applauded the Gold Wing, the British press greeted it with cynicism. Soon termed a two-wheeled car or 'Lead Wing', *Bike* magazine was particularly scathing, prompting Honda to withdraw their advertising, and refusing test bikes for a year. It

would take some time before it was fully accepted, but eventually the Gold Wing would become one of Honda's most important models, and one of the few with a cult following.

For 1976, the GL1000K1 was essentially unchanged. There was also a GL1000LTD Gold Wing Limited Edition, in candy brown, with gold accents, and for Britain, Rickman produced 52 Gold Wing Executives, one for each week of the year. Setting the Executive apart from the regular Gold Wing was a black finish, a frame-mounted fairing, and Lester cast aluminium wheels.

Detail refinements on the 1977 GL1000K2 were mainly aimed at improving comfort and reducing noise. There was a dual contoured seat and higher handlebars, but more updates occurred with the 1978 GL1000K3. To improve mid-range power the carburettors were slightly smaller (31mm), the valve timing shorter, and there was more ignition advance. The engine response was significantly improved, although the claimed power was reduced slightly to 78hp.

Chassis updates included a longer-travel front fork with revised damping, and FVQ shock absorbers. The front brakes came from the CB750F2, the wheels were Comstar, and there was a totally revised instrument layout which included an additional instrument panel built into the top of the dummy fuel tank. The dry

The release of the six-cylinder CBX in 1979 created even more controversy than the Gold Wing. *Mick Woollett*

# CBX: THE POWER AND THE GLORY

By the mid-1970s, Honda motorcycle development was in the doldrums. Preoccupied with car manufacture, apart from the Gold Wing there was nothing really new and other manufacturers were gaining ground. Honda had lost its performance image, and needed a knockout motorcycle, one that would make everyone gasp. They needed the fastest motorcycle in the world, and their response in 1978 was the six-cylinder CBX1000.

The CBX project leader was Shoichiro Irimajiri, designer of the famous racing sixes, and his influence saw the six-cylinder design prevail over a four-cylinder. The in-line six-cylinder, with double overhead camshafts and four valves per cylinder owed its genesis to the racing sixes, and took Irimajiri one and a half years to complete. Inside the one-piece cylinder head the two 25mm intake and 22mm exhaust valves were inclined at 63°. The valves were operated by twin overhead camshafts, with valve adjustment by shims sitting above buckets. Each hollow camshaft was in two halves, joined at the centre by an Oldham coupler, with a 9.5mm Hy-Vo chain driving the exhaust cam from the crankshaft. A similar chain drove the intake camshaft from the exhaust. The three-ring 64.5mm flat-topped pistons provided a very moderate 9.3:1 compression ratio, and with a 53.4mm stroke the capacity was 1,047cc. The forged crankshaft ran on plain bearings, with a 34mm Hy-Vo primary drive to a jackshaft behind the cylinders running the alternator and ignition. This helped minimise engine width, as did chamfered outer crank webs. Engine width was 594mm, only 50mm more than the CB750. The cylinders were also canted forward 33°, and the inlet manifolds for the six 28mm Keihin CV carburettors angled to the centre to allow room for the rider's knees. Ignition was by three double-ended coils with three transistorised igniters, while drive from the five-speed transmission was by a large, 630 chain. The CBX motor produced 105hp at 9,000rpm, considerably more than any other production motorcycle in 1978. The exhaust system was a six-into-two, but during its development Irimajiri was sent to record the sound of F-4 Phantom jet fighters and replicate it in the exhaust system. Although they successfully managed this, Tadashi Kume, Director of R&D, vetoed the Phantom exhaust saying: 'We cannot build motorcycles that sound like jet fighters.'

This impressive engine hung from a braced steel frame, with a slender swingarm pivoting in plastic bushes. The front fork was a spindly 35mm, and the FVQ shock absorbers faded under hard use. The braking system was also marginal, with twin 276mm front discs with floating calipers and a single 295mm rear disc. While Irimajiri went to considerable effort to reduce weight, including magnesium

engine covers, 19 and 18-inch Comstar wheels with aluminium spokes, and forged aluminium handlebars and footpegs, the dry weight of the CBX was a considerable 247kg. The styling of the CBX by Norimoto Otsuka was also one of Honda's most successful. The open cradle frame allowed the motor to dominate, and each component was carefully chosen to ornament, and exalt, the six-cylinder masterpiece. A large motorcycle, most components were unique to the CBX, and were cleverly scaled up in size to provide the impression of a smaller machine.

The CBX certainly met Honda's performance expectations, *Motor Cycle* achieving an impressive 136.53mph (219.68km/h). This was vindicated by a ride on a CBX by the author late in 1978. Despite having no fairing, the CBX was easily the fastest machine available at that time as it just left a Z1000 Kawasaki in its wake in a top-speed test on a deserted back road. Supremely smooth, the sound of the six accelerating hard through the gears is inimitable. *Cycle* magazine in America tested a pre-production CBX, this flying through the standing start quarter mile in 11.552 seconds at 117.49mph (189.04km/h). *Cycle* was criticised in some circles for testing a hand-assembled prototype, but in their customary manner they summed up with: 'The CBX is an immensely flattering bike with perfect elegance and total class, and history will rank it with those rare and precious motorcycles which will never, ever be forgotten.'

Unfortunately, the CBX landed smack in the middle of a Superbike war. It was fast enough, and powerful enough, but the power only emphasised its underlying weakness. Weight, width, and a frame and suspension that were barely adequate. Some of these handling problems were addressed for 1980, but lower lift and

Top: The failure of the CBX as a sportsbike saw it mature into a grand tourer for 1981. The front brakes included ventilated discs and twin piston calipers. *Author*

Middle: Completely dominating the CBX, the 24-valve six-cylinder motor was a wondrous piece of work. *Cycle World*

Bottom: Also included in the specification of the 1981 CBX was Pro-Link rear suspension and detachable saddlebags. *Cycle World*

shorter overlap camshafts saw the power reduced to 98hp. Chassis improvements included air assistance for the front fork (still 35mm), a 16mm (up from 14mm) swingarm pivot, now supported in a needle roller bearing on the drive side, and ball bearings opposite. The wheels were reversed Comstars, the rear width increased from 2.15in to 2.50in, and the final drive chain a smaller 530. The Showa FVQ shock absorbers were now adjustable for compression and rebound damping, but the CBX (this year assembled in Marysville, Ohio) was still heavy, and no longer as quick and as fast. The Superbike crowd continued to shun the CBX. Honda's own, cheaper, CB900F was almost as fast, and handled better, so the CBX was refocused, into a sport tourer for 1981, the CBX1000SS.

In its adaptation into a sport tourer, the CBX gained a vastly improved chassis, but lost much of the elemental appeal of the original. The six-cylinder engine was tuned for more mid-range power, with new higher lift camshafts (8.0mm on the intake and 7.5mm on the exhaust), a more horizontal mounting of the carburettors, and a revised exhaust system. The power of the black-painted motor was still an impressive 100hp at 9,000rpm, but it had a lot more weight to propel.

Chassis updates began with an increase in steering head angle (to 29.5°), and wider-spaced 39mm fork legs. At the rear was a single shock absorber Pro-Link rear suspension, based on that of the Motocross bikes but with the linkages underneath the aluminium swingarm to provide room for the battery and electrical components. The front brakes were also updated, with twin piston calipers and twin 296mm ventilated cast discs. The reversed Comstar wheels also had wider rims (2.50 x 19 and 2.75 x 18in), and completing the specification was a fairing, similar to the CB900F2, engine protection bars, a more luxurious seat, and removable saddlebags. The result was a very large motorcycle, rolling on an extreme, 1,535mm wheelbase, and weighing 250kg. It was still reasonably fast though, with the Italian magazine *Motociclismo* achieving a top speed 127mph (205km/h), but didn't offer enough to woo the touring crowd. The colours were changed to white for 1982, but the sport touring bikes were even less popular than the original, and were no longer offered for 1983.

Unlike many Japanese motorcycles, the CBX has enduring appeal. It may not have lived up to expectations, but it was the most stylish six-cylinder motorcycle ever, and the embodiment of the most aggressive marketing policy in Honda's history. Since 1980, there has been a CBX club (The International CBX Owners Association), and the CBX has become an allegory for Honda. Honda didn't need to build a six, but their corporate persona required a six for emotional, rather than engineering reasons. It may have been a sales disaster for Honda, but it has become a monument to Honda's capability.

The Gold Wing grew to 1,200cc for 1984, with the Aspencade including a factory fairing and luggage. *Cycle World*

1,182cc (75.5 x 66mm). The valve system included hydraulic lifters, while the clutch featured a diaphragm spring. With a 9.0:1 compression ratio, smaller inlet valves (36mm), new camshafts, and with a return to Keihin 32mm carburettors, the power went up to 94hp at 7,000rpm.

The chassis was modified to provide an impression of lightness and nimbleness belying the considerable weight of the fully outfitted touring GL1200. A new double-cradle steel frame placed the engine further forward, there was upgraded suspension and smaller, 16 and 15-inch wheels. These provided quicker steering response with other chassis changes seeing improved mass centralisation and better handling. The front fork was now 41mm, with TRAC on both fork legs

resulting in the GL1200 steering and handling like a much smaller bike. This was also the final year for the unfaired GL, so well-designed and functional was the factory-fitted fairing and luggage of the Interstate and Aspencade.

There were only detail updates to the Interstate and Aspencade for 1985. Touring riders never seemed totally happy with the gearing and this year saw new first and fifth gears, along with a lower secondary drive. To commemorate Honda's 25 years in America, and the Gold Wing's tenth anniversary, the GL1200L Gold Wing Limited Edition was produced. Loaded with equipment, this set a new standard for luxury motorcycling. The engine was shared with the Aspencade, but computerised fuel

Commemorating 25 years of
American Honda, the 1985 Gold
Wing Limited Edition included
electronic fuel injection. *Cycle World*

injection (CFI) replaced the bank of Keihin
carburettors. Designed to improve throttle response,
cold starting and fuel economy, the injected bikes
didn't run as well as the carburetted versions.
Accessories included electronic cruise control, trip
computer, and an on-board air compressor, with
auto-levelling rear suspension (ALRS) to compensate
for load. The Limited Edition proved so popular that
there was another series for 1986, the GL1200SE-i
when the Gold Wing motor received hydraulic valve
tappets, while revised valve timing boosted the mid-
range power.

The final year for the flat-four Gold Wing was 1987,
and there were only two models, the Interstate and
Aspencade. The Aspencade incorporated some of the

features of the earlier SE-i, including cruise control and
the driveshaft bevel gears were now helical, rather than
straight-cut. After 13 years the charismatic flat-four
Gold Wing engine ended, having earned an enviable
reputation for reliability. As time wore on, Gold Wing
development became increasingly conservative. Now
considered by many to be the last 'real' Gold Wings,
the final GL1200 represented the end of an era, but a
new age was beginning.

## SIX CYLINDERS

With the flat-four engine at the peak of its
development, Honda cautiously canvassed loyal Gold
Wing supporters regarding the direction they should

Right: Introduced in 1988, the GL1500 six-cylinder Gold Wing lasted more than a decade with only minimal updates. This 20th Anniversary model appeared in 1995. *Cycle World*

take with its replacement. They found the market demanded more power, smoothness, features and luxury, expanding the parameters of American-style touring and becoming the definitive two-wheeled luxury platform.

As Shoichiro Irimajiri was now the head of American Honda, it wasn't surprising to see the inspiration coming from the first M1 prototype of 1973. Irimajiri was the six-cylinder M1 project leader, and over a four-year developmental period, Honda built more than 60 prototypes, including 20 separate engines.

The GL1500 engine was completely new, with dimensions of 71 x 64mm providing 1,520cc. While both the flat-four and flat-six layouts provided perfect primary and secondary balance, the crankshaft layout for the six allowed for 60° crankpin spacing rather than 90°. Whereas the original GL1000 had been designed as a high-performance engine, gradually softened over the years, the GL1500 was envisaged as a touring engine from the outset. The single overhead camshaft, two-valve per cylinder layout was retained, the two camshafts still being driven by toothed rubber belts. The primary drive was now by helical gears at the rear of the crankshaft, with a counter-rotating wet multiplate clutch. The gearbox shafts were still mounted underneath the crankshaft for a lower centre of gravity. There was also an electric reverse gear operated by the starter motor for easier low-speed manoeuvrability. Helical gears drove the trademark counter-rotating alternator, and the only chain was a Hy-Vo spinning the oil pump. Another improvement was the more accessible air-cooled 546-watt alternator. The earlier oil-cooled alternator required removal of the entire engine to replace it in the event of failure, a common occurrence if overloaded with electrical accessories. The six-cylinder engine was only 63.5mm longer than the four, and weighed 118kg, up 10kg.

Following the lack of acceptance of the earlier computerised fuel injection system, the GL1500 relied on carburettors, complemented by a sophisticated and extremely complicated electronic engine management system. Two 36mm Keihin downdraft diaphragm-type carburettors bolted to a high six-tube manifold were controlled electronically. There were eight sub-systems monitoring air and engine temperature, manifold pressure, altitude, rpm, and gear position to manage the intake and ignition. Central to the induction system was a liquid-heated intake manifold with engine coolant routed through the inlet manifold to stabilise intake temperature. Computers took care of cruise control and the ignition, with two different advance curves available. With a compression ratio of 9.8:1 the power was 95hp at 5,000rpm, but the engine pulled cleanly from 700rpm until the redline.

The frame was influenced by the newer generation sports bike frames and consisted of two huge, rectangular 35 x 80mm box-section steel main load-bearing members, with a tubular steel engine cradle and rear section. The downtubes were removable to allow easier engine servicing, and the engine was rubber mounted. To improve high speed stability, the front wheel was 18-inch, with a 16-inch on the rear. The vented dual front 296mm discs bolted directly to the hub, and as on the previous Gold Wing, the braking system was unified. The rear brake pedal activated the right front and rear 316mm disc twin-piston calipers, while the handlebar lever operated only the left front disc. The front 41mm TRAC-equipped fork lacked air adjustment, while the vertically mounted rear twin shock absorber suspension only received air-assistance on the right. The inherent advantages of the horizontally opposed cylinder layout and the under-the-seat fuel tank were immediately evident with the GL1500. Despite its size and weight of 360kg, the GL1500 handled with lightness at walking pace speeds, yet could be hustled through the mountains and fast sweepers without wallowing or grinding the undercarriage excessively.

Underneath the fully enclosed ABS bodywork was possibly the most complex equipment ever seen on a motorcycle, but it didn't detract from reliability. Serviceability was the only impediment, with rear wheel removal a major operation. The GL1500 rewrote the parameters for touring motorcycles, and was hailed as the most significant touring machine since the first Gold Wing of 1975. For a first-year model the GL1500 was surprisingly trouble free. This was the last Gold Wing produced in Japan.

Now an American-built model only, after two years with minimal development, for 1990 there was a host of mechanical improvements to the GL1500, as well as a higher-specification model, the SE. There were updates to the gearbox to improve shifting, and the Pearl White SE included an improved ventilation and sound system. Celebrating ten years of Gold Wing at the Marysville plant saw three variants for 1991, all with commemorative 'Anniversary Edition' badges.

This year also saw a return of the 'stripper' Interstate, the previous GL1500 continuing as the Aspencade, while the SE remained at the top of the range. There were few changes to the Gold Wing line-up for 1992, but for 1993 the valve rocker arms now spun on needle roller bearings to reduce valve train friction and noise. Only colour changes distinguished the 1994 versions, and for the Gold Wing's 20th anniversary in 1995, the seat was lowered by 30mm. All 1995 models received distinctive anniversary badges.

Even 20 years on, the Gold Wing continued to be extremely popular. Despite being one of the most expensive machines on the market, sales of the three versions of the Gold Wing saw it become Honda's best seller, and the second best-selling motorcycle in the USA during 1995. Thus there were no changes for 1996, but for 1997, many of the upgraded engine and transmission components of the Valkyrie made it to the Gold Wing. This included higher-quality crankshaft main bearings, pistons, rings, valve springs, con-rod

Large and expensive, the Rune was an exotic limited-edition custom motorcycle that looked unlike anything else. *Honda*

# THE VALKYRIE RUNE

One of the most amazing production Honda motorcycles was the Valkyrie Rune (NRX1800). The Rune (meaning 'mystery' or 'secret' in ancient Anglo-Saxon) appeared out of four concept models overseen by American Honda motorcycle design chief Martin Manchester. From the T1 (Valkyrie hotrod), shown at the 2000 *Cycle World* Long Beach Show, T2 (retro custom), T3 (street dragster), and later T4, the T2 became the basis for the production Rune that appeared for 2004. Under Large Project Leader Masanori Aoki, the Rune was envisaged as an expensive ($24,490) limited-production piece of rolling art. Production was to be around 1,200 bikes in total, one for each Honda dealer. This limited production idea wasn't new for Honda, but their last similar effort was the NR750 of 1992.

Powered by the 1,832cc Gold Wing engine, but with six 32mm throttle bodies instead of two, the Rune incorporated a number of distinctive features. The unusual trailing link front fork, with twin upper shocks actuated by pushrods and links, was inspired by the

Zodia concept bike of 1995. The rear suspension included a single-sided swingarm and single shock absorber, the lay-down shock's upper mount contained within the swingarm rather than the chassis, in a manner similar to the RC211V MotoGP racer. The wire-spoked wheels (with optional chrome) were 18 and 17 inches, and the triple disc braking system included the combined braking system of the VTX1800. Even the chromed radiator, harking back to 1932 Fords, was designed to complement the styling. The frame was an aluminium beam type, and everything was finished to an impeccable standard. From the 1,750mm wheelbase to the 350kg dry weight, the Rune was a large-scale motorcycle. Although the ride was surprisingly good for such a big machine, the Rune's primary appeal was its appearance. Here was a custom motorcycle with the fit and finish of a quality production machine. As *Motorcycle Cruiser* said: 'Because we are always riding new and seemingly always better bikes, it's rare to come across a model that will make us envy its owners. The Valkyrie Rune is such a machine.'

with the traditional flat-six engine layout and conventional suspension. Extending the parameters for a touring motorcycle, at the time the GL1800 was the largest-capacity series-production motorcycle in the world. This was to be Honda's most important new model for 2001, and pivotal to Honda's goal in achieving its three-year plan of market dominance in each segment of the motorcycle market.

Responding to the general perception that the GL1500 was more automotive than motorcycle, the GL1800 reiterated its motorcycle emphasis. Project leader Masanori Aoki came from a sporting motorcycle background, with the two-stroke NSR250, the sporting CBR250RR and the CBR400RR to his credit. Central to the design was a new 1,832cc, 74 x 71mm liquid-cooled, horizontally opposed 'pancake' six-cylinder engine. Lighter than the GL1500 by 1.1kg, this also featured a completely new cylinder head design. Honda's market research showed Gold Wing owners wanted to ride their motorcycles, not work on them, and that outright horsepower was of less importance than on-the-road performance. Thus the GL1800 retained a single overhead camshaft on each bank of cylinders, and two parallel valves per cylinder. All the valves were positioned directly under the camshaft, the shim-under bucket system requiring valve adjustment intervals every 30,000 miles. The camshaft drive was no longer by toothed rubber belt, but a thinner, silent-type cam chain with automatic tensioner. These design changes were to create a more compact engine, provide more leg room, and allowed the seat to be moved further forward. The GL1800 therefore rode on a slightly shorter wheelbase (1,691mm) than the GL1500.

Other engine updates included the water pump mounted behind the engine, driven directly from the crankshaft, and a 1,100-watt alternator. The electric reverse gear no longer required operation through a separate lever, but was engaged by controls on the handlebar. Instead of the complicated multi-computer-controlled induction system of the GL1500, the GL1800 had a pre-programmed PGM-F1 electronic engine management system. The injection system included two 40mm throttle bodies and six Keihin injectors, with four nozzle tips per injector. As with all Gold Wings, the 25-litre fuel tank was positioned below the seat. Twin exhaust catalysts reduced emissions, and the GL1800 was one of the most environmentally friendly large-capacity motorcycles

available. The engine was solidly mounted in the frame, and positioned lower and further forward than the GL1500. With a 9.8:1 compression ratio the power was a moderate 118hp at 5,500rpm.

The chassis was considerably improved over the GL1500, the box-section dual spar aluminium frame using the engine as a stressed member. Weighing 11kg less than the earlier steel design, the frame was engineered for an optimum balance between rigidity and flex so as to provide excellent handling along with maximum ride comfort. This concept of tuned flex in frame design was relatively new. Honda was already known for their emphasis on weight distribution for optimum handling, the more-forward engine location also providing improved ergonomics, and negating the necessity for the earlier tiller-like handlebars.

A lighter, cast aluminium single-sided swingarm (Pro Arm) improved rear wheel accessibility, and there was a single shock absorber with a Pro-Link rising rate linkage. The 45mm front fork was similar to the Valkyrie, and no longer had TRAC anti-dive, instead incorporating a hydraulic anti-dive system with a secondary master cylinder on the left fork leg, activated when either the front brake lever or rear brake pedal was applied. There were also new 18 and 16-inch wheels, with wider rims, fully floating 296mm front discs, and a 316mm ventilated rear disc. The three Nissin brake calipers were triple piston type, with a new proportional braking system that coupled all three brake calipers through a secondary master cylinder and a proportional control valve. An anti-lock braking system (ABS) was optional.

New bodywork continued the theme of the earlier Gold Wing, but the riding position was more sport-touring than before. There was also considerably more equipment, extending from a sophisticated cruise control to larger-capacity integrated trunk and saddlebags. Other updates aimed at bringing the Gold Wing into the 21st century included a new analogue and digital instrument and display panel. The result was a considerably more up-to-date motorcycle that continued the Gold Wing tradition while adding sporting capability. In the words of *Cycle World*: 'With a sportbike-style aluminium beam frame and single-sided swingarm, and 118 free-revving horsepower on tap, best not to mess with a well-ridden 1800 on a twisty road. Maybe they should have named it Sport Wing?'

The GL500 Silver Wing Interstate
offered full touring equipment,
but was extremely
underpowered. *Cycle*

# 5 NEW HORIZONS

By the mid-1970s, Honda was expanding beyond many existing motorcycle design parameters. Although they continued to build on the CB750's success, the Gold Wing indicated they were prepared to move outside mainstream design layouts. They were prepared to gamble, endeavouring to leave no stone unturned in their quest to fill every conceivable niche in the motorcycle market. Continuing the path of innovation initiated during the 1960s, many of the late 1970s designs were startling and unusual. It began with the new Hawk and Dream twins, and was followed by the CX500 and CBX1000. There was an element of risk associated with many Honda designs of this period. Some were extraordinary and successful, while others were short-lived failures, loved by the press and ignored by the public.

## NEW HAWKS AND DREAMS

There had been a time when nearly every second motorcycle sold was a CB250 or a CB350 twin, and these humble machines reached the non-enthusiast market unlike anything else. Not surprisingly, other manufacturers began developing similar machines, and the Kawasaki Z400, Yamaha 360 and Suzuki GS400 were soon muscling in on Honda's traditional lucrative territory. These manufacturers also offered high-performance two-strokes. While Honda was left with the superb four-cylinder CB400F, this failed to appeal to the masses, and despite its sophistication still couldn't match the two-strokes. The ageing, and extremely staid CB360 didn't sell like the CB350, and Honda's response were new 250 and 400 twins, the CB250 and CB400T for 1978. The 400s were called Hawks in America, while the 250 was known as the Dream in Europe, continuing the nomenclature of an earlier era.

Powering these new Hawks and Dreams was an advanced all-new 360° parallel twin engine. While retaining a single overhead camshaft, driven by a Hy-Vo chain, the cylinder head included three valves per cylinder (two 26mm inlet and one 32mm exhaust on the 400). The engine dimensions were extremely oversquare (70.5 x 50.6mm for the 400 and 62 x

New for 1978, the CB400T was
intended to replace the CB400F
and CB360. *Motorcycle Trader
collection*

41.4mm for the 250), encouraging high revs. To quell
vibration there were two chain-driven balance shafts,
rotating in the opposite direction to the one-piece
crankshaft now running in plain bearings. Primary
drive was by straight-cut gears, to a five-speed gearbox,
and the ignition was CDI. Also innovative was the

exhaust system which included a power chamber
underneath the engine. The new engines were quite
highly tuned, the 395cc CB400T featuring twin 32mm
Keihin carburettors to produce 40hp at 9,500rpm.

The chassis was significantly updated over the earlier
CB360, with the welded steel backbone frame

including the engine as a stressed member, and vastly improved suspension. The CB400TII included a single 280mm front disc brake and 19 and 18-inch Comstar wheels. While the 167kg CB400T performed acceptably, the similar CB250T's performance was barely adequate. *Motor Cycle Weekly* achieved a top speed of only 87.8mph (141.3km/h). For America there were three versions of the CB400: a sports CB400TII, an economy CB400TI (with spoked wheels and drum brakes), and the CB400A with a detuned engine (28mm carburettors). This had a semi-automatic two-speed transmission, and was excruciatingly slow, becoming the CM400A Hondamatic custom in 1979, lasting until 1981.

While the largely unchanged CB400T Hawk continued in America for 1979, joined by a CM400T cruiser, the dumpy styling was unpopular in Europe where an updated CB400N and CB250N Super Dream were offered. Now with a six-speed gearbox, and CB750F-inspired styling, the power of the CB400N was increased to 43hp at 9,500rpm. There was a dual front disc brake, and while capable of nearly 106mph

Below: Replacing the excellent, and highly
successful, CB500S for 2004 was the CBF500,
with more aggressive styling. *Honda*

(170km/h), the CB400N still vibrated. More successful, especially in Britain, was the 27hp CB250N. Although *Bike* magazine stated: 'The CB250N is a bit of a bore,' it was smoother and cheaper, and looked almost identical to the 400. The CB400N was seen as a poor replacement for the charismatic CB400F, but the CB250N was a sales success.

By 1980, the Euro-styling and six-speed transmission made its way to the American CB400T Hawk. Tightening environmental controls saw smaller, 30mm carburettors, the kick-start was deleted, and the power was reduced to 35hp. Still with a single front disc, the CB400T continued for one more year, now with a dual-piston front brake caliper. This year also saw the CM400C custom, with a stepped seat, shorter mufflers and pull-back handlebars. The European Super Dreams and Super Hawks received a black-painted engine from 1981, and dual-piston brake calipers, new-style Comstar wheels, and lubrication improvements for 1982. This included an exterior oil pipe to pressure feed the cylinder head bearings.

With Kawasaki and Suzuki stretching their entry-level twins beyond 400cc Honda bored the 400 twin to 75mm for the American versions. Now displacing 447cc, there were initially three new models for 1982, headed by the CB450T Hawk. Additionally, there was the CM450C custom, the economy CM450E, CM450A Hondamatic and CB450SC Nighthawk. All

the 450s now included an oil cooler (previously reserved for the Automatic) in front of the engine, and cylinder head lubrication improvements.

As Honda began to concentrate on V-fours and V-twins, the 450 twin line-up diminished after 1983. That year the CB450SC Nighthawk replaced the Hawk as the sporting twin, receiving cast alloy wheels. There were no 450s offered in the USA for 1984, but the 450 Nighthawk reappeared for 1985 and '86. Encouraged by the success of the CMX250C single-cylinder Rebel, a similar CMX450C appeared for 1986. The custom style included a long, low look, with wire-spoked wheels. The 450 Rebel may have looked new, but as *Cycle* magazine observed: 'Deep inside is a tough little engine that was a high-tech jewel when engineers wore bell bottoms.' The 447cc twin also made it to the European CB450N for 1985. With 32mm carburettors and a 9.3:1 compression ratio, the power was 44hp at 9,000rpm. Chassis updates included revised styling, a 35mm front fork, and cast alloy 18-inch wheels. The front brake was upgraded to double 231mm discs. This unremarkable machine weighed in at a porky 187kg, and could barely top 87mph (140km/h). A new lightweight perimeter-style steel frame for the 450 saw the CB450S for 1986. The weight was reduced to 168kg, and this lasted until 1990. Even when it was conceived, the Hawk engine was a curiosity, a twin trying to be a four. By 1990, it was merely an obsolete novelty.

Eventually, as Honda endeavoured to fill every possible niche in the market, a new 500cc water-cooled parallel twin appeared. This double overhead camshaft eight-valve 499cc (73 x 59.6mm) twin produced 57.2hp at 9,500rpm. The crankshaft was 180°, there was a gear-driven counterbalancer, the carburettors were 34mm flat-slide VP (FireBlade-style), and the valve adjustment was bucket and shim. Launched for 1994 as a commuter, the 170kg CB500 soon earned an enviable record for reliability. Honda established CB500 Cup racing, uprating the CB500 to the 60hp CB500S. The CB500 cup became one of the most popular racing categories in Britain, launching the careers of many of today's established stars (including 2004 Superbike World Champion James Toseland who won the CB500 Cup in 1997). An indication of its incredible reliability was a 24-hour CB500 Cup race at Le Mans in 1999, where every entry finished without breaking down. A superb and enjoyable all rounder, after ten years, the CB500 was updated into the 2004

The CX500 was ugly, but eventually earned a reputation for solid reliability. *Mick Woollett*

CBF500, with new styling, a steel backbone frame and monoshock based on the 600 Hornet, a 41mm fork (instead of 37mm), and larger tyres. There was also optional ABS and integrated luggage, and the CBF500 remained one of the best budget mid-range motorcycles available. This bike could provide more fun than anyone could rightfully expect for the modest outlay.

# V-TWINS

## The CX500 and CX650

One of Honda's most startling efforts of the late 1970s was the CX500. This liquid-cooled 80° transverse V-twin featured pushrod-operated four-valve cylinder heads and shaft-drive – features most often associated with touring models, but the CX500 almost defied categorisation. The CX500 could do just about anything, but was universally declared extremely ugly, earning the nickname the 'plastic maggot'.

As with many Honda designs, the CX500 was not only different, it was a brilliant concept. The idea of a transverse V-twin wasn't new, with Moto Guzzi having used it for the past decade, but Honda looked at it in a fresh light, envisaging the CX500 as a smaller companion to the Gold Wing. Automotive-like, the crankcase was cast with integral cylinders and featured a single high camshaft driven by a Hy-Vo chain. Short pushrods operated the four valves per cylinder, and the cylinder heads were skewed to provide room for the rider. The bore and stroke were 78 x 52mm, with primary drive by straight-cut gears to the multi-plate clutch (acting as engine balancer), and a five-speed gearbox. Carburetion was by a pair of 35mm Keihin

Although providing more performance than the 500, the GL650 Silver Wing was unsuccessful. *Cycle*

CV carburettors, and the power was 50hp at 9,000rpm.

A spine frame held the engine at two points as a stressed member, with ugly pressings supporting the swingarm, while the Comstar wheels permitted the use of tubeless tyres. The CX500 had a single front disc brake in America (twin discs in Europe), and a very ugly headlight and instrument nacelle. No lightweight at 200kg, it was greeted with some scepticism. *Bike* magazine saying: 'If looks could kill, this one should be six feet under.' Problems more serious than the unfortunate styling soon emerged. The cam chain tensioner failed, and was modified four times in the first two years, but most of these were ineffective. Some early bikes also had incorrect crankshaft bearings, but despite these problems the CX500 earned a reputation for an extraordinarily long life. It became a favourite with London despatch riders, and Honda also had so much faith in the design they commissioned Jerry

Griffith to convert one into an AMA Grand National dirt track racer. The motor was turned 90° and installed in a flat-track frame, but it wasn't very successful.

While the CX500 continued largely unchanged in Europe for 1979, with a fly screen added to the ugly headlamp cowling and metal surrounds for the radiator instead of plastic, it became a Custom and a Deluxe in America. This Custom (Honda's first Custom street bike) would last until 1982. The low-maintenance layout was particularly suited to the custom idea, and the Custom outsold the standard CX500 ten to one in America. It was developed further with the GL500 Silver Wing for 1981. There was a new chassis, still retaining the engine as a stressed member, but with a single shock absorber Pro-Link rear suspension system. The engine was slightly uprated with two Keihin 34mm CV carburettors, and was mounted lower. A unique feature of the Silver Wing was the modular seat/rear

Below: Massive and complicated, the CX500C Turbo was a technological marvel. *Mick Woollett collection*

Bottom: After one year, the Turbo evolved into the improved CX650C, but the turbocharging fad was short lived. *Honda*

# TURBO POWER

Turbocharging was the fashion in the early 1980s, and all the Japanese manufacturers felt it was *de rigueur* to ride this bandwagon. While Suzuki and Yamaha built turbocharged air-cooled 650cc fours, and Kawasaki a 750, Honda again steered a different path by using the water-cooled CX500 as a basis. When it was released in 1982 the CX500TC was a technological marvel, with computer-controlled electronic fuel injection and ignition, and the highest specification chassis available. The entire engine was strengthened, with the compression ratio lowered to 7.2:1 to prevent detonation at high boost pressure. A tiny, 50mm, IHI turbocharger provided boost of 17.4psi, and the motor produced 82hp at 8,000rpm. This gave incredibly high rpm performance, but the CX500TC was noticeably sluggish at low engine speeds.

The high-specification chassis included a larger front fork (37mm) with TRAC on both legs, larger diameter (270mm) front discs with twin-piston calipers, a Pro-Link aluminium swingarm, and wide 18 and 17-inch Comstar wheels. The bodywork was hand-laid glassfibre, and underneath it lay a maze of wiring and plumbing. Not only was the CX500TC bewilderingly complex, it was excessively heavy at 239kg. It didn't meet with unanimous acceptance, and *Cycle* magazine found 'the CX500TC a handful, offering no functional advantage over a CB900F.'

After one year, the turbo was redesigned to alleviate the considerable shortcomings. The resulting CX650T was based on the CX650, the motor featuring 32mm and 28mm valves, and a slightly higher, 7.8:1 compression ratio. The turbocharger compressor was larger, and the boost slightly lower at 16.4psi. Along with a simplified engine management system, this resulted in a considerable power increase to 100hp at 8,000rpm. The turbo lag was reduced, but the CX650TC was still a tricky motorcycle to ride fast. While the chassis layout was unchanged, the suspension was more adjustable, and the weight was still a considerable 235kg. As *Cycle* magazine said: 'The Honda Turbo isn't a bike for the average rider, but has become a splendid touring bike.' After one year the CX650TC disappeared, although unsold stock was still available for several more years in some markets. The turbo

revolution was one of the shortest in motorcycling. By 1984, there was no justification for expensive, heavy, and complex machinery that provided no performance advantage over conventional motorcycles.

trunk design which could be configured three ways; a dual seat with no trunk, solo seat with a small trunk, or a solo seat with large trunk and backrest.

Alongside the GL500 Silver Wing was the GL500I Silver Wing Interstate. This incorporated the factory-integrated Interstate fairing and saddlebags along with twin front disc brakes. While the GL500 was overweight at 196kg, the Interstate weighed 226kg,

which was too much for the 500cc engine to cope with. Although offering an overweight and underpowered touring motorcycle at a premium price was hardly the recipe for success, the GL500 Silver Wing and Interstate continued for 1982 largely unchanged. For 1983 the engine was bored and stroked (82.5 x 63mm) to 674cc to create the GL650 Silver Wing, Interstate and CX650C Custom. There were larger valves (32mm

One of the best
balanced small
Hondas was the
1980 CB250RS.
*Mick Woollett*

# MISCELLANEOUS SINGLES

By 1980, the successful XL250 dirt bike motor was adapted for street duties with the superb CB250RS. The 74 x 57.8mm four-valve single had twin-chain driven counterbalance shafts, a higher, 9.3:1 compression ratio, and a 30mm Keihin CV carburettor. The power was 26hp at 8,500rpm and the cam chain tensioner was now fully automatic. This motor was slotted into an abbreviated frame, and high-quality components included light alloy 18-inch wheel rims and a small front disc brake. Tastefully restrained in styling, the 134kg CB250RS was one of the most charismatic Hondas of the era. It was also faster and more charming than the best-selling CB250N. *Bike* magazine managed 91.4mph (147.1km/h), stating: 'The RS has made the transition from dirt bike to lightweight sportsbike with real aplomb.' Unfortunately, the CB250RS was another model loved by the press and enthusiasts but shunned by buyers, although it remained available in some markets, with a fairing and saddlebags by 1985.

After the demise of the CB250RS, the next interesting four-stroke 250 was the CBX250 of 1984. Powering this was a single overhead camshaft four-valve RFVC single, with dimensions of 75 x 56.5mm. The 28hp CBX250 featured 16 and 18-inch Comstar wheels, remote reservoir shock absorbers, and an integrated fairing. More interesting was the double overhead camshaft CBX250RS and Clubman of the same era. With a longer stroke (72 x 61.3mm) RFVC four-valve engine boasting 31hp, these were high-specification motorcycles. Both had wire-spoked wheels with alloy rims, the GB250 Clubman going a stage further, with a solo seat, black finish, and gaitered forks, in the style of a classic British single of the 1950s. Weighing a moderate 129kg (125kg for the Clubman), these high performance singles were available, primarily in Japan, for many years. The 250cc street single reappeared for 2004 in the guise of the CBF250. The air-cooled double overhead

Below: Offering high performance in a compact package, the CBX250RS was a superb motorcycle. *Honda* Bottom: Another adaptation of a trail bike motor in a street chassis was the unsuccessful FT500 of 1982 and '83. This is the 1982 version. *Motorcycle Trader collection*

Below: The GB500 Tourist Trophy emphasised a nostalgic theme. This is a 1987 Japanese market model. *Peter Herbert*

camshaft four-valve engine had new dimensions (73 x 59.5mm), and with a 9.3:1 compression ratio and 32mm carburettor, produced 20hp at 8,000rpm. With sporty styling, the 138.5kg CBR250 also had quality suspension, including a 37mm front fork, and a mono-shock swingarm. Honda also produced the superb Dream 50 racer. Powered by a 7hp 49cc double overhead camshaft single, the 71kg Dream 50 was a homage to the RC110 and CR110 racers of 1962. Although fitted with up-to-date Showa suspension and a single front disc brake, the styling replicated the earlier racers, right down to the 18-inch wire-spoked wheels.

Endeavouring to build a niche out of the nostalgia of the big single 'thumper', for 1982 Honda created the FT500C out of the successful XR/XL500 dirt bike. In America it was called the Ascot, after the half-mile dirt track at Ascot Park in Southern California. It was a spurious association, and while the FT500 was styled like a dirt tracker it was very street orientated. The 498cc (89 x 80mm) single was first introduced in 1979 in the XL/XR, and included up-to-date features such as a four-valve cylinder head and twin counterbalancers. One balancer rode on a shaft in front of the crank, with the other on the transmission mainshaft, linked with a

single-row chain. In the transition to street duties an electric start was added (there was no kick-start), the carburettor was increased to 43mm (35mm for America), and the electrical system upgraded to 12 volts. The valve sizes were 35mm and 30mm in the RFVC (radial four valve) cylinder head, and the dual exhaust headers exited into a single muffler. The compression ratio was a low 8.6:1, and a modest 35hp was produced at 6,500rpm.

The tubular steel frame was similar to those of the off-road models, the leading axle front fork was a stout 37mm, and there were disc brakes front and rear. The rear suspension was by twin gas-charged shock absorbers, and the cast alloy wheels 19 and 18-inch. Although the weight was a reasonable 159kg, the five-speed FT500 was still underpowered relative to other 500s, and struggled to attain 90mph (150km/h). There were only minor changes to the FT500 for 1983, including graphics and an improved electric start, but there was no market for the underpowered single and it wasn't offered for 1984.

After the failure of the FT500, rather surprisingly Honda produced another 500cc street single in 1985, the XBR500, and domestic GB500 Tourist Trophy. The GB500 endeavoured to recreate the classic British look with a two-into-one exhaust and simplified equipment. The engine was the shorter stroke dry-sump version (92 x 75mm) of the 1983 XR500, the radial valve cylinder head having 36mm and 31mm valves. There were gear-driven counterbalancers to quell vibration, and with a 39mm CV carburettor, the power was 44hp. The 157kg XBR featured a choice of 'Boomerang' Comstar or wire-spoked wheels and while a favourite of the press, this didn't translate into sales. For 1989, Honda decided to sell the GB500 Tourist Trophy in America, based on the Japanese version, but with minor updates. While this was undoubtedly handsome, it was considerably overpriced at $4,198, and lasted only two years.

The European CX500E Sports of 1982 featured Pro-Link rear suspension and more agreeable styling. *Author*

intake and 27mm exhaust) and the carburettor size increased to 35mm. Chassis updates included cast aluminium wheels, and a stronger frame and front fork. Although an improvement over the anaemic 500, the GL650 was still too heavy at 217kg, with the Interstate even heavier at 240kg. These 650s only lasted one year.

Meanwhile, the CX500 continued to sell a steady 3,500 units a year in England, becoming a more sporting model in 1982 with the CX500E. But for an automatic cam chain tensioner and different rocker covers, the 496cc engine was largely unchanged. The updated chassis included a box-section swingarm, air-assisted Pro-Link rear suspension, 18-inch 'Boomerang' style Comstar wheels, dual 276mm front disc brakes with twin piston calipers, and a disc brake at the rear. The wheelbase increased to 1,495mm and the weight went up to 207kg. *Bike* magazine summed it up as 'too heavy, too slow, and too ponderous.' For 1983, the CX650E replaced the 500, the power increased to 64hp at

8,000rpm. TRAC was incorporated in the left fork leg, but the 208kg CX650E was very similar to the CX500. The CX650E lasted until 1985, but while it was efficient, this wasn't a machine that stirred the senses.

# NARROW-ANGLE V-TWINS

## *The VT500, VLX, VT750, and VT1100*

Seemingly wanting to fill every possible niche, and build every conceivable engine configuration, for 1983 Honda produced a pair of longitudinal V-twins, the VT500 and VT750. There were three 500s: the VT500C Shadow, VT500FT Ascot, and European VT500E, with one 750, the VT750C Shadow. These were radical designs, and another case of Honda gambling in the marketplace. Unlike their own new V-fours, Honda chose a narrow-angle vee, overcoming the problem of primary imbalance by offsetting the crankpins. The VT500 was 52° twin (71 x 62mm) and

The VT500E motor looked air-cooled but was actually water-cooled. The enclosed front disc made wheel removal difficult. *Honda*

the VT750, 45° (79.5 x 75.5mm), both featured water-cooling, single overhead camshafts, and three valves per cylinder. Each camshaft was driven by an individual Hy-Vo chain, one on the left and one on the right side of the engine. The VT500 included screw-type valve adjustment and the VT750 hydraulic valves. The 750 also featured dual spark plugs per cylinder. To achieve the perfect primary engine balance of a 90° twin, the 500's crankpins were offset 76°, and the 750's 90°. While this effectively subdued vibration, it didn't quell it completely. Unusually for a Honda, the crankcases were vertically split, with the cylinders and heads milled from common castings. Primary drive was by straight-cut gears, and an innovative one-way Sprague-clutch with a diaphragm spring feeding the power to a six-speed gearbox and a shaft final drive. With a pair of 34mm downdraft Keihin carburettors between the cylinders, the 500 produced 50hp at 9,000rpm, and the 750, 70hp at 7,500rpm.

This unusual motor was housed in a traditional full-cradle steel frame with a box-section twin Showa FVQ shock absorber swingarm. The two cruisers featured a leading axle fork and alloy Comcast wheels (19 and 15-inch for the VT750 and 18 and 15-inch for the VT500). 18-inch Comstar wheels graced the VT500E, with the dubious inboard ventilated front disc brake shared with other models of this era. The 52hp VT500ED seemed to be a fresh take on the CX500 idea, weighing a reasonable 177kg and providing superior performance. The VT500E lasted until 1989, with a revised EF model. Apart from the usual cosmetic changes, the EF also featured many updated components, including cylinder heads, big-end bearings, gearbox, and driveshaft. Despite these developments, the VT500E remained just another boring motorcycle.

The VT500 Ascot was an extension of the FT500 Ascot theme, and a hybrid model. The 18-inch wheels were cast alloy, as was the leading axle fork and there was a normal single front disc brake. Styling

V-twin cruisers have been a staple diet in the Honda line-up since 1983, and the most popular has been the VT1100. This is a 1994 example, which is very similar to the current version. *Australian Motorcycle News*

considerations saw an impractical tiny, 9.5-litre fuel tank and Harley-style two-into-one exhaust system. Like the European VT500E, buyers stayed away from the VT500 Ascot, and it was available long after production ended in 1984.

Far more successful was the VT750C Shadow. *Cycle* magazine called the VT750C 'the most radical Honda ever built,' Honda correctly anticipating the expanding market for cruisers. The engine was downsized to 700cc (76.5 x 75.5mm) for 1984, the VT700C continuing until 1987 with only minor updates. While Honda was struggling with their problematic high-profile V-fours in 1984, the VT700C was their most popular model, sales seeing them grab 60 per cent of the US market that year. The motor grew to 800cc (79.5 x 80.6mm) in 1988 with the VT800C Shadow. This only lasted a year, but the VT750C Shadow made a return in 1998.

The most significant cruiser was the VT1100C of 1985, Honda for the first time venturing into Harley-

Davidson territory by following the American notion that bigger is better. Manufactured in Ohio, the liquid-cooled 1,099cc (87.5 x 91.4mm) 45° V-twin followed the lines of the VT750 with 90° staggered crankpins, three valves per cylinder (32mm intakes and 40mm exhaust), and dual spark plug ignition. Other similarities included individual Hy-Vo chain-driven single overhead camshafts, hydraulic valve adjustment, and shaft final drive, although the gearbox was five-speed. Where the VT1100 really differed was in its overall dimensions, the VT1100C riding on a huge 1,610mm wheelbase and weighing 240kg. So began the life of one of Honda's most popular models in America, which continued in 2004 with only minor updates. There was a small redesign for 1987, with more Harley-esque styling and increased bottom-end power. From 1995, the VT1100C ACE (American Classic Edition) was available. The engine included a single-pin crankshaft, while styling cues saw deeply valanced

Another Honda success story has been the VT600C VLX cruiser, styled to look like a rigid frame. This is a 1994 Shadow Deluxe. *Australian Motorcycle News*

mudguards. Other variants included the Shadow Spirit, Shadow Aero, and Shadow Sabre. Solid and reliable, even the release of the new wave of VTX-powered cruisers hasn't killed the VT1100.

Honda departed from their usual cruiser style with the VT600C VLX Shadow of 1988. The 52° V-twin 583cc engine (75 x 66mm) was based on the VT500, but included screw and locknut valve adjustment, a single-pin crankshaft instead of offset pins, a simpler cable clutch, a four-speed gearbox and chain final drive. The frame was styled to look as if it had a rigid rear end, but included a cantilever single shock absorber swingarm. There were gradual updates over the years, including stronger crankcases from the XRV750 Africa Twin in 1991 and retuning with restyling for 1999. In 1990, with the demand for cruisers now low, this was Honda's only cruiser, and it was another model with a long shelf life, still remaining in the line-up for 2004.

Eventually, the V-twin cruiser re-established itself, with Honda releasing the VT750C ACE Shadow for 1997. The styling was deliberately nostalgic, with deep mudguards and a stretched fuel tank, while the three-valve 745cc (79 x 76mm) engine was a larger version of the 52° VT600 rather than a resurrection of the earlier 45° VT750. With a five-speed gearbox, and the chain final drive of the VT600, the swingarm was more conventional and included twin rear shock absorbers. The range of VT750s soon expanded to include a stripped-down version, sold as 'The Black Widow' in England, and as the 'Shadow Spirit' in the USA. The power was a moderate 42hp and this was about as good as a mid-range cruiser came. Continually updated over the next few years, the VT750C Shadow (Shadow Aero in the USA) received engine revisions, including a single 34mm Keihin carburettor and a new exhaust system for 2004. The peak power was slightly lower, there was shaft final drive, and some styling updates.

Below: In 1997, Honda released this VT750C ACE Shadow, and it continues today as one of their most popular models, in many parts of the world.
*Australian Motorcycle News*

The only 750 Cruiser available in America for 2004 was the Shadow Aero, replacing the retro ACE 750 Deluxe and Shadow Spirit.

# TAKING AN ALTERNATIVE V-TWIN PATH

*The VT250F, VTR250F, XLV750R, Transalp and NTV650, The VT250F and VTR250F (from 1983)*

While Honda was intent on creating a new definitive motorcycle blueprint with their new V-fours in 1982 (see Chapter 7), one of the machines that evolved out of the new V-four was the twin-cylinder VT250F of 1983. Virtually half a VF500F, the VT250F was the world's first liquid-cooled 90° V-twin. The double overhead camshaft eight-valve 248cc (60 x 44mm) motor used the same 11:1 pistons, 23mm and 20.5mm valves, 32mm Keihin carburettors, and planetary gear-change mechanism. The engine produced an impressive 35hp at 11,000rpm, and was installed in a tubular steel frame similar to the VF400F. Also similar was the Pro-Link rear suspension, 16 and 18-inch Comstar wheels, and the dubious front inboard ventilated disc brake. Standard equipment included a sports fairing, but there was an optional sports pack with a chin cowl and rear seat cover. The VT250F was a beautifully balanced little machine, if somewhat heavy at 149kg. In 1984, it became the VT250FII, with a full fairing, and continued to be very popular. The VT250F wasn't available in the USA, but for 1988 it made a surprising appearance as the garish VTR250, with 16 and 17-inch cast alloy wheels, and still with the inboard disc brake. The frame was now a steel beam type. The final version was the 1990 VTR250, with a 17-inch front wheel and a conventional front disc brake. In the meantime, the VT250 evolved into the 40hp VT250 Spada, with a beam aluminium frame, for Japan in 1989. Weighing only 135kg, this superb little machine eventually became available in export markets. One of many variants only available in Japan was the 1992 Xelvis.

Below: Evidence of Honda's commitment to unconventionality, the Pacific Coast was a less successful model however. *Cycle*

Bottom: Virtually half a VF500F, the VT250F was one of the most advanced 250s available in 1983. *Author*

# THE PACIFIC COAST

During 1989, Honda extended their automotive approach to motorcycles with the Pacific Coast. This was designed to appeal to a wider range of buyers, and the engine and chassis disappeared under the all-compassing bodywork. The rubber-mounted 800cc V-twin engine came from the VT750 Shadow cruiser. Carburetion was by two Keihin 36mm downdraft CVs. As the engine was difficult to access, maintenance-free features included a sealed battery, hydraulic valve adjusters, automatic cam chain tensioners, and a hydraulic clutch. There was shaft-drive and the frame was similar in design to that of the GL1500, with two rectangular steel main spars. The 41mm front fork included TRAC, and the wheels were 17 and 15-inch front and rear. Although no lightweight at 262kg, the Pacific Coast was surprisingly agile, mainly due to the low centre of gravity and low seat height (765mm). The automotive influence in the design of the bodywork included a rear section that imitated a car trunk. Not very popular, the Pacific Coast was deleted in 1991, making a surprising return from 1994 until 1998. Envisaged as a lifestyle motorcycle, the Pacific Coast was ahead of its time, but lacked charisma.

Below: The 2000 model VTR250 could almost be mistaken for a mini-Ducati Monster. *Australian Motorcycle News*

Bottom: Designed to emulate the Paris–Dakar racers, the Africa Twin wasn't as capable in the dirt as it looked. *Honda*

This was an unusual model that combined several 1980s retro elements, including a tubular steel frame, 16-inch wheels, dual shock suspension, and a chin fairing. The 250cc V-twin also powered a V25 Magna

Custom (or VT250), and the VTR250 continues more than 20 years on with only minor updates. The 2004 version featured a tubular steel Ducati-style frame, a 41mm fork, and at only 139kg, was an excellent beginners' motorcycle.

# THE XVL750R AND AFRICA TWIN (1984–2003)

The popularity in Europe of the Endurance desert races such as the Paris–Dakar Rally led to a wave of large-capacity dual-purpose motorcycles. Honda was running modified XL600s in these desert events, but for 1984 created the XLV750R out of the 45° V-twin

An NX650 in its perfect environment – dirt back roads. *Australian Motorcycle News*

three-valve VT750. Retaining the 90° staggered crankpins, the compression ratio was reduced to 8.4:1, the valves were smaller (30mm intake and 38mm exhaust), the carburettors were downsized to 33mm, and there was a five-speed gearbox. Apart from the bright red engine cases, the most significant difference was the cooling which was changed from water to a combination of air and oil. Output was 61hp at 7,000rpm. While retaining shaft final drive, the XLV750R received a rectangular section aluminium frame, 43mm leading axle fork, a hydraulic disc brake with a twin-piston caliper, and Pro-Link rear suspension. The wheels were 21 and 17-inch, and the XLV certainly looked like a real desert racer, but at 193kg only the brave would venture off-road.

Honda's success in the Paris–Dakar Rally with the factory NXR750 (83 x 72mm; 789cc) twin led to the XRV650 Africa Twin in 1988. With an engine similar to that based on the NTV650, the XRV650 was more conservatively styled than the XLV750R, but was soon replaced by the XRV750 Africa Twin. Released for 1990, the XRV750 featured a new single overhead camshaft three-valve 52° V-twin, displacing 742cc (81 x 72mm). With two 36.5mm Mikuni carburettors the power was 59hp at 7,500rpm. The frame was similar to the Transalp, but the more suitable off-road suspension included a 43mm front fork. There were twin 276mm front disc brakes, and as the weight was 210kg the Africa Twin was even less suited to real desert duties than the earlier XLV750R. With its twin headlights, and desert racer styling, the XRV750 was more show than go. The Africa Twin received a revamp for 1993, with a new semi-double cradle frame. The result was a reduction in weight to 202kg, and a lower seat. It then lasted until 2003 with only minor styling updates.

## THE TRANSALP (FROM 1987)

A less radical approach to the Paris–Dakar replica was the Transalp (XL600V), introduced in Europe for 1987 and the USA for 1989. With a 583cc (75 x 66mm) 52° V-twin based on the VT500, the Transalp included a five-speed gearbox and chain final drive. The engine breathed through two 32mm Mikuni carburettors, and with each cylinder ignited by twin spark plugs, it produced 55hp at 8,000rpm. The frame was a square-

## THE NX650 DOMINATOR (1988–2003)

Another crossover model in the vein of the Transalp and Africa Twin was the NX650 Dominator single. The air-cooled 644cc (100 x 83mm) four-stroke cylinder engine was based on the XL600 trail bike, with a single overhead camshaft radial four-valve cylinder head. It was a dry-sump unit, carrying the oil in the frame backbone, and included an electric start. With an 8.3:1 compression ratio, and a 40mm Keihin carburettor, the power was 45hp at 6,000rpm. Many chassis components were similar to the Transalp, including the square-section steel frame and swingarm, 41mm front fork and the Pro-Link rear suspension. Braking was by a single front disc with dual-piston caliper, and with its low front mudguard, the NX650 was still more suited to street or light trail duty. Weighing only 152kg, this it did with aplomb.

While the NX650 Dominator wasn't offered in the USA after 1989 (there was a smaller NX250 instead), it survived in various guises for other markets for several more years with only an occasional styling makeover. Some versions had the front brake under a plastic shroud, and for 1993 there was a larger fuel tank and more integrated fairing. A spin-off for 1998 was the naked SLR650, with 19 and 17-inch wheels, and for 2000, the NX650 evolved into the street Vigor, with the motor detuned to 39hp. There was still a high-rise exhaust and long-travel suspension, but the Vigor lacked the Dominator's appeal. In latter years the NX650 was produced in Italy, but through to its demise it remained a competent and highly enjoyable, if somewhat expensive, all-rounder.

motorcycle that did a lot of things well, if nothing spectacularly and has remained a consistent seller. After several seasons with only minor updates, the Transalp was revised for 1994. The fairing and headlight were restyled but the engine and running gear were still much as before.

A third-generation XL650V Transalp appeared for 2000, upgraded in design and configuration. Now with the 647cc 52° V-twin of the Deauville, but fitted with 34mm carburettors and producing 54hp, the most striking feature of the Transalp was its stunning new bodywork. With 256mm dual front disc brakes, the Transalp was no lightweight at 191kg, but continued the Honda tradition of mass centralisation. As a result, the XL650V was a supremely efficient and an enjoyable adventure motorcycle.

# THE REVERE, HAWK GT (BROS) AND DEAUVILLE (FROM 1989)

Sometimes the parts bin approach can reap dividends, and one example was the excellent Hawk GT (NT650), or Bros for Japan. In Europe this machine was the Revere (NTV650), but with its shaft-drive was less sporting. This crossover machine, targeted somewhere between the boulevard and racetrack, took the Transalp 52° V-twin, bored it to 647cc (79 x 66mm) and placed it in a VFR-style aluminium frame. The liquid-cooled engine retained three-valves per cylinder and the offset crankshaft, and featured a five-speed gearbox. There was also a 399cc (64 x 62mm) Bros for Japan, and both the Hawk GT and Bros had chain final drive. With a moderate 9.2:1 (9.4:1 on the Hawk GT) compression ratio, and 36.5mm slant-type CV carburettors, the power of the Revere was 60hp at 7,500rpm, and the Hawk GT 55hp at 8,500rpm. This engine was solidly mounted in an aluminium twin-spar frame, with a single-sided swingarm, 17-inch cast alloy wheels and a 41mm non-adjustable fork from the 550 Nighthawk. The front brake was only a single disc, but this was adequate to stop the 181kg Hawk GT, and 188kg Revere. There were minor differences between the US Hawk GT and the Japanese Bros, the latter receiving a closer ratio gearbox and larger front disc brake. With a chassis

section single steel downtube, full-cradle type, with a 41mm leading axle fork and Pro-Link rear suspension. This mild-mannered adventure tourer featured high handlebars and a tall seat, and although the alloy-rimmed wheels were 21 and 17-inch enduro style, the Transalp wasn't really an off-road motorcycle. The 174kg Transalp performed best on smooth dirt roads where the rear wheel could slide predictably. This was a

able to handle much more power, it wasn't surprising to see the Hawk GT developed into a competitive racer. Two Brothers Racing won a national 750cc championship with their highly modified racer. The Hawk GT was available from 1989 until 1991 virtually unchanged, and while it received very favourable press and was welcomed by the hard-core enthusiast, this didn't translate into sales. Now though, the Hawk GT and Bros, with the RC31 designation, are cult classic motorcycles.

Although the Hawk GT and Bros had a limited life, the Revere continued until it was replaced in 1998. This reliable, if unexciting, middle-of-the-road machine earned a loyal following, many owners fitting them with fairings and panniers. As they did with the Gold

Wing, Honda decided there was money in providing factory-fitted accessories, equipping the Revere with an integrated fairing and panniers to create the NT650V Deauville for 1998. With a longer muffler for the two-into-one exhaust, the engine produced 55hp at 7,750rpm. For 1999, the Deauville received an anti-theft ignition, but it continued for the next few years largely unchanged. An updated Deauville appeared for 2002 with larger panniers, the engine revised to reduce vibration, and a combined brake system with three-piston brake calipers on the front. There were minor styling updates, and although unkindly termed the 'Dullsville', the 228kg Deauville continued to provide exceptional touring ability, as long as the rider wasn't in too much of a hurry.

Below: Inspired by the NS500 Grand
Prix racer, the three-cylinder MVX250F
was Honda's first attempt at creating a
high-performance 250cc two-stroke.
*Honda*

# UNCONVENTIONAL TWO-STROKES

Honda remained loyal and committed to the four-stroke street bike longer than any other Japanese manufacturer. Adhering to the four-stroke for 32 years, the H100 two-stroke was released in 1981, followed by the MB50 and MB8 in 1982. The MB50 was the only two-stroke street bike ever offered in the USA, and it included Comstar wheels and a single front disc brake. More interesting was the MVX250F of 1983, inspired by the new NS500 Grand Prix racer of 1982 and designed to take on the successful Yamaha 250LC. Unlike the 112° V-three NS500, the MVX250F was a 90° V-three with a bore and stroke of 47 x 48mm. The two outer cylinders were horizontal, and the third cylinder vertical. To overcome any imbalance, the crankpins were in line, with a heavier central con-

rod, 9mm inner flywheels and 15mm outer flywheels. On the left of the crank was the electronic ignition pick-up, with the water pump drive and clutch on the right. The crankshaft ran in four ball bearings, induction was regulated by reed valves, and the carburetion was by a trio of 20mm square-slide Keihin downdraft carburettors. With an 8:1 compression ratio the power was 40hp at 9,000rpm. A large radiator situated on the front frame downtubes cooled each cylinder individually.

Although the six-speed engine was quite a radical design, the welded tubular steel frame was very conventional. It included a Pro-Link box-section swingarm, and Comstar wheels were 16 and 18-inch front and rear. The front brake was Honda's unusual enclosed disc with twin-piston caliper, and while the MVX250F was acceptably light at 138kg, its performance was disappointing. While capable of running with the 250LC, the new Yamaha RX250 with a power valve overwhelmed it. There was also some

Below: While beautifully
executed, the NS400 was
another example of Honda's
unsuccessful unconventionality.
*Honda*

Below: High-performance 250cc two-strokes have continued to be
popular, especially in Japan. This 1991 NSR250R had a banana-shaped
'gull' swingarm. *Australian Motorcycle News* Bottom: The 2003
NSR150 SP was resplendent in Repsol livery and featured a mono-
shock Pro-Arm. *Australian Motorcycle News*

speculation about its reliability, *Two Wheels* magazine stating: 'It's a brand-new model, so who knows how developed and sorted it really is?' After a year the MVX250 was replaced by the twin-cylinder NS250R, while the MVX250 evolved into the NS400.

One of Honda's production two-stroke gems was the NS400R of 1985 and '86. The 57 x 50.6mm triple displaced 387cc, and followed the same layout as the MVX250, but with two ATAC systems on the front cylinders. Carburetion was by three 36mm Keihins, and with a 6.7:1 compression ratio the power was 51hp at 9,000rpm. Beautifully detailed in Rothmans livery and with dozens of alloy castings, the NS400 suffered from a peaky engine that made it difficult to live with. With its alloy frame and swingarm, bolted up tangential spoke racing-style 16 and 17-inch wheels and hydraulic rear shock spring preload, the handling was superb. Unlike the MVX250, the brakes were conventional 256mm discs, with dual-piston calipers. The 37mm air-assisted fork had TRAC, and the NS400R was respectably fast, with *Performance Bikes* achieving 134.2mph (215.93km/h). Unfortunately, it had to compete with the larger-capacity Suzuki RG500 and Yamaha RD500LC, and despite its superb execution, the NS400 was lost in no-mans land, between the 500s and 350s.

Announced early in 1984, The NS250R was envisaged as a basis for the unsuccessful racing RS250R. The engine was a 90° V-twin (56 x 50.6mm), and now incorporated ATAC (automatic torque amplification chamber) on the exhaust. The 37mm front fork included TRAC, and while the wheels were Comstar (16 and 17-inch), the brakes were conventional discs. Over the next few years the NS250R gained an aluminium frame, and evolved into the 45hp NSR250R with a beam frame for 1987. The engine dimensions were now the same 54 x 54.5mm as the GP bikes. The NSR250R remained an important model, particularly in the domestic line-up, receiving a banana-shaped 'gull' swingarm for 1991, and a single-sided swingarm for 1997. The power on some

versions was as high as 64hp at 11,500rpm, and with state-of-the-art equipment the 134kg NSR250 was a formidable sporting streetbike. Alongside the NSR250R from 1989 was the single-cylinder NSR125 (produced in Italy) and the NSR150. These also provided high-technology entry-level motorcycling, and continue to do so largely unchanged, often in colours replicating racing teams. Later versions of the NSR150 SP also included a single-sided Pro-Arm. The little 59 x 54.5mm 149cc reed-valve single produced 39.5hp at 10,500rpm, which the 122kg NSR125 SP was capable of 90mph (150km/h).

Mick Grant on the NR500 at the Donington test. Although pleased with the test, Grant was still 2½ seconds off the 500cc lap record. *Mick Woollett*

# 6 GRAND PRIX RETURN:

## FOUR-STROKES TO TWO-STROKES (1979–91)

By 1976, the era of the four-stroke Grand Prix racer was on the wane. The four-stroke MV Agusta was barely competitive, and new noise regulations for 1977 ensured its death knell. It was in the midst of this sombre outlook that Honda, champion of the four-stroke, decided to develop a four-stroke 500cc Grand Prix racer. Surprising nearly everyone, Honda made the announcement at the end of 1977 that they were preparing to return to Grand Prix racing. It was an extremely audacious decision. Honda had been out of Grand Prix racing for a decade and was seemingly unaware of the progress in two-stroke development. The Yamaha and Suzuki 500cc four-cylinder two-strokes were producing around 120hp at 11,000rpm, with a brake mean effective pressure of nearly 150psi. Four-stroke BMEP had long since peaked at around 200psi, and as a four-stroke was also restricted to four-cylinders it would need to produce an inconceivable 280psi at comparable revs. The only way a four-stroke could match the two-stroke's double power strokes per engine cycle was to double the revs, to around 22,000rpm. Honda simply believed they could do it.

## THE NR500 (1979–82)

Kawashima entrusted the design of the NR500 engine to Shoichiro Irimajiri, with Takeo Fukui the project leader. Irimajiri was assisted by a young graduate, Suguru Kanazawa, and much time was spent considering how to increase engine speed and valve area. Irimajiri then decided to instigate development of the NR's most distinguishing feature; oval pistons. FIM regulations stipulated the number of cylinders, but not their form, and four oval cylinders could provide the benefits of the eight-cylinder engine that Honda really wanted to build. Even if Honda had built an engine out of two RC164 250cc fours they would have had a V8 that produced nearly 100hp, without water-cooling. Amid much scepticism, Irimajiri tested an experimental single cylinder. This functioned sufficiently well for the project to proceed.

Mick Grant confers with Honda team boss Gerald Davidson during the NR500 test at Donington Park in August 1979. *Mick Woollett*

disappointing 80hp at 14,000rpm. By the time the engine (now the OX) was installed in the chassis it was producing nearly 100hp at 17,000rpm.

This chassis was almost as radical as the motor. Designer Kamiya wanted a monocoque chassis, and constructed this out of sheet aluminium. Every effort was made to reduce frontal area, and the chassis included the engine as a stressed member and acted as a lower fairing and mount for the side radiators. Several fairing combinations were tried, including one with the nose separated from the body. The most serious disadvantage of the monocoque design was that to access the carburettors the engine and rear half had to be separated from the front end. To further reduce frontal area, provide a lower centre of gravity, and quicken the steering, the NR500 had 16-inch wheels front and rear. This forced Michelin and Dunlop to develop new tyres. More unconventional features included Comstar wheels and an upside down Showa telescopic fork with external springs and the fork tubes offset ahead of the front axle. With the Nissin brake calipers positioned in front of the fork, the front-end geometry went against established practice. Compared with the rest of the specification, the rear suspension was surprisingly conventional, Honda using a single shock absorber and cantilever swingarm. To minimise chain tension variation as the suspension compressed, the swingarm pivoted on bearings in the monocoque that were in line with the rear sprocket.

The first complete motorcycle was ready for testing by April 1979, and the Honda International Racing Company (HIRC) was established to run the GP programme from England. UK racing team manager Gerald Davidson was to head the programme, with experienced test riders Mick Grant and Japan's first World Champion, Takazumi Katayama. After a tentative practice session at Donington, they were entered in the final two GPs of 1979. Even the experience of Grant and Katayama couldn't disguise the NR500's deficiencies. The NR500 was extremely slow, the aluminium frame kept cracking, and at Silverstone in August, the two NR500s qualified 38th and 41st. Honda's humiliation was complete when Grant crashed at the first turn and Katayama retired after two laps. The nightmare continued at the French Grand Prix three weeks later. Although the power was increased to 108hp, and the weight reduced by 10kg, neither qualified and although they joined the grid, Grant and Katayama were ordered back to the pits.

The NR500 engine was a water-cooled V-four, the 100° angle between the cylinders slightly wider than the optimum 90° to provide room for the carburettors. Drive to the double overhead camshafts was by a train of gears from the crank on the right side of the engine. The pistons on the NR500 were not quite oval, and consisted of two straight sides and two curves. They were 93.4 x 41mm, requiring two con-rods for support. The stroke was 36mm, and the 82mm long one-piece con-rods included a 12mm gudgeon and 26mm big-end. Also like the 1960s racing engines the crankshaft was built-up, with roller bearings. The valves were arranged in two rows of four (18mm inlet and 16mm exhaust), with a reasonably wide included angle of 65°, and each pair of inlet valves fed by a twin-choke 30mm downdraft carburettor. To speed up burning in the wide combustion chambers there were two 8mm spark plugs per cylinder, fired by an electronic CDI ignition. Lubrication was by conventional wet sump, and there was a six-speed gearbox and dry multiplate clutch. The first engine, designated the K-0, was running in April 1979, but piston ring problems saw it produce a

For 1980, the NR500 was completely redesigned, with a Ron Williams frame and 18-inch wheels. Early in the season the brakes were Lockheed, but by the British Grand Prix Brembo front brakes were fitted. Katayama finished 15th on this machine. *Mick Woollett*

Honda's engineers worked hard to make the NR500 competitive for the 1980 season. Parts of the machine, including the front wheel and handlebars, were taken to a Shinto shrine to be blessed with speed. The engine (designated 1X) had a narrower included valve angle of 55°, and eventually 40°. The valves were increased to 19mm and 17mm with the power increased incrementally until it reached 118hp at 19,000rpm by January 1980. The monocoque chassis was also scrapped, and a Maxton frame commissioned from British designer Ron Williams. Along with the tubular steel frame, still using the engine as a stressed member, came a return to the more traditional 18-inch wheels. A Marzocchi front fork replaced the earlier upside down type, and the radiator moved to the front of the motor, but the NR500 was still heavy at close to 150kg. After the ignominy of 1979, Davidson persuaded Honda to race the NR500 in some European International races before attempting GPs. An encouraging third place at Misano resulted in Katayama's entry for the Finnish GP at Imatra. He qualified last but conflict within the team meant he didn't race. Katayama's results in the final two races were more heartening. The disturbing fragility of the engine seemed to be overcome when Katayama finished the British GP in last place, following this with a 12th place at the Nürburgring. It was enough to bring a smile to the faces of the Honda development team, and encouraged them to install a Tamaka-designed frame with Pro-Link rear suspension for an International race at Misano towards the end of 1980.

By this stage many engineers involved, including Kanazawa, doubted the NR500 would ever be competitive. *Cycle* magazine was invited to test the bike, and was given a souvenir connecting rod. They commented 'the NR500 is the bravest technological attempt we've ever seen. But we do think it may not have a future.' Despite these doubts, NR500 development continued in preparation for the 1981 season. The incorporation of magnesium engine castings and carbon fibre wheels saw the weight reduced to around 130kg. Engine development (now the 2X) included a reduction in the cylinder angle to 90°, with the forward cylinders almost horizontal. The

Left: Freddie Spencer provided the NR500 with its most impressive GP performance, placing fifth in the 1981 British Grand Prix, before the motor expired. *Mick Woollett*

Below: Two NR750s were entered in the Australian Swann series in November 1987, with Malcolm Campbell winning one race. Here, Campbell readies for the track. *Author*

gear camshaft drive was now between the cylinders and the water pump moved from behind the crank on the left, to the front. The included valve angle was reduced further, to 38°, and the carburettors were complex 30mm flat-slide, designed by Seiki Ishii.

These improvements saw the NR500 achieve its only victory, in a damp 200km race at Suzuka in June 1981. Ironically, this victory was masterminded by Youichi Oguma, one of the chief proponents in the quest for a change in direction to two-strokes. Riders Kiyama and Abe managed to beat the factory two-stroke Yamahas and Suzukis by racing with one less fuel stop. While this victory didn't prevent the decision to build the NS500 two-stroke, it did provide the NR500 with a brief reprieve. Rising American star Freddie Spencer tested the NR500 at Suzuka, and elected to race it at the Champion Spark Plug 200 at Laguna Seca. There, he astonished everyone by winning his heat race, beating reigning 500 champion Kenny Roberts. The NR500 broke its valve springs as Spencer revved it to

22,000rpm in the main races, but this performance was good enough for Honda to enter Spencer on the NR500 for the British Grand Prix. Again Spencer surprised the pundits. He qualified ninth and was up to fifth before the motor characteristically expired. Spencer was timed at 144mph (232km/h), the same speed as Barry Sheene's Yamaha.

While the NR500 didn't race again in 1981, continued development saw the fourth-generation motor (the 3X) produce 130hp at 18,500rpm by the end of the year. The 90° V-four was tipped back a further 20°, the valve angle reduced to 30°, there was an aluminium frame, and the swingarm and wheels were carbon-fibre. Ron Haslam rode it in three GPs in 1982. Although it now weighed 135kg and produced 132hp, it was too late for the nearly ready, then never-ready 'New Racer.' A final version was exhibited at the 1983 Tokyo Show, and at Cologne in 1984, with a carbon-fibre frame and swingarm, but it wasn't raced. While incredibly difficult to ride, and with no flywheel

# THE NR750

Undeterred by the failure of the NR500, during 1983 and '84 HRC developed an oval piston 250cc turbocharged GP engine. Two types were tested, a parallel twin and a V-twin, eventually producing 165hp at 17,000rpm, and limited only by the cooling of the oval pistons. During 1984, planning began for the next-generation oval piston engine, and HRC director Takeo Fukui surprised everyone when he announced the NR750 Endurance and Formula 1 machine early in 1987. Directly descended from the final version of the NR500, but with a narrower, 85° angle between the cylinders, the NR750 also had a plain-bearing crankshaft. Like the NR500, the crankpins were in line. The included valve angle between the four inlet and four exhaust valves was 36°, with the dual-throat 28mm Keihin carburettors pointing upwards. The cast pistons used three rings, and as with the NR500, each piston was supported by two titanium con-rods. The stroke was 42mm. On the right side of the crankshaft was a gear drive for the camshafts, and the six-speed gearbox was removable through a side plate behind the one-way Sprague clutch, similar to the 500cc GP bikes. In a conservative state of tune for endurance racing, the power was around 155hp at 15,000rpm.

The 750cc engine was installed in a chassis similar to the all-conquering RVF750, with an aluminium beam frame, a 43mm Showa fork, and single-sided swingarm with Showa shock

absorber. Weighing only 158kg, the NR750 was lighter and more powerful than the RVF750, and was entered in the 24-hour race at Le Mans on 19–20 April. Piloted by Australian ace Malcolm Campbell and two journalists, Gilbert Roy of France, and Ken Nemoto of Japan, Campbell qualified second fastest. In the race the NR750 lasted only three hours, until a big-end bolt loosened, blocking an oil way and seizing a piston. The NR750 subsequently made an appearance in the Australian Swann series towards the end of 1987, ridden by Campbell and Rob Scolyer. Now producing 160hp, Campbell won one race and finished the series third overall. Just like the NR500, the NR750 retired with one race victory, and it also reappeared four years later.

As soon as it appeared, the NS500 triple was competitive. The early 1982 examples had a tubular steel frame. *Mick Woollett*

effect due to the high internal friction of the straight-sided pistons, the NR500 served a very useful purpose for Honda. It may have been unsuccessful on the race track, but the knowledge gained regarding high rpm four-strokes, back-torque limiting clutches, and gear camshaft drives would later be applied to production engines. While cynics at the time dismissed the NR500, it is now acknowledged as a technological masterpiece.

# THE NS500 AND RS500 (1982–87)

In July 1981, Oguma travelled to the Belgian Grand Prix to examine the two-stroke competition. He reported back to Shinichi Miyakoshi, the director of Motocross development, who was responsible for the Elsinore and championship-winning CR motocrossers. Honda's GP two-stroke era had begun, but Honda's development philosophy was that they had to be different. Being different cost Honda dearly with the NR500, but this time they were on to a winner.

Miyakoshi and Oguma believed the current crop of four-cylinder 500s were too complex, too heavy, and the motorcycles too unwieldy. They went for a radical solution, a V-three, with the central cylinder horizontal and the outer cylinders vertical. While ultimately producing less power than the fours, Honda believed a lighter, more compact machine with a smaller frontal area was a superior solution. Their other radical feature was to use reed valves rather than disc valves. Reed valves were popular on motocross machines because they broadened the torque curve, but were eschewed in Grand Prix racing as they restricted ultimate power. Honda may have been forced down the two-stroke path, but no-one could accuse them of copying.

The NS500 engine had the cylinders spaced at 110°, and the bore and stroke was 62.6 x 54mm. Unlike the Suzuki and Yamaha fours, there was a single crankshaft, reducing friction, and with the reed valves feeding into the crankcase at the base of the cylinder, the engine was barely wider than a twin. The cylinders were scaled down 250 motocross cylinders, with five

Spencer finished second in the Nations GP at Misano on the NS500, and went on to finish third in the championship. *Mick Woollett*

transfer ports and one exhaust port. The engine was turned backwards with power going to a clutch on a jackshaft, incorporating a balancer, behind the crankshaft. Three forward-facing 34mm Keihin carburettors nestled in between the cylinders, and the exhaust ports pointed to the rear of the bike. The ignition was total loss, running from a pack of dry-cell batteries on the left. This brilliant engine was initially housed in a tubular steel frame, the rear suspension featuring a near-vertical shock absorber with a linkage attached to the aluminium swingarm. The wheels were aluminium Comstar, a 16-inch front making a return. Development proceeded extremely quickly, with a prototype running by the end of the year. Initial impressions were disappointing – the engine only produced 108hp initially, and the narrow powerband was between 9,800rpm and 11,000rpm. Although it weighed only 128kg it was doubtful the NS500 could compete with the more powerful Yamahas and Suzukis. Honda wanted their young American Superstar Freddie Spencer to head their GP effort, and Spencer was sufficiently impressed by the size of Honda's operation

to go with it. Spencer brought along his ace tuner Erv Kanemoto. Kanemoto was hugely experienced, and would go on to help four Honda riders win seven titles, but he was sceptical a new triple could beat the established fours.

One thing was evident from the outset. After suffering three years of scorn and ridicule resulting from the NR500, Honda would stop at nothing in their determination to win races and the World Championship. They lured 500cc World Champion Marco Lucchinelli into the team alongside Spencer and Katayama, and each separate team had two machines. The power was now up to 120hp and Miyakoshi's faith in the competitiveness of a smaller, compact racer, was vindicated. On its first outing in Argentina Spencer finished third, with Lucchinelli and Katayama fifth and sixth. Lucchinelli almost won at the next race in Austria, crashing while in the lead on the last lap, but at the Belgian GP at Spa Spencer provided Honda with their first 500 GP win in 15 years. Katayama won in Sweden, and Spencer again at the San Marino GP at Mugello, with Spencer finishing third in the World

Mid-way though the 1982
season the NS500 received
an aluminium frame.
*Mick Woollett*

more forward in the chassis, and the wheels were 16-inch front and rear.

The 1983 racing season turned out to be another struggle between two racing giants, reminiscent of the Hailwood and Agostini days. This time the roles were reversed, with Spencer's lighter and more manageable three-cylinder Honda battling the more powerful, but less agile, rotary-valve Yamaha of Kenny Roberts. They shared six Grand Prix victories apiece, and the championship went down to the final race after Spencer's aggressive riding in Sweden resulted in Roberts running off the track. Spencer won Honda's first 500cc title when he finished second to Roberts at San Marino.

It was fortunate for Honda that the development of the NS500 peaked early in the 1983 season, enabling Spencer to establish a comfortable points lead after the first three GPs. Towards the end of 1983 the Yamaha was vastly improved, and the NS500's superior handling and manoeuvrability less pronounced. Honda needed more power, and already HRC had plans for a four-cylinder machine. In the meantime, the NS500 continued to win races and provide good results. Randy Mamola and Spencer won GPs on it during 1984, and Mamola, Wayne Gardner and Ron Haslam filled the podium on many occasions during 1985. Even during 1986, now with 140hp, a full-beam aluminium chassis and 17-inch Comstar wheels, Raymond Roche achieved respectable results with the light (113kg) NS500. In the wet 1987 French Grand Prix Pier Francesco Chili rode an NS500 to second. The production RS500 was also extremely successful, living on until 1988. In 1986 it received a beam aluminium chassis and 16 and 18-inch six-spoke magnesium wheels. Weighing 125kg and producing 130hp, these production RS500s were the mainstay of the privateer Grand Prix rider until the early 1990s.

Championship. From the outset Spencer and the NS500 were a formidable combination, perfectly suited to each other.

While the NS500 surprised the pundits, it wasn't perfect. There were many engine seizures, some ignition problems, and the flat-sided expansion chambers were too restrictive, contributing to a power deficiency. The early steel frame positioned the engine too far backwards, so for Assen there was a new aluminium frame. Updated Nikasil cylinders, revised porting, and a choice of 34mm, 36mm or 38mm cylindrical slide Mikuni carburettors saw the power rise to 125hp. A carbon-fibre rectangular section swingarm and carbon-fibre and magnesium composite wheels contributed to a reduction in weight, to only 120kg.

In September, Honda Racing Corporation was formed, and sensing a championship victory, HRC produced an updated NS500 for 1983. The riders this year were Spencer, Lucchinelli, Katayama and Haslam, with the latter the chief tester. Haslam tested three versions, including a prototype RS500 production racer. With more carbon-fibre, an ATAC valve, self-generating ignition, and circular cross-section expansion chambers, the lighter (115kg) NS500 was more powerful (130hp) than before. The engine was

## THE NSR500 (1984–86)

While the NS500 was a brilliant package, it was inevitable that Honda would follow the four-cylinder route. And typically of Honda, they wanted to do it differently. As there was no alternative to a V-four, Honda decided on a radical chassis. It was a return to the NR500 scenario where Honda's development team, headed by a project leader, would pursue an independent path with total determination, however illogical.

Brilliant and extremely talented, Freddie Spencer was groomed by Honda when he was only 19 years of age. At Daytona in 1981 Spencer had a special RS1000 and was leading by a huge margin until the engine blew. *Mick Woollett*

The NSR500 V-four engine (54 x 54.5mm) featured similar design characteristics to the NS500 in that it included a single crankshaft and reed valve induction. The cylinders were arranged at 90° for perfect primary balance, with the vertical bank inclined forward about 10°. There were five transfer ports and the ATAC mechanically controlled variable volume exhaust. The crankshaft rotated forwards, with power transferring to a jackshaft, and the crank was extremely light to assist rapid direction changing and acceleration. With two dual throat 34mm cylindrical slide Keihin carburettors it immediately produced 140hp, but the light flywheels allowed the engine to over-rev as the tyre broke traction. In their quest to be different, Honda's engineers also moved the fuel tank underneath the engine, routing the exhaust pipes above the power plant and exiting under the seat. Influenced by the ELFe Endurance racer Honda supplied RS1000 engines as it was believed that by placing the weight of the fuel underneath the engine this would lower the centre of gravity. Unfortunately, the weight was too low, inhibiting turning, and despite baffles in the underslung fuel tank, there was also the problem of the fuel surge under braking and acceleration. The aluminium frame held the solidly mounted motor in three locations, and the wheels were Comstar carbon-fibre (16 and 17-inch) with a Michelin radial tyre on the rear. The front brakes were 300mm steel, and at the rear was a small carbon disc. Although it ran on a short, 1,375mm wheelbase, the weight of nearly 135kg was disappointingly heavy, and it was a mechanic's worst nightmare as access to the engine was difficult under the hot exhaust pipes.

Although in its race debut at Daytona in March 1984, Spencer finished second, the Grand Prix season started badly. During practice for the South African GP the Comstar carbon-fibre rear wheel collapsed, but Spencer managed to win the next race at Misano. It was then that serious problems with the NSR500 really became evident. A crash in the Transatlantic race at Donington, caused by a fuel surge pushing the front wheel, was followed by the Austrian GP at Salzburgring where Randy Mamola on an NS500 triple slowed to let Spencer through into second place. The two Honda riders were booed by 80,000 spectators.

Fearing humiliation at the new Nürburgring circuit, Spencer elected to ride the year-old NS500, and won. Acutely embarrassed, as they always believe new is better, Honda produced a new NSR500 for Spencer at

# FAST FREDDIE

Supremely talented, Freddie Spencer was only 21 years old when he provided Honda with their first 500cc World Championship. Born in 1961 in Shreveport, Louisiana, the religious Spencer was groomed by his parents from the age of five to become a motorcycle racer. By the time he was 11 he had won ten state motorcycling championships. Switching from dirt to tarmac when he was 12, Spencer showed an incredible ability to learn tracks quickly. In 1978 he teamed up with the brilliant tuner Erv Kanemoto and soon set the racing world in the USA alight. When only 17 years old, Spencer won the 1979 AMA 250 Expert series, earning him a Honda Superbike ride for 1980. After an astonishing foreign debut in the Transatlantic Trophy series, when he beat many established stars on the Kanemoto Yamaha 750, Spencer became Honda's star rider, heading the American racing programme for 1981. When he won his first GP in 1982, Spencer was the youngest Grand Prix winner at that time.

After winning a hard-fought championship with Kenny Roberts in 1983, Spencer responded with one of the most amazing seasons ever in 1985, winning both the 250 and 500 titles. It was an extraordinary achievement, but a hand injury sustained in a minor fall at the 1985 British Grand Prix triggered a tendonitis injury which forced his retirement early in 1986. Spencer made several belated comebacks, retiring from GP racing in 1989, but making a surprising return on a factory Yamaha in 1993. Back in the AMA series, Spencer went on to win three more US Superbike nationals, with a final victory in 1995, before retiring from racing in 1996. Spencer subsequently founded a successful Honda-backed performance riding school at Las Vegas. With 27 GP victories, all on Hondas, Spencer will always be remembered as the only rider to win the 250cc and 500cc double in a season.

the French GP. Spencer vindicated Honda's faith in the V-four, comfortably winning the race, and following this with a victory in Yugoslavia. But there were still problems with the NSR500, Spencer favouring the NS triple to win in Belgium. A crash on the V-four at Laguna Seca ended Spencer's championship hopes, but Mamola rode the difficult NSR500 to victory in its final race at Silverstone before it disappeared back to Japan. Although the NS500 of Mamola and RS500 of Raymond Roche provided Honda with some credibility, the 1984 season was one they wished to forget. The combination of explosive power and unpredictable handling was one that only a master rider like Spencer could manage.

For 1985, Honda's engineers licked their wounds and produced a conventional NSR500 for Spencer. The fuel tank was located above the conventional Cobas-

style beam aluminium frame, and the swingarm, a rectangular box-section type, connected to a Showa shock absorber with a Pro-Link system. While retaining the single crankshaft, reed valve V-four layout, the engine was completely redesigned to make it lighter and more compact. The firing order was revised, the jackshaft behind the crankshaft removed, the crankshaft being rotated anti-clockwise. The power increased to close to 144hp at 11,500rpm, and the weight was 119kg. Honda also produced a 250 twin for Spencer, concurrently with the NSR500. Spencer was so impressed with the 250 he asked for a 500 which was simply a larger version.

This is what Honda provided, and despite the exhaust pipes splitting, Spencer won at Daytona. The engine was initially positioned too far back in the chassis, pushing the front wheel, but by the start of the European GP

versions of the engine were tried, each with different exhausts and cylinders, providing different power characteristics. This was the last year with low level exhausts, and a four-into-two exhaust system was also tried in an effort to tame the wicked power delivery that was destroying tyres early in the race. Mid-way through the season the ATAC system was also replaced by a new exhaust valve arrangement similar to the Yamaha YPVS. The power was 152hp at 11,800rpm, the chassis was redesigned, with a longer swingarm, and the wheels were generally 17-inch front and rear. The front brake discs were increased from 310mm to 320mm, and the TRAC could be removed from the 43mm Showa fork if required. The weight was unchanged at 119kg.

On paper the redesigned NSR500 should have been a winner. Rising Australian star Wayne Gardner was drafted alongside Spencer, but when Spencer retired while leading the opening race in Spain, Gardner was left to spearhead Honda's hopes. Gardner's riding style was completely different, and he found the marginally improved NSR500 uncomfortable. Designed for Spencer, the motor had a very narrow powerband, something Gardner, coming from the world of four-strokes wasn't used to. Gardner also struggled with the forward weight bias and lack of chassis stability which didn't worry Spencer. Spencer didn't return during 1986, and in his absence Gardner bravely fought with the NSR500. Suffering from chronic understeer, Gardner did his best to keep the ill handling NSR500 with the ever-improving Yamaha of Eddie Lawson, managing to win three GPs. Gardner ended second in the championship, but Honda was extremely disappointed not to win the title after their spectacular performance in 1985.

season there was a new chassis with the engine further forward and a steeper steering head angle. The NSR500 now turned more easily but at the expense of stability. Spencer was also using a new, 16-inch Michelin radial front tyre, and from the second round in Spain proved hard to beat on the NSR500. He won seven GPs to convincingly take the 500cc World Championship. Spencer was at the peak of his career, but it had taken an enormous effort to win two championships.

For the 1986 season, Honda again redesigned the NSR500. The engine looked similar, but was tipped forward, and moved forward, to put more weight on the front wheel. New castings made it 25mm narrower than before. All the internal parts were redesigned and the only unchanged component was the clutch. This resulted in a 5 per cent reduction in weight, and a 10mm shorter wheelbase. During the season three

## THE RS250R-W (1985), RS250R (1984–5) AND NSR250 (1986)

At the same time as Honda was developing the NS500 triple, they produced a production racing RS250, based on the street two-stroke NS250. The engine was a 90° 56 x 50.6mm reed valve V-twin, with ATAC and heavy street bike crankcases. With 34mm Keihin carburettors, the claimed power was 66hp at 11,500rpm. A lightweight square-section aluminium frame compensated for the heavy engine, and the weight was

Honda produced the RS250R-W for Spencer in 1985, and he rewarded them with their first 250cc World Championship in 18 years. *Alan Cathcart Archive*

around 100kg. By basing the racer on a street bike, Honda completely miscalculated, and the RS250 was a disaster. Slow, and unreliable, it seldom finished a race during 1984.

Undeterred, Honda produced three 250 GP racers for 1985. The production RS250 featured smaller crankcases, the vertical cylinder turned 180°, and a twin spar aluminium frame. A special version of the RS250 was provided for semi-works riders Anton Mang and Fausto Ricci, while Spencer received a very special RS250R-W for his bid to win two crowns in a season.

The RS250R-W was based on the NSR500, the 90° V-twin sharing the 54 x 54.5mm bore and stroke. The vertically mounted reed valves flowed directly into the crankcase, while the front cylinder tilted further forward. The Nikasil cylinders had two exhaust and five transfer ports, and were fed by a dual-throat cylindrical 38mm Keihin carburettor positioned behind the engine, above the gearbox. ATAC chambers were included on the titanium exhaust pipes. Unlike the production RS250, the RS250R-W gearbox was removable for ratio adjustment, through the right side of the crankcase. In the quest to save weight, many components were magnesium, including the crankcases, and the RS250R-W produced 75hp.

The aluminium beam frame was also lighter than that of the RS250, and although the swingarm was longer, the wheelbase was 38mm shorter. The fork sliders and triple clamps were magnesium, and with aluminium 16 and 17-inch Comstar wheels the weight was right on the FIM minimum of 90kg. In the hands of Spencer at his peak, this phenomenal machine made a mockery of the 250cc competition during 1985. Although many doubted Spencer could pull off two World Championships, after winning the first GP in South Africa he was virtually unbeatable. Spencer won seven of the first nine GPs. With the World Championship sewn up he then concentrated on the 500 title.

Spencer abdicated from the 250 class for 1986, Honda turning the RS250R-W into a less exotic racer, the NSR250, and lent a number to selected riders. Yamaha made their 250 into a factory special, and the Honda was now outclassed. Although the power was still 75hp, the weight was up to 100kg. The crankcases and carburettors were now aluminium, and there were minor changes to the rear shock absorber mount. While Sito Pons, Dominique Sarron, and veteran Anton Mang shared victories the title was lost to Carlos Lavado on the Yamaha.

Below: After the disappointment
of 1986, Honda had two new
World Champions for 1987; Toni
Mang and Wayne Gardner.
*Two Wheels*

# 1987 CHAMPIONS: WAYNE GARDNER AND TONI MANG

Wayne Gardner continued a tradition of Australian riders heading to Europe when he won the 1980 Castrol Six-Hour production race, and decided on a career as a professional racer. Born in Wollongong in 1959, the tough fitter and turner soon showed his ability and determination in England, finally earning a ride with Honda Britain in 1982. A meteoric rise, and a significant victory in the 1985 Suzuka 8-hour race, saw him with a factory 500cc ride for 1986, and becoming Australia's first 500cc World Champion in 1987. Unlike many other World Champions Gardner was aware of the importance of public relations, raising the profile of motorcycle racing in Australia, and enabling other Australian riders to follow his example. Although he was never again consistent enough to win a world title, Gardner continued to win GPs until his retirement in 1992. One of his most astounding victories was in the 1990

Australian GP, when he won with a broken wrist and a broken fairing that threatened to fall off at any time. After retiring from motorcycle racing, Gardner successfully raced touring cars in Australia and Japan.

When Anton (Toni) Mang received a Honda contract for 1985 he was a veteran. Born in Inning am Ammersee in Bavaria, in 1949, he was initially attracted to skiing, becoming a Junior European ski-bob champion when he was 16. A toolmaker by trade, he took to motorcycle racing with childhood friend Sepp Schlögl, a brilliant motorcycle engineer and tuner, who remained with Mang throughout his racing career. The winner of four 250cc and 350cc World Championships for Kawasaki he struggled to be competitive after Kawasaki's withdrawal from Grand Prix racing at the end of 1982. Then, in 1987 at the age of 38, Mang surprised everyone by winning his fifth World Championship. He was undeniably the fastest and most consistent 250cc rider in the world that year, but a slow recovery from a broken collarbone after a crash at the 1988 Yugoslavia GP prompted his retirement from Grand Prix racing. As Germany's most successful ever motorcycle racer Toni Mang won 44 GPs spanning a decade.

Wayne Gardner had a new
NSR500 for 1987, and won the
World Championship. *Two
Wheels*

# THE NSR500 (1987–91)

The failure of 1986 prompted Honda to carefully
scrutinise the NSR500's shortcomings and endeavour
to overcome them with a new design. Influenced by the
success of the NS500 triple, the angle between the
cylinders was increased to 112° to allow the two round
slide 34mm or 36mm twin-choke Keihin carburettors
to sit within the vee, rather than behind the cylinders as
before. As on the NS500 and 1984 NSR500, a balance
shaft was fitted behind the crankshaft, running from
the primary gears on the left to the clutch on the right.
On the 1987 engine this was to cancel secondary
imbalance, but another advantage was that it allowed
the motor to rotate forwards, helping to load the front
tyre under acceleration and overcome the understeer.
The relocation of the carburettors allowed more space
for the exhausts, with the rear exhausts sweeping under
the seat. While the power valve system was similar to
the final 1986 version, the operation was now electrical

rather than mechanical. The engine was solidly
mounted in the aluminium frame, and the swingarm
was similar to before, but cut and tapered at each end,
increasing the wheelbase to 1,375mm. The new engine
produced close to 160hp at 12,000rpm, and the
NSR500 weighed 125kg. In 1987, Honda provided the
NSR500 to three teams, Rothmans sponsoring Spencer
and Gardner, and HB sponsoring Niall McKenzie.
Although still not perfect, the NSR500 was good
enough for Gardner to dominate the 1987 GP season
with seven victories. Spencer reappeared on several
occasions, but he only finished one race, in seventh
place at Sweden. Gardner was riding at his peak, but
was never really satisfied with the machine. Despite
this, the determined Gardner rarely finished off the
podium, and had the title wrapped up with one round
to go.

Not content with evolutionary development, a new
set of engineers at HRC redesigned the NSR500 for
1988. The engine incorporated an electronic control

The 1989 NSR500 was a wicked machine, but Eddie Lawson managed to give Honda another World Championship. *Alan Cathcart Archive*

that tied exhaust-gate height and throttle angle, and while this slowed acceleration the harsh throttle transition disappeared. Honda also introduced a programmable ignition curve, allowing different curves for different situations. Shinichi Tsunoda created a new chassis, believing a lower centre of gravity was the solution to the single crankshaft gyro effect. The engine was slightly more powerful and compact, but the lowered engine and swingarm pivot, with near horizontal unbraced swingarm, resulted in a machine that was virtually unrideable. The NSR now squatted under power, producing unwanted mid-corner attitude changes. Other problems also emerged, the quest for lightness leading to brake fade as the lighter rotors overheated. After seven different frames during the season, and bravely trying to tame the wild NSR early in the season, Gardner managed to win four GPs, including three in a row mid-season. But the NSR500 exhibited all the characteristics of independent development without an overall sense of integration.

Despite Gardner's best efforts, it wasn't enough to snatch the title from Eddie Lawson and the Yamaha.

After the disastrous 1988 season, Honda produced a completely new NSR500 for 1989. While the motor now produced 170hp, with cylindrical slide Keihin carburettors the powerband was wider. The chassis was redesigned to incorporate tuned flex. During the year there were 13 frame updates, plus a 50 per cent stiffer upside down Showa front fork, and carbon brakes. The swingarm was also now banana-shaped on the right to clear the exhaust pipes, and there was a return to a 16-inch front wheel on occasion to improve the change of direction. While Honda's engineers worked on overcoming the NSR500's deficiencies, a further shock was in store for 1989. World Champion Eddie Lawson persuaded Honda to let him ride the NSR500 in a Kanemoto satellite team, with full factory backing. Honda was reluctant to agree, but 'Mr Yamaha' Lawson came with the Number 1 plate. Gardner was not impressed, but he still headed the official HRC

Big and brutal, the VF1000F didn't capture the big bike market as Honda envisaged. *Motorcycle Trader collection*

# 7 V-FOUR VICTORY

For nearly a decade, Honda tantalised the world with their exotic racing four-cylinder machines before they unleashed the CB750. Then, content to ride on the wave of the CB750's success, motorcycle development stagnated as Honda concentrated on building their automotive empire. Eventually time ran out for the CB750, and while there was another generation of air-cooled four-cylinder motorcycles, Honda knew its days were numbered. Increasing emission and noise regulations demanded a change in direction, and this appeared in 1982 with the V-four 750 VF750S and Sabre. The appearance of the V-four wasn't unexpected. Since 1979, Honda had been racing the NR500, and while this was a failure on the track, they learnt much from its development. Also at this time, Honda was being seriously challenged by Yamaha in the USA, and wanted to respond with a vengeance.

## THE VF750C MAGNA AND VF750S SABRE (1982–2004)

The choice of a liquid-cooled 90° V-four was an obvious solution for a new generation of engines. The 90° cylinder angle provided perfect primary balance, and the layout enabled the short-stroke (70 x 48.6mm) motor to be extremely compact. Liquid-cooling ensured there was no problem cooling of the rear cylinders, and at only 414mm wide the motor could be mounted lower in the frame. Many features came from the CX500 twin, including horizontally split crankcases incorporating the cylinders. The one-piece crankshaft was supported by four plain bearings, and the VF750 (V45) had a 360° crank, with each pair of pistons rising and falling together, much like two Ducati twins side-by-side. With 26mm and 23mm valves, the four-valve cylinder head design was new, with a narrower (38°) included valve angle, allowing a flat-topped piston for a reasonably high compression ratio of 10.5:1. Double overhead camshafts were driven by Hy-Vo chains from the centre of the crank, and the valve actuation changed from Honda's usual bucket and shim to a Suzuki-style screw adjustment. Primary drive was by split straight-cut gear to a

Powered by a water-cooled 750
V-four engine, the VF750S was a
radical departure from
established production layouts.
*Motorcycle Trader collection*

hydraulically operated multiplate clutch and six-speed gearbox with shaft final drive. A chain from the main transmission shaft drove the oil and water pumps, and there were 32mm Keihin VD32 carburettors angled at 45°, with horizontal float chambers. The power was a respectable 78hp at 9,500rpm, but with its shaft drive the VF750 was undoubtedly envisaged as a cruiser rather than a sports bike.

The Magna and Sabre featured different chassis, both with conventional steel double-cradle frames, but the Magna cruiser included a 37mm leading axle front fork with TRAC and dual rear shock absorbers. With cast alloy 18 and 16-inch wheels and a low 759mm seat, this was successfully launched in America, *Cycle* magazine noting 'the V-fours signal a giant step forward.' The VF750S Sabre was a less satisfactory incarnation. The chassis included a 37mm

centre-axle front fork with TRAC and a Pro-Link single shock absorber rear suspension, but the wheelbase was a huge 1,562mm, and the weight a considerable 224kg. Rolling on 18-inch wheels front and rear, the VF750S didn't handle particularly well, but the most disconcerting feature was the ugly and awkward electronic instrument panel. The VF750S didn't receive much of a welcome in Europe, but in America *Cycle* magazine commented: 'The Honda Sabre says the future of street motorcycling is as bright and incandescent as we've ever seen it.' The magazine was correct in their assumption, but in the meantime the VF750 was extremely troubled. Problems manifested themselves almost immediately, with early bikes failing to idle evenly, resulting in 40 official bulletins sent to alleviate the problem. Other engine problems, particularly camshaft and

The VF750C Magna was re-
introduced in 1994 with the
VFR750 motor, which lasted until
2003. *Australian Motorcycle
News*

transmission, indicated the development of the new V-four was a little hasty.

The Sabre and Magna lasted only until 1983 before downsizing to 700cc for the USA in 1984 to defeat the tariff barrier for motorcycles of more than 700cc. A shorter stroke (45.4mm) provided 698cc, and there were shorter con-rods (115.6mm instead of 117.2mm). A range of Hondaline touring accessories was also available for the Sabre, but the VF700C Magna was much as before, continuing until 1987 with styling updates and a continual lengthening of the wheelbase to provide a more custom look. The 1987 model had an unusual four-into-four exhaust system and an aluminium disc rear wheel. The Sabre also continued as a 700, the VF700S, for 1984 and 1985. The VF750C Magna made a brief reappearance in 1988, but this sold poorly, despite its excellent engine and chassis. The

failure was blamed on the extreme styling, the quartet of bazooka exhausts combining elements of a dragbike with the Japanese interpretation of an American hot-rod. Like most motorcycle manufacturers, Honda floundered in America in the late 1980s. Revitalised interest in the Magna convinced Honda to create a new VF750C Magna, this appearing in 1994 with a motor based on the VFR750. In many respects the new Magna was a continuation of the earlier concept. The engine retained the 360° crankshaft, not the 180° VFR type, 34mm carburettors, a five-speed gearbox, a cable-operated clutch and chain-driven camshafts. The valve actuation was the VFR bucket and shim type, and to increase the visual impact the engine received enlarged cylinder fins. In an effort to reduce costs the final drive was by chain. The Magna continued with only minor updates until its demise in 2003.

Below: Complex and heavy, the dense 1982 FWS1000 was not beautiful, but it was very effective, providing Honda with the AMA F1 Championship. *Mick Woollett*

# THE FWS 'WATER WHALE,' RS850R AND RS920R

At the beginning of 1980, American Honda announced a five-year plan for their involvement in US road racing. While this was initially centred on the CB750F Superbike and RS1000 F1 machines, the release of the VF750S Sabre encouraged Honda to develop a racer from it for the 1982 season. Constructed with an unlimited budget, Honda took a set of VF750S crankcases and cylinder heads, substituted gears for the chains, and bored and stroked the motor to 78 x 53.5mm to give 1,024cc. The sprague clutch was similar to the NR500, and power was more than 150hp. This engine was placed in a steel cradle frame as a stressed member, with an aluminium swingarm and rising-rate linkage. Much of the chassis equipment came from the NR500 3X, including the 16 and 18-inch Comstar wheels with magnesium hubs and aluminium spokes. The front discs were gripped by four-piston calipers, and the 41.3mm Showa front fork included TRAC. Complex and heavy (around 173kg), the FWS1000 demonstrated that if you threw enough money at something it would win races. The rumoured cost was $1 million per bike, and Freddie Spencer and Mike Baldwin blitzed the opposition in the 1982 AMA F1 series although they didn't win at Daytona. Honda Britain also provided an FWS for Joey Dunlop at the Isle of Man, and

Ron Haslam at Donington after the TT, but the heavy FWS didn't perform as well as in America. Honda rolled the FWS out again for Baldwin at Daytona in 1983, but he could only manage fourth.

For 1983, European Endurance racing and the TT F1 World Championship, a second-generation FWS was produced. No longer 1,000cc, the 75 x 48.6mm engine displacing 859cc, these RS850Rs produced 132hp at 11,500rpm. TT regulations required 32mm carburettors, but the engine included the usual racing components, such as gear camshaft drive, and a wet clutch. Two versions were produced, one with an aluminium frame for Joey Dunlop in the TT F1 series and another with a tubular steel frame. Both versions were extremely compact, rolling on a 1,420mm wheelbase, but they still weighed 171kg.

After an inauspicious debut at the Le Mans 24-hour race, Dunlop provided the aluminium-framed RS850R with an incredible victory at the Isle of Man. Wayne Gardner took the British F1 title on the steel-frame RS850R, and Honda then produced a 920cc version to enable Dunlop to take the TT F1 title. This he did in spectacular fashion, leaving the field for dead on a wet track, and initiating the Dunlop/Honda V4 era of absolute domination of pure road racing. To cap off a highly successful year; Raymond Roche, Guy Bertin and Dominique Sarron rode an aluminium-framed RS920R to victory in the Bol d'Or. In this final year of 1,000cc racing the FWS came of age.

Although it was revolutionary for 1983, the VF750F was an incomplete package and tainted by unreliability. *Cycle World*

# THE VF750F INTERCEPTOR (1983–85)

After only a year the troubled VF750S Sabre evolved into a true sporting model, the VR750FD, or Interceptor in the USA. The impetus for the Interceptor came from new regulations for AMA Superbike racing, dropping the limit from 1,025cc to 750cc. Most of the V-four engine was unchanged, but different cams, a larger airbox and freer-flowing exhaust system contributing to an increase in power to 86hp at 10,000rpm. The motor included reinforced crankcases, was rotated backwards 15° to allow for more front wheel travel and a shorter wheelbase, and the shaft drive was eliminated. This meant the engine now rotated forward rather than backwards, improving the handling in tighter corners. The gearbox was only a five-speed, and incorporated the FWS sprague clutch to reduce wheel hop when downshifting at high rpm. The engine was no longer rubber mounted in the frame as on the VF750S, and it all added up to be a package more suitable as a basis for a Superbike racer.

While the motor was similar to its predecessor, the chassis was the most radical ever for a production bike. Designed for Superbike racing, the rectangular-section steel frame was a perimeter style, similar in design to the second-series 1982 NS500. The frame was intentionally designed as a styling feature, and was painted silver to replicate aluminium. The swingarm was cast-aluminium with a single-shock rising-rate Pro-Link rear suspension system. The adjustable 39mm front fork retained TRAC on the left leg, with a brace to tighten the front end. The VF750F was also the first production bike with a 16-inch front wheel. While American Interceptors received 16 and 18-inch Comcast wheels, European examples included gold 'Boomerang' style Comstars. The brake calipers were Honda's new twin-piston design, the styling of which was very revolutionary. Displaying the frame and motor, and incorporating a small fairing around the rectangular headlamp, there was also a belly pan underneath the engine. The instrument panel was more conventional, but the weight was still a considerable 221kg. The styling hasn't stood the test of time, but it influenced a whole generation of 1980s motorcycles.

Honda wasted no time in enlarging the V-four for the VF1100C cruiser of 1983. This was much more successful than the 750, but only lasted until 1986. *Honda*

Not only did the VF750FD Interceptor look different, its function set a new standard for production motorcycles. *Cycle* magazine was effusive in its praise, claiming: 'As a sport bike it's nearly perfect. The VF750F excels in every area; engine performance, steering, suspension, ground clearance, brakes and tyres.' It was faster than other 750s too, with *Which Bike?* achieving a two-way top speed of 132.64mph (213.42km/h). In Australia, Malcolm Campbell and Rod Cox won the Castrol Six-Hour race for box stock production bikes but unfortunately the VF750F didn't live up to its initial promise. Soon after its release there was a recall to replace faulty handlebars, but more serious problems soon emerged when many VF750Fs began to suffer camshaft failures. It took several modifications to overcome the problem of premature camshaft wear, including redesigned oil lines and a special tool to hold the camshaft during valve clearance adjustment. It was really only a minor problem, but consumer confidence never really recovered. Sales stalled (only 80 VF750Fs were sold in the UK in 1985), and ultimately Honda was forced back down the in-line four road. The VFR750F was also downsized into the VFR700F in America for 1984 and '85. But by now it was too heavy, and its handling, once setting the class standard, was considered ponderous and heavy.

All along, Honda was developing the V-four into a devastating racer, and for the 1983 AMA Superbike series the newly formed HRC built specialist racers. Regulations required a stock frame and swingarm, but the engine featured a wet/dry sump system, with the sump divided into two sections. The front sump received the returning oil from the engine and sent it to the oil cooler. As on the FWS, the camshaft drive was by gears, with bucket and shim valve adjustment replacing the screw type. The titanium valves were 28mm and 25mm, and the con-rods were also titanium. The clutch was dry and the one-way drive was moved to the end of the crankshaft where it was easily removed if required. Just about everything on the VF750F Superbike engine was special, including the 34mm magnesium-bodied CV carburettors.

While the frame needed to be stock, Honda fitted the FWS Showa fork, with milled alloy legs. TRAC was included in both legs, and the front brakes included Nissin four-piston calipers with 34mm and 27mm pistons. The wheels were the familiar racing Honda Comstar, and the 180kg racer produced around 120hp. It was enough for Spencer to win the Daytona Superbike race, but while the VF750F won the first six rounds in the AMA Superbike Championship, Mike Baldwin and Steve Wise couldn't defeat Wayne Rainey and his Kawasaki, on a fraction of Honda's budget. For 1984 there was no stopping the VF750F racers in America, Fred Merkel dominating the Superbike series. He continued this in 1985, despite missing three races due to injury.

# THE VF1100C V65 MAGNA AND VF1100S V65 SABRE (1983–86)

While the 750cc V45s had their problems, it didn't stop Honda enlarging the V-four to 1,098cc with the VF1100C V65 Magna cruiser for 1983. The engine layout mirrored the 750, but everything was scaled up. With a bore and stroke of 79.5 x 55.3mm, the new crankcases were wider, and the cylinder head included larger (30mm and 26mm) valves. The clutch was a diaphragm spring type, and the V65 retained the six-speed gearbox and shaft final drive. When it came to the chassis, both V65s were similar to their V45 brethren, but the V65 motor was a powerhouse, with 116hp. The best thing about the motor though was its mid-range punch. As *Cycle* magazine summed it up: 'Its

Below: Attractive, but expensive, the
VF400F was a fine handling machine.
*Australian Motorcycle News*

horsepower translates immediately into a gut-wrenching rush unmatched by any other production street machine.' The V65 Magna was a huge success in America, leading to the less-popular V65 Sabre in 1984. For the Sabre the carburettors went up from 32mm to 36mm, but this huge, 241kg, motorcycle had an identity crisis. It wasn't a cruiser, sports bike, or tourer, and was discontinued after 1985. Despite its sales success, the Marysville-built V65 Magna didn't last beyond 1986, as Honda shifted their cruiser emphasis to the twin-cylinder VT1100C.

# THE VF400F

Always prepared to take on the two-strokes, Honda released the VF400F as its RD350LC YPVS-beater in 1983. The VF400F motor was a scaled-down VF750F, the six-speed 55 x 42mm 16-valve unit (20.5mm and 18mm valves) breathing through four 32mm Keihin carburettors to produce an impressive 53hp at 11,500rpm. The red-painted frame was displayed in much the same manner as the VF750F, but was tubular steel. Also similar was the 16-inch front wheel, and Pro-Link rear suspension, but unfortunately, Honda decided to equip the VF400F with the inboard ventilated single front and rear disc brakes which they favoured in 1983. The weight of 173kg was considerably more than the competitive two-stroke, but the performance was similar, *Bike* magazine achieving 109.77mph (176.62km/h). The VF400F's most serious disadvantage was its cost, £1,895 in 1983, when the Yamaha was £200 less. The VF400F soon disappeared.

One of the best balanced
motorcycles of the mid-1980s, the
VF500 was praised by the press,
but there were reliability problems.
*Motorcycle Trader collection*

# THE VF500F

More successful than the VF400F was the VF500F, arguably the best balanced of all the early V-fours. Either two VT250Fs side by side, or an enlarged VF400, the 60 x 44mm displaced 498cc. The valves were 23mm and 20.5mm, the camshafts provided more valve lift, and the camshaft was a double-row roller type to reduce friction. The main bearing and rod journals were increased over the 400, and with four 32mm CV Keihin carburettors the power was an impressive 70hp at 11,500rpm. This little gem of an engine was installed in a VF750F-style rectangular steel perimeter frame, with an aluminium swingarm with Pro-Link. The 37mm front fork included TRAC on the left leg, and unlike the VF400F, the brakes were conventional discs, dual on the front, with twin-piston calipers. The wheels were 16 and 18-inch, Comstar in Europe and Comcast in America, and while the weight was considerable for a

500 at 184kg, the mass centralisation of the VF500F was right. The standard VF500F included a chin spoiler, but there was also a fully faired VF500FII.

*Cycle* magazine was always effusive in its praise of the VF500F, claiming: 'Its marvellous engine, chassis that works well everywhere, and classic balance of power and weight, makes it almost the perfect motorcycle.' Unfortunately, the VF500F was another insufficiently developed model, suffering crankshaft breakage on early examples, forcing a recall in America and Germany. For 1984 and '85 in America there was also the V30 Magna. This featured chain final drive like the VF500F, and the tubular steel frame and twin-shock rear suspension of other Magnas. Even in 1986, Honda showed faith in the VF500F by redesigning the engine to provide more mid-range power. The carburettors went down to 30mm and the camshafts were milder, but this still couldn't save it.

As the VF1000F failed to win buyers, Honda transformed it into the sport-touring VF1000FII Bol d'Or for 1985. *Motorcycle Trader collection*

# THE VF1000F, VF1000FII AND VR1000R

While the V-four became an 1100 in the V65 Magna cruiser, when it was enlarged as a sporting model for 1984 it became the VF1000F Interceptor. To keep the size manageable, the VF1000F motor was an enlarged VF750F unit rather than downsized VF1100C. The crankcase casting was from the 750, but with steel cylinder liners to allow the fitting of 77mm pistons. The stroke was stretched to 53.6mm and the con-rods were 2mm longer, with 2mm larger gudgeons. The valve sizes went up to 30mm and 26.5mm, and the double overhead camshafts were driven by roller chains. With four 36mm Keihin carburettors the power was up to 116hp at 10,000rpm.

The VF1000F chassis was also based on the VF750F,

but the motor was 20mm lower, the steering slightly quicker, and the Pro-Link set-up included needle bearings instead of bushes. The front fork was 41mm, with four-way adjustable TRAC in the left fork leg, and the wheels 16-inch on the front and 17-inch on the rear, although an 18-inch rear was optional. As on the VF750, US versions had Comcast wheels, while Europe had Comstars. The overall dimensions were larger than the 750, and the weight 233kg. Unfortunately for the VF1000F, its release coincided with the Kawasaki GPz900R and Yamaha FJ1100. The Kawasaki was faster and more sporting, while the Yamaha was a superior tourer. The VF1000F lasted only one year in America, but continued in Europe until 1987. In 1985 it had been updated into the VF1000FF, with a revised cam drive and cooling system, and also an 18-inch front wheel. The frame was redesigned, with the steering head angle raked out to 29°, and there was a new front fork.

Although the first production V-four with gear-driven overhead camshafts, the huge VF1000R was too heavy, and a disappointment. *Motorcycle Trader collection*

Below right:One of the most spectacular Honda racing machines was the 1986 RVF750. This machine provided Joey Dunlop with yet another world F1 title. *Alan Cathcart Archive*

In an effort to broaden the VF1000F's appeal, much had been done with the CBX1000 when sales stalled, the sporting emphasis was softened, and for 1985, the touring VF1000FII Bol d'Or was created, with a full fairing, alongside the VF1000FF. The engine included the VF1000FF updates, but added an oil cooler. Although it was intended the VF1000FII would tackle the BMW R100RS, Honda neglected to include optional luggage. As a result the 245kg VF1000FII was just another heavy Honda without anything to really endear it. The most surprising thing about the huge Bol d'Or was that it won the 1985 Isle of Man Production TT, admittedly in the hands of TT specialist Geoff Johnson.

Another 1,000cc V-four that didn't live up to expectations was the limited-edition VF1000R.

Intended to continue where the fantastic CB1100Rs left off, Honda really miscalculated with the VF1000R. Intentionally styled after the conquering RS850R, the VR1000R was unleashed in 1984 with the expectation to succeed in Production racing, but this didn't happen. While the engine was spectacular, and the first production Honda with gear-driven overhead camshafts, was, as *Revs* magazine in Australia succinctly summed up: 'Put simply, the chassis/suspension package is unable to cope with the blinding speed the motor is capable of.'

Central to the VF1000R was the 998cc V-four packing a then thunderous 122hp at 10,500rpm. The camshaft timing was wilder, and the compression ratio slightly higher at 10.7:1. The chassis followed the lines of the VF1000F, but with NS500 racing-style 16 and

# SPECIAL 750S: THE RS AND RVF (1984–87)

With Endurance and F1 regulations limiting the capacity to 750cc for 1984, Honda created the RS750R. The engine was largely that of the 1983 US VF750F Superbikes, but for two additional alloy radiators, and with no chassis restrictions the eight works bikes received alloy frames. They also reverted to an 18-inch front wheel. These 160kg, 132hp racers were smaller, faster and more agile than the earlier RS, and were also totally reliable. In every series they contested they were dominant. Wayne Gardner won every race he entered in the British F1 Championship, Joey Dunlop took the World TT F1 title, and Gerard Coudray and Patrick Igoa the Endurance World Championship.

While Roger Marshall gave Honda the 1985 British F1 title on an RS750, this year saw a new-generation bike for Endurance racing, the RVF750. The engine was now producing 135hp at 11,000rpm, but the most significant development was a new twin-spar aluminium frame. This was known as the Diamond frame, because the engine was set in place as a stressed member. The front fork was now a 43mm Showa, the front wheel was 17-inch, and the weight 159kg. Although the two RVFs failed at their first appearance, the Le Mans 24-hour race in April, Gardner then rode a spectacular race at Suzuka to claim victory. The year finished on a high note for the RVF with Dunlop's fourth consecutive TT F1 title, and another win for Coudray and Igoa in the Endurance World Championship.

While the production V-fours were struggling to find a market, the racing versions continued to be more dominant. By 1986, the RVF750B was unquestionably the finest four-stroke racing motorcycle in the world. Still using a five-speed gearbox based on the earlier VF750F, and a 360° crankshaft, the ignition was now Matsuba electronic instead of Kokusan, and there were round exhaust headers instead of oval. The power of Dunlop's F1 machine was 137hp at 13,000rpm, with the Endurance version producing 132hp. The frame was strengthened and included a single-sided swingarm to speed up wheel changing during endurance races. The weight of the F1 bike was 152kg, compared with the Endurance 164kg. Although only five machines were built, the revised RVF was as dominant as before. Dunlop took his fifth TT F1 title, and the Endurance version won every round of the championship.

Honda elected not to run the RVF during 1987, providing factory V-fours only for the Suzuka 8-hour and 24-hour Endurance races. Now based on the new VFR750, with a narrower engine and six-speed transmission, the 1987 RVF was a racer with a different character. The earlier models were known for their easy riding characteristics and their wide powerband, but the 1987 version was designed for GP riders. There was more forward weight bias, and while retaining the 360° crank the engine was peakier. This year the wheels were 17-inch front and rear, and while it won the Bol d'Or, this was the RVF's only significant victory this year. For 1988, the RVF was less exotic, but no less efficient, and was based on the production RC30.

153

The author's 1986 VFR750F, a great bike
only let down by the 16-inch front wheel
and unsatisfactory suspension. *Author*

17-inch Comstar wheels. The rear Bridgestone
140/80VR17 was the first radial tyre fitted to a
production motorcycle. There were some very nice
features on the VF1000R, including an endurance-style
quick-release front wheel, but the VF1000R was
handicapped by its size, weight, and high centre of
mass. The wheelbase was a lengthy 1,505mm, and the
weight a massive 238kg. Although very fast,
*Performance Bikes* achieved 150.2mph (241.7km/h),
there was no way this monster motorcycle was a
Production racer. The VF1000R was also available in
the USA for 1985 and '86, and was identical but for a
lower and longer hump-backed fuel tank. *Cycle*
magazine wasn't very impressed with the VF1000R,
concluding: 'Slow, top-heavy, and threatening, this
motorcycle gives Superbikes a bad name.'

## FROM VF TO VFR

Despite the racetrack domination of the superb RS and
RVF750, sales of all early incarnations of the V-four
were disappointing. Honda came perilously close to

abandoning the V-four altogether, putting their faith
back in the in-line four CBX750. They then decided to
persevere with the V-four by adapting many of the
racing RVF features on a production model. The result
was the VFR750, one of Honda's finest production
motorcycles of any era. This soon evolved into the even
more impressive VFR750R, or RC30, and a range of
400cc versions. All along, the V-four continued to form
the basis of Honda's four-stroke racing programme.
Eventually, the V-four succumbed to the popularity of
the new CBR in-line fours, but always maintained its
position as an important model in the line-up.

## THE VFR750F (1986–89)

Although only three years old, new 750s from Suzuki
and Yamaha rendered the VF750F obsolete, and the
second-generation V-four, the VFR750FG, was a huge
leap forward. About the only feature retained was the
bore and stroke (70 x 48.6mm), and the redesigned
engine was 20 per cent lighter and included a 180°
crankshaft and gear drive for the camshafts. All the

internal components were lighter, with the valve clearance adjusters moved from the valve end to the fulcrum end. This allowed for the four carburettors to be grouped at a closer, 52° angle with straighter intakes. With four 36mm carburettors, and a 10.5:1 compression ratio, the power was increased substantially, to 105hp at 10,500rpm. The gearbox was now a six-speed, instead of the previous five-speed.

Complementing this new engine was an equally radical chassis. Following the example of the RVF750, the main frame was constructed of 28 x 60mm aluminium box section tubing. Weighing only 14kg, it was claimed to be 50 per cent stiffer than the VF750F, and included a box-section aluminium swingarm. The engine was tipped back slightly in the frame, and the steering head angle reduced from 28.2° to 27.5°. Honda's obsession with reducing weight saw lighter, 16 and 18-inch wheels, a 37mm front fork (instead of 39mm), forged aluminium handlebars, and thinner brake discs. The rear shock absorber included a Pro-Link rising-rate linkage, and the weight of the VFR750F was reduced to 198kg.

With subdued styling and a semi-sporting riding position, the VFR750F wasn't a hard-edged sporting motorcycle like some of its competitors. However, it was a tremendous all-round street bike, let down only by the 16-inch front wheel and inadequate short travel suspension. In the search to reduce costs Honda skimped on the suspension quality, compromising the overall package. But the engine was a dream. Silky smooth through until its 11,000rpm redline, providing plenty of mid-range power, it exorcised the camshaft gremlins. Despite its suspension inadequacy, the VFR750F was a vast improvement on its predecessor; and the best street motorcycle available in 1986, *Superbike* proclaiming it 'damn near perfect.' *Two Wheels* said: 'It's not spectacular, just a good honest beast. It's so easy to ride that the VFR is Number One.' The VFR750F also raised the ante regarding speed for 750s, *Performance Bikes* managing 147.6mph (237.5km/h). For the USA the VFR750F was downsized to 700cc, with the VFR700F and F2 Interceptor for 1986 and '87. The F and F2 were similar, but the F2 featured the European colours and rectangular instruments. The VFR750FH continued for 1987 unchanged except for a digital ignition system, and became the VFR750FJ for 1988. Arguably the definitive model, improvements extended to 17-inch wheels front and rear, and larger 296mm front discs.

Joey Dunlop was not only a great road racer, but he did much of his own preparation. Here, he works on his Honda 125 at the 2000 Isle of Man, only a month before his tragic death. *Mac McDiarmid*

# TT MASTER: JOEY DUNLOP

Acknowledged as one of the greatest of all road racers, and the most successful TT rider, Joey Dunlop started racing in his native Northern Ireland in 1969. He won his first TT in 1977, going on to win 26 TTs in the next 25 years; with three TT trebles. His best ever TT lap at 123.87mph (199.31km/h) set in the 2000 Senior TT saw him the fourth fastest rider in TT history. It wasn't only at the Isle of Man Joey Dunlop was spectacular. He also won 24 Ulster GPs, 13 at the North West 200, and five World TT Formula One Championships. His exploits earned him an MBE and an OBE for his services, not only to motorcycling, but for humanitarian missions to Bosnia and Romania, travelling alone to provide food, clothes and toys for unfortunate children. Always 'one of the boys', Dunlop was a hero for many. Father of five children, for years he combined racing with running a pub in Co Antrim. He died in July 2000, 48 years old, on a Honda RS125 in the pouring rain at Tallin, in Estonia, but will never be forgotten.

Primarily produced for the Japanese market, the VFR400 was almost a miniature RC30. *Australian Motorcycle News*

stroke lap record set on an RVF750 a year earlier. This bike (known as the 6X) was subsequently sent to Britain and raced by Geoff Johnson to second place, behind the RVF750 of Dunlop, in the 1986 TT F1 race. For 1987, Dunlop had a VFR-based F1 machine, and while he failed to take the World title, he did win the F1 race, his tenth TT.

As the RC30 wasn't homologated for Superbike racing in America, Honda continued to campaign VFR750F-based machines. Wayne Rainey took the AMA Championship in 1987 with Bubba Shobert continuing the VFR's dominance during 1988. Even into 1989, the VFR Superbikes were competitive, privateer John Ashmead winning the Daytona Superbike 200-mile race that year.

## THE VFR400R AND RVF400 (FROM 1986)

Alongside the new-generation VFR750F was the VFR400R (NC21) for 1986. The 59hp engine was a miniature VFR750 unit (55 x 42mm), with a 180° crank and gear-driven camshafts, while the frame was also an alloy twin-spar type. The 16 and 18-inch wheels were three-spoke Comstars and the total weight was quite high at 182kg. There was also an unusual naked version, the VFR400Z. The NC21 became the NC24 for 1987, and while it was similar to the NC21 in appearance, the engine had a 360° crankshaft and an updated chassis that included the Pro-Arm single-sided swingarm. The NC24 was the first production Honda with this feature and it was finished in Rothmans replica colours.

For 1989, the VFR400R was upgraded into the NC30, a shrunken RC30, and one of Hondas' most spectacular smaller models. Still with the RC30-style 360° crank tiny, 8mm spark plugs, and with 30mm carburettors the power was 59hp. This superb handling motorcycle became a cult machine in Japan, and as it looked almost identical to the RC30 it was the best-selling of all the V-fours. Small, uncomfortable, difficult to live with, and heavy for a 400, the 164kg NC30 was extraordinarily fast, *Performance Bikes* managing 140mph (225km/h). While the NC30 was primarily a Japanese market model, thousands were exported to other countries as grey market imports, further fuelling their cult status. For 1991, the NC30 received upgraded suspension, including a 41mm cartridge fork

The three-piece fairing featured integrated indicators, an adjustable windscreen, and a clock and fuel gauge in the instrument panel. Upgraded suspension included a beefier 41mm fork, and the engine received larger intake and exhaust valves, and a slightly higher, 11:1 compression ratio to boost mid-range torque. While the weight went up to 203kg, *Superbike* continued in their praise, stating: 'The best 750 available, no question.' The VFR750F continued into 1989 as the similar FK.

Not surprisingly, with its RVF pedigree, the VFR750F was easily transformed into a competitive Superbike racer. HRC offered a full racing uprating kit, boosting the power to 130hp, with racing Showa suspension and 17-inch racing wheels. They also produced special Superbike racers for the US Superbike series. For the third year in a row Fred Merkel won the AMA Superbike Championship, but only just from Wayne Rainey on a similar machine. Their racing VFRs, with 360° cranks, 28.5mm and 25.5mm titanium valves, and 34mm magnesium-bodied carburettors, produced 135hp and weighed 146kg. This same engine was used in a VFR Superbike by Wayne Gardner at Suzuka when he broke his own four-

*A classic, and still magnificent today. Few motorcycles can emulate the purposefulness of the RC30, or match its race success.*
Australian Motorcycle News

and a remote reservoir rear shock absorber. The front brakes included four-piston calipers, and the wheels were 17-inch front and rear. The 1992 version received fully adjustable suspension, and the 1993 colours replicated the Suzuka 8-hour RVFs. Replacing the NC30 in Japan for 1994 was a mini-RC45, the RVF400 (NC35). A very high-specification machine with headlights shaped more like the RVF Endurance racer, the RVF400 had a 41mm upside down fork, four-piston brake calipers, and 17-inch wheels front and rear. With a lower compression ratio and smaller (29mm) carburettors, the power of the Japanese restricted RVF400 was 53hp at 11,500rpm, and the weight was 165kg.

## THE VFR750R (RC30)

Only rarely does a company build a bike that resonates its soul, but the VFR750R, or RC30, encapsulated Honda's spirit. The idea was to create a street-legal TT F1-style machine, which could be homologated for Production racing, and the RC30 is one of the few legendary, classic, Japanese motorcycles. Released in

mid-1987, the VFR750F also formed the basis for Fred Merkel's World Superbike Championship-winning machines of 1988 and '89. Each RC30 was produced by one of three four-man teams at HRC, producing only 60 bikes a week, and the quality was unsurpassed.

While the technical specifications, including the bore and stroke, looked similar to the VFR750F, the RC30 engine was very close in specification to the factory RVF racers. The crankshaft was 360°, and the con-rods and valves titanium. There were new cylinder heads with needle roller-mounted camshafts which acted directly on the valve stems, and the intake port tilted 6° higher to provide a straighter intake path. The camshaft gears were also more compact, and the intake valves 2.5mm larger, although the 38° included valve angle was retained. The 11:1 pistons were two-ring racing style, carburetion was by four 38mm Keihin CV carburettors, there was a close-ratio six-speed gearbox, and the claimed power was 112hp.

The twin-spar aluminium chassis followed the lines of the RVF, with an ELF-patented single-sided swingarm, and 17 and 18-inch wheels. A single 36mm nut retained the rear wheel, while an eccentric provided chain

# SUPERBIKE SUPREME: RACING THE RC30

With the creation of the World Superbike series for 1988, the RC30 had a raison d'être. In the early days of this championship the competition was underdeveloped and Honda's entry was unofficial. Fred Merkel, riding for the Italian Rumi team, eventually won the first World Superbike Championship despite a series of engine failures and only two race wins. For 1989, Merkel, Stéphane Mertens, and Roger Burnett received RC30s from HRC, and this year the RC30 won the most races. Merkel took his second World Superbike title, but it would be the RC30's last. The RC30 was soon outclassed by the ever-improving Ducati and Kawasaki, and there were no more race wins in this series for the Honda after 1990. However, long after most other teams had relegated the RC30 obsolete, in Australia, Troy Corser provided it with a surprising series win in the 1993 Australian Superbike Championship.

The RC30's competitive life was much longer on the Isle of Man, and in F1 racing, where its impeccable reliability was more important than outright speed. From 1988 through until 1993, the RC30 was the machine to beat. RC30s won the Production Class B, F1, and Senior TT in 1988, and it was the same in 1989, although Steve Hislop had an RVF750 for the F1 race. Hislop won three TTs that year, and Carl Fogarty took the 1989 TT F1 title. Fogarty had two TT victories in 1990 together with another TT F1 cup. In 1991, to ensure their tenth consecutive TT F1 title, Honda shipped two 1989 model RVF750s, each with a squad of HRC mechanics, one for Hislop, and the other shared by Fogarty and Dunlop. It was on one of these terrifyingly fast RVFs that Hislop set a new lap record of 124.4mph (200.16 km/h). Needless to say, Hislop won both the F1 and Senior TTs. With Hislop and Fogarty defecting from Honda, Phil McCallen was Honda's hope at the TT in 1992. He won the F1 race on an RC30, and received an RVF for 1993, rewarding Honda with a win in the Senior TT, while Nick Jeffries provided the RC30 with yet another F1 victory. The RC45 was now waiting in the wings, but this was a fitting end to a magnificent chapter of racing dominance.

The RVF continued to race in the longer-distance Endurance events during 1988, winning the Le Mans 24-hour race and the Bol

d'Or, but not entering enough races to take the title. Honda was defeated at the Suzuka 8-hour in 1988, but returned in 1989 with a dramatically revised RVF750, providing Dominique Sarron and Alex Vieira with victory after Mick Doohan collided with a backmarker while in the lead. Vieira went on to win the Endurance Cup in 1989. Doohan and Gardner were back on a factory RVF750 in the 1990 Suzuka 8-hour race. Undoubtedly the fastest and most developed four-stroke racer in the world, the RVF weighed only 138kg in sprint trim, and produced over 140hp at the gearbox. Suspension included a 43mm Showa inverted fork, and the RVF was timed at 275km/h (171mph). Although the RVF embarrassingly ran out of fuel at Suzuka, Vieira won the Endurance Cup with wins at Le Mans and the Bol d'Or.

Despite the Endurance series regaining World Championship status for 1991, Honda, after a decade of dominance decided not to contest the series. But after three humiliating losses in the Suzuka 8-hour, they provided an RVF750 to GP regulars Doohan and Gardner, enlisted the services of the experienced French endurance squad, and restored Honda's honour in this premier event. Gardner returned to Suzuka in 1992, this time with GP hopeful Daryl Beattie, winning again and culminating in an extraordinary career of success at Suzuka. Rule changes ensured 1993 was to be the final year for the RVF750. Honda's determination to win saw Doohan and Beattie, with Eddie Lawson and Satoshi Tsujimoto provided with the best the factory could offer. But crashes by Doohan and Lawson ended Honda's hopes of the RVF retiring in a blaze of glory.

adjustment. The front fork was 43mm, with external damping adjustment and a quick-release front wheel. From the 310mm front brakes with four piston calipers, to the wide, 5.5-inch rear wheel, everything about the 185kg RC30 was state-of-the-art for 1988. Small and

compact, the wheelbase of 1,407mm was also the shortest of any production 750. Always a limited production model, the glassfibre was hand laid and the fuel tank was aluminium. A total of 1,000 RC30s were produced for Japan and sold by lot. These had smaller

headlights and 77hp engines. For 1989, approximately 300 were produced for the US market. These had larger twin headlights and carried the RC30 designation on the tail section. American engines also received air injection for the front two cylinders to reduce emissions, and had smaller-diameter exhaust pipe collars to reduce noise. They also came at a premium price of $14,998. A second series of RC30s was produced for 1990, with a deeper sump and with many components from the optional race kit fitted as standard. Total production was 3,000, and while not much faster than a stock VFR750F, the RC30 lived up to all expectations. Capable of 158mph (254km/h) when tested by *Performance Bikes*, there

were some early engine problems, but these were soon overcome. Now the RC30 is rightly considered the archetypal sporting Honda.

## THE VFR750F (1990–97)

After four years, the VFR750F was completely redesigned, and the VFR750FL (RC36) appeared for 1990. This fourth-generation V-four engine included bucket and shim valve actuation and a narrower, 32° included valve angle. The valves were 27.5mm and 23mm, carburettors 36mm Keihin, and the gear camshaft drive was retained, as was the 180°

For 1994, the VFR750F received new NR750-inspired styling, but continued the same theme.
*Australian Motorcycle News*

crankshaft. There was less emphasis on outright power, but the new engine still produced 104hp at 10,500rpm.

The more compact cylinder head, and thinner radiator, allowed the engine to be moved forward 34mm and lowered 5.5mm in the new 80 x 30mm aluminium box-section frame. The steering head angle was decreased from 27.5° to 26°, and the swingarm was a single-sided Pro-Arm like the RC30. Also new was the cartridge 41mm fork, and wider, 17-inch wheels. Still a sport-touring motorcycle rather than an out-and-out sportster, the VFR750FL, with its upright riding position and protective fairing, continued where the earlier VFR had left off. The new bodywork also housed twin headlights and a faired sidestand. Despite a weight increase, to 216kg, the VFR750FL maintained its position as the best real-world street bike available, but at a price. *Superbike* magazine found it difficult to justify £6,200 when other Japanese 750s cost considerably less, but they countered by saying it 'was one of the best bikes ever produced.' *Cycle* magazine

was also impressed, claiming: 'It's a pentathlete in a world of single event specialists.'

There were few updates for the 1991 VFR750M, but VFR750FN developments for 1992 included a tinted windscreen, spring preload adjustment for the front fork, and rebound damping adjustment for the Showa rear shock. In response to cries for more top-end power, the carburettor velocity stacks were shortened by 18mm, and the intake ports were reshaped as there were new valve seat angles for smoother gas flow. The exhaust canister volume was increased, and the gain was 3hp. The VFR750FN was still good enough for *Cycle World* to say: 'Yep, Honda's VFR750 is the pick of the litter' in a ten-bike 750cc comparison test. The final VFR750 in this series was the FP of 1993, similar to before, but for new paint.

Honda claimed there were 500 changes for the NR750-styled 1994 VFR750FR. While the motor was much as before, there were reshaped ports, different cams, and smaller, 34mm semi-flat-slide carburettors similar to those on the CBR900RR. The exhaust was now a lighter, 4-2-1 type, and the power was increased slightly, to 107hp. While the chassis was similar to before, the frame, swingarm and wheels (the rear narrower) were all lighter, and the weight was reduced to 209kg. The most noticeable change was to the bodywork, with louvred ducts on the side of the fairing. The exaggerated styling didn't meet with unanimous acceptance, but there was no denying the VFR750FR continued as the finest all-round motorcycle available.

## THE RVF750R (RC45) (1994–99)

With the announcement that Endurance racing motorcycles were to be production based for 1994, and the exotic RVF750 ineligible, Honda needed something to replace the ageing and now uncompetitive RC30. The result was the RC45, developed from the ground up as a joint Honda/HRC project. Central to the new design was an all-new 90° V-four, still with a 360° crankshaft, but with the spring-loaded gear cam drive moved to the right, eliminating one crankshaft and one camshaft journal. This reduced friction and allowed the engine to be narrower. There was a new bore and stroke of 72 x 46mm, and the four valves inclined at a narrower, 26° included angle. The intake valves were

The RC45 replaced the RC30 for 1994, but initially it couldn't replicate its predecessor's success.
*Australian Motorcycle News*

2mm larger, and the ports steeper and straighter, with valve adjustment by the usual bucket and shim. The compression ratio was 11.5:1, and the con-rods were titanium. The fully mapped PGM-F1 electronic fuel injection was similar to the NR750, with a pressurised 7-litre airbox and four 46mm throttle bodies, but in stock form, the power wasn't earth-shattering at 118hp at 12,000rpm.

The twin-spar aluminium chassis was also all-new, and included a redesigned single-sided swingarm, 20.3 per cent stiffer than that of the RC30, and able to accommodate a 6-inch wide rear wheel. The 41mm Showa fork was an upside down type, the first for a production street Honda, but rather surprisingly, the front wheel was a 16-inch, and the rear a 17-inch. The front brakes were 310mm floating discs from the NR750, with Nissin four-piston CBR900RR calipers. Extremely densely packaged, the RC45 was also heavier than the RC30, at 189kg. The result was underwhelming, and disappointing for many.

Compared with the RC30 the RC45 was much larger, and less nimble. Timed at 156mph (251km/h) by *Motorcyclist* magazine, in outright performance the RC45 was bettered by Honda's own considerably cheaper CBR900RR. Certainly the handling was fantastic for a road bike, but the price tag of £17,780 was difficult to justify. *Cycle World* said: 'Considering its price, the RC45 is a letdown in terms of outright acceleration and top speed. As an exotic streetbike it doesn't live up to expectations.'

# THE VFR800FI (1998–2001)

After four years virtually unchanged, but still acknowledged as one of the finest all-round streetbikes available, for 1998 the VFR750F made way for an updated VFR800FI. The V-four engine was now based on the RC45, with a side-mounted gear train,

Automotive in execution, one of Honda's
longest running models was the European-style
ST1100 tourer. *Australian Motorcycle News*

# TOURING EUROPEAN-STYLE: THE ST1100 AND STX1300 PAN-EUROPEAN (FROM 1990)

Continuing to expand the boundaries of motorcycle function and engine design, for 1990 Honda released a European-style tourer, fitting somewhere between the CBR1000R and the Gold Wing. Conceived by Honda Germany, the ST1100 was a joint effort between Honda Japan and Honda Europe. Continuing Honda's fascination with the V-four, the ST1100 90° V-four was swung around, with the crankshaft inline fore and aft, as on the Gold Wing and earlier CX500/650. The motor was also very automotive like in its execution, with twin overhead camshafts driven by toothed rubber belts. The 73 x 64.8mm V-four displaced 1,085cc, and the four valves per cylinder, set at a shallow 32°, featured bucket and shim adjustment. The crankshaft was a 360°, and the engine included some unusual features; notably the front-mounted clutch and rear-mounted generator spinning opposite the crankshaft to eliminate the rocking effect, and there were three driveline dampers. The five-speed gearbox was also a cassette-type that could be removed with the motor in the frame. Small, 32mm carburettors contributed to an emphasis on mid-range power, as the ST1100 was limited to 100hp due to Germany's power limit.

Housing this large engine was a conventional double downtube round-section steel perimeter frame, with the right side of the

For 2003, the ST1100 evolved
into the ST1300 Pan European.
*Motorcycle Trader*

swingarm containing the driveshaft. The 41mm cartridge fork
included TRAC in the left leg, and there was a single rear shock
absorber. The wheels were a sporting 18 and 17-inch, and the
ST1100 was equipped with a wind tunnel-designed fairing and
integrated luggage. Although designed as a sport-tourer, the
ST1100 was still a large motorcycle, weighing in at 268kg. As *Cycle*
magazine commented: 'It needs a Jenny Craig diet and better
suspension.'

The ST1100 continued as a popular and reliable motorcycle
for many years. There was an ABS option and traction control in
1992, a wider windscreen in 1995, a higher output alternator
and TCS linked brakes in 1996, and a second-generation ABS II in
1997. With the ABS came a larger, 43mm front fork. After 12
years of minimal development, for 2002 the ST1100 became the
more powerful (116hp) Pan-European. With this came all-new

bodywork and a larger, 20.8-litre fuel tank with an additional 8.2
litres just above the swingarm pivot. After one year, the STX1300
(or ST1300 in America and Australia) Pan-European replaced the
ST1100. With a 1,261cc (78 x 66mm) motor with electronic fuel
injection (with 36mm throttle bodies), and chain-driven
camshafts, there were two engine counterbalancers, and the
power went up to 126hp at 8,000rpm. The generator was moved
to between the cylinders, and the 60mm shorter engine was
mounted 20mm lower and 40mm more forward in a new twin-
spar aluminium frame. A new swingarm saw the wheelbase
reduced to 1,490mm from 1,555mm. The front fork was
increased to 45mm, and the style of the fairing made similar to
the previous Pan-European. The weight went up to 276kg, but
ergonomically the STX1300 was superior to the ST1100, as the
seat was adjustable.

Everything on the NR750R was of the highest quality, but it was so expensive very few could experience it. *Australian Motorcycle News*

# ULTIMATE EXOTICA: THE NR750R (RC40)

After 13 years of development, the oval piston technology of the racing NR500 and NR750 finally became a production reality with the limited-production NR750R. Marketed as an extraordinarily expensive collector's bike, primarily to be seen and not ridden, the NR750R's purpose was to showpiece Hondas' achievement with oval-piston technology. By the time the NR750R was released, oval piston cylinders were outlawed by the FIM so the NR750R was always going to be a novelty.

Based on the 1987 Endurance racing NR750 (see Chapter 6), the production engine differed in that it was a 90° V-four. The pistons were 101.2 x 50.6mm, and the stroke 42mm, giving 747.7cc. Inside the motor was a myriad of special components, from the eight titanium con-rods to the nickel-plated and Teflon-coated pistons. Each piston ring required 27 machining operations, the spark plugs were 8mm, and the eight 30mm chokes featured a single fuel injector. A departure for Honda was the incorporation of PGM-F1 electronic fuel injection. Fully mapped, with seven sensors and a 16-bit CPU, this also included a

self diagnostic function. There were gear-driven double overhead camshafts, eight valves per cylinder, set at an included angle of 29°, and with an 11.7:1 compression ratio and an 8-4-2-1-2 stainless-steel exhaust system the power was 125hp at a very moderate 14,000rpm.

The NR750R chassis was more conventional than the motor, with the usual aluminium beam frame and single-sided swingarm. The front fork was a 45mm upside down type, and the specially designed wheels 16 and 17-inch. Weighing 222.5kg, and rolling on a 1,433mm wheelbase, the NR750 was never going to be a svelte sportster. But it was crafted with the most incredible attention to detail and built out of the highest quality materials. The carbon-fibre body panels were individually hand-made in numbered sets, and the production was extremely limited, at around 200, two to three a day for one year. The ridiculous price of £38,000 ensured it remained a rare commodity. As the NR750 couldn't be homologated for racing, Honda prepared a 180kg, 155hp record-breaking machine for Loris Capirossi to ride at the Nardo test track in southern Italy. In August 1992, Capirossi set new flying mile, flying kilometre and standing start mile and 10km records, with a fastest speed of 299.825km/h (186.311mph).

eliminating one crankshaft journal, and spring-loaded split gears to reduce noise. Other RC45 features were the 26° included valve angle, and the 72mm bore. The stroke was lengthened to 48mm to give 781cc, and the crankshaft was still 180° as on earlier VFRs. As the engine was designed to fit in a pivotless frame (like the VTR1000F Firestorm), the crankcases included the swingarm pivot and mounts for the footpegs and Delta-Link suspension. Despite these updates the new engine was 15mm narrower and 2.5kg lighter. Also inherited from the RC45 were the metal composite cylinder sleeves, and PGM-F1 electronic fuel injection. There were four 36mm injector bodies, and with an 11.6:1 compression ratio the power was increased to 110hp at 10,500rpm. Cooling was provided by two VTR1000F-style side radiators.

To reduce weight, the pivotless frame consisted of two triple box-section aluminium spars and a welded cast alloy steering head. The motor was a stressed member, and the frame, without any downtubes, was 3.5kg lighter than on the VFR750F. The VFR800FI retained the single-sided Pro-Arm, now mounted directly on the rear of the engine, with a Delta-Link rising rate system anchored to a bracket on the rear of the engine. The conventional 41mm cartridge front fork and single shock absorber featured HMAS, and the rear five-spoke wheel was now a 5.5 x 17-inch. The braking system was also the Dual CBS (combined braking system) of the ST1100 CBS-ABS, with three three-piston brake calipers and two independent hydraulic systems.

Along with the updated engine and chassis, was a CBR1100XX Super Blackbird-inspired fairing, and the styling was intentionally more aggressive than before. Despite the increased sophistication, the weight of the VFR800FI was reduced slightly, to 208kg. And the VFR800FI continued to set the standard for this type of motorcycle, with *Motorcyclist* still claiming: 'Perhaps the best streetbike yet loosed upon an unsuspecting universe.' At least until the next generation.

Below: Although he didn't manage to win a World Superbike Championship on the RC45, Aaron Slight was a stalwart campaigner. In 1999 he finished fourth. *Author*

# ANOTHER SUPERBIKE CHAMPION: RACING THE RC45

Unlike the RC30, the RC45's racing career began inauspiciously. During 1994, Doug Polen and Aaron Slight couldn't manage a win in either the AMA or World Superbike championships, although they did provide the RC45 with a win in the important Suzuka 8-hour race. The Honda team came with massive Castrol sponsorship, but despite a 25mm longer swingarm, the RC45 suffered handling problems all season. The power was 143hp at 14,000rpm, but the Castrol RC45 was completely outclassed by the Ducati 916 in the 1994 World Superbike Championship.

A completely revamped RC45 was provided for Aaron Slight in 1995, and with Honda providing a succession of new motors and a double exhaust, a special seven-spec gave Slight the RC45's first World Superbike victory. Slight ended up third in the championship. Even the addition of World Superbike Champion Carl Fogarty to the Castrol Honda team for 1996, and a new F-spec motor mid-season, failed to make the RC45 a winner. Fogarty found the RC45 difficult to ride, claiming it didn't suit his style. Although Fogarty won a double at Assen, and Yuichi Takeda and Takuma Aoki won at Sugo, Slight was the most consistent finisher during the season, ending second overall.

Former 250cc World Champion John Kocinski switched to the RC45 for 1997, the engine now producing 180hp at 14,750rpm with two injectors per cylinder and 46mm throttle bodies. Continual refinement by Neil Tuxworth and the Castrol team resulted in the best all round package this year, as evidenced by Kocinski's nine wins. Slight's three victories also provided Honda with the Constructors' Championship.

Colin Edwards joined Slight in the Castrol Honda team for 1998, and detail engine improvements (including a 13.5:1 compression ratio) saw the power up to around 184hp at 15,000rpm. There was a new exhaust system with the exhausts on opposite sides, and the new frame was less stiff side to side. Along with a new Showa 47mm upside down fork, the most noticeable update was a double-sided swingarm (heavier by 1kg). The RC45 was good enough to provide Slight with five wins, and Edwards a double at Monza after Slight's engine uncharacteristically expired

The RC45 racer in its final version of 1999. Despite handling problems Edwards savoured some glory by finishing second in the World Superbike Championship. *Author*

on the last lap as he was challenging to pass. The series went down to the final race, with Slight four and a half points adrift of Fogarty at the end.

For 1999, its final season, the RC45 was honed into the fastest V-four four-stroke racer ever. On its day it was also the finest. To reduce internal friction, the wet sump motor was converted into a double sump, semi-dry type. With RC45 production finished, the cylinder heads were VFR800, and the 13.5:1 pistons were two-ring, also to reduce friction. With an Akrapovic exhaust, the power was up to an incredible 191hp at 15,150rpm. Nakamoto's HRC team and chief mechanic Adrian Gorst worked on improving the handling, with new Showa suspension and an asymmetric double-sided swingarm. The brakes were Nissin instead of Brembo, with six-piston calipers on the front. Although plagued with inconsistent handling from one race to the next, Edwards finished second in the World Superbike Championship, taking five victories along the way.

At the Isle of Man the RC45 continued where the RC30 had left off. Steve Hislop won the F1 and Senior TTs in 1994, while Phillip McCallen won every F1 and Senior TT between 1995 and 1997 (except Joey Dunlop's 1995 Senior win, also on an RC45). Ian Simpson continued with a double in 1998. The RC45 was also moderately successful in the USA. Ben Bostrom took the 1998 AMA Superbike Championship, and Miguel Duhamel won the 1999 Daytona 200.

The reliability of the RC45 also meant it continued to shine in Endurance racing, with Doug Polen and Christian Lavielle winning the 1998 title. But of all events, the Suzuka 8-hour was always the most important to Honda. Here the RC45 continued to dominate. Slight and Polen won in 1994, and Slight, teamed with Tadayuki Okada, won in 1995. After a one year hiatus, Tohru Ukawa and Shinichi Itoh won in 1997 and '98. They narrowly lost to Okada and Alex Barros in 1999. It may have been time for the new RC51 twin, but for Honda, the RC45 had done its job.

For 1993, the CBR1000F received a linked braking system and a reshaped fairing, but the style was unchanged. *Australian Motorcycle News*

# 8 LIQUID-COOLED

## INLINE-FOUR DOMINATION: THE 1980s AND '90s

After failing to change the course of motorcycle design with their V-fours, Honda surprised everyone by returning to the in-line four for 1987. A shrinking demand for motorcycles demanded a reduction in production costs, and the seeds were sown in November 1985 when the CBR250 was exhibited at the Tokyo Motor Show. This 16,000rpm liquid-cooled 16-valve in-line four was canted forward, and housed in a beam-type aluminium frame, indicating larger displacement CBRs were likely in the near future. But as was typical of Honda, when they appeared they represented a new take on the traditional layout. For the first time for Honda, the engines were totally buried under efficient AirFlow bodywork.

## THE CBR1000F AND CB1000 (1987–99)

The impetus for the creation of the CBR1000F came from the success of other Japanese large displacement fours, notably the Kawasaki GPz900R. Honda's last open class four was the 1983 CB1100F, but much had changed in the intervening four years. Previously, Honda had adopted a radical approach to motorcycle development, but now they reverted to conservatism. There was nothing really new about the CBR1000F Hurricane, but the CBR1000F was a Renaissance motorcycle. Like the Renaissance Man, the CBR1000F was a machine of many talents.

Central to the CBR1000F was an all-new water-cooled four-cylinder engine with the cylinders nearly upright (canted forward 12°). The bore and stroke of 77 x 53.6mm was more oversquare than the comparable Kawasaki, and the Hy-Vo chain drive for the double overhead camshafts was in the centre. Displacement was 998cc, and the engine was tuned for high horsepower. The four valves per cylinder were a large, 30mm intake and 26.5mm exhaust, and the carburettors 38.5mm Keihins. These were the largest carburettors ever for a production four-cylinder motorcycle. Finger-style valve followers were mounted on ball ends, with screw-type adjusters. The motor was very compact, with the chain-driven alternator mounted on the cylinders, and included a counterbalancer driven off the primary gear to cancel

The CBR1000F of 1987 established a new four-cylinder lineage. Although a traditional layout, Honda provided full-coverage bodywork. *Motorcycle Trader collection*

secondary vibration. Right from the outset Honda was intent on producing the fastest Superbike, and the six-speed CBR1000F produced 135hp at 9,500rpm.

This powerful engine was rigidly mounted in a perimeter-style steel chassis, made up of two 30 x 60mm box-section members, and with familiar Pro-Link rear suspension. The wheels were 17-inch front and rear and the front fork 41mm with a more compact TRAC anti-dive. Honda made no attempt to make the engine visually attractive, deciding to enclose the entire unit with full coverage ABS AirFlow bodywork. Whether this was done for functional or economic reasons was debateable, but it certainly made the CBR1000FH distinctive. And it was extremely fast, *Performance Bikes* achieving 162.3mph (261.1km/h). While no lightweight at 222kg, the CBR1000F was functionally superior, with *Cycle World* claiming: 'With the Hurricane 1000, Honda has simply built the best all-round sportbike in the world.'

While sagging sales caused by sky-rocketing insurance rates saw the CBR1000F not offered in the USA for 1989, there were a few updates to the CBR1000FK elsewhere. Emphasising sport-touring, the restyled fairing included a new headlight, providing improved weather protection, and a vent in the base of the windscreen was claimed to decrease turbulence. There were fairing protectors in case of a tip over, and an anti-lock braking option. Although bikes sales dropped 40 per cent in the USA during 1989, Honda released the updated CBR1000F in America for 1990. Focusing less on brute power, this year saw a new, lower frame, wider wheels with radial tyres, and a cartridge Showa fork. The weight went up to 246kg, but the CBR1000F was still the most refined litre Superbike available. For 1991, the CBR1000FM had a higher screen and ducts to reduce turbulence. There were few updates for 1992, and the CBR1000F wasn't offered in the USA this year, but it reappeared for 1993 (CBR1000FP) with new bodywork and a linked braking system. The fairing featured a steeper nose, moving the headlight weight backwards. Other updates included more compact 38mm carburettors, while the

Honda took a different approach to the big-bore naked standard motorcycle, using the water-cooled CBR1000F motor in the CB1000. *Australian Motorcycle News*

linked brakes featured three-piston brake calipers. The downside of the integrated braking system was a rise in the overall weight, to 250kg. Although replaced by the CBR1100XX in 1997, the CBR1000F continued until the CBR1000FX of 1999. In some markets this was still available in 2000.

Also new during 1993 was the CB1000 'Project Big One', a naked standard motorcycle which took a detuned CBR1000F motor and placed it in a tubular steel double-cradle frame with twin remote reservoir shock-absorber rear suspension. The front fork was a non-adjustable 43mm, and the wheels were 18-inch front and rear. This was a very large motorcycle, with the largest swingarm of any Honda, a 1,540mm wheelbase, and weighing 235kg. Unlike the competitive Suzuki and Kawasaki which featured large four-cylinder air-cooled engines, Honda took the liquid-cooled CBR engine, painted it gloss black, with polished cam and side covers, and tidied up the plumbing. The motor produced 98hp, courtesy of smaller, 34mm carburettors, smaller valves milder

cams, a 10.5:1 compression ratio, and its own four-into-one exhaust system. Unlike the CBR1000F, the gearbox was a five-speed. Styled like an early 1980s Superbike, the CB1000 was designed to take you back in time, while providing modern features.

# THE CBR600F, CBR400F AND RR, CBR250RR AND CB-1 (1987–2000)

At the same time as the CBR1000F was released, it was accompanied by the CBR600F (and CBR400F in Japan). The CBR600F followed the example of the CBR1000F. There was nothing really new, but the result redefined the middleweight sportsbike category. Prior to the CBR600F, mid-range motorcycles were not really considered as an alternative to large-displacement Superbikes by serious sporting riders. But the CBR600F provided almost unimaginable performance for its time,

A miniature FireBlade, the high-specification CBR250RR was built primarily for the Japanese market. *Australian Motorcycle News*

it was so perfectly balanced, with handling and braking in harmony with its power, that 600cc motorcycles became legitimate high-performance sporting machines. This situation continues today, and the CBR600F has been a consistent best-seller.

The 60 x 52.4mm CBR600F motor (55 x 42mm; CBR400F) was similar to that of the CBR1000F, but was canted forward 35°. There was no engine balancer, and the alternator was mounted on the crankshaft. This required the engine to be positioned quite high, also putting the centre of mass higher than usual. As Honda had found from their GP racing programme, this was desirable for handling. The camshafts were driven by chain (gears on the CBR400F), and with 24mm and 21mm valves (22mm and 19.5mm, CBR400F), 32mm carburettors, an 11:1 compression ratio, and a four-into-one exhaust system; the power was a then class-leading 85hp at 11,000rpm. As with the CBR1000F, the engine was mounted in a steel frame (the CBR400F had an aluminium frame) as a stressed member, but the rear suspension unit was tucked in above the gearbox to concentrate the mass further. The front fork was 37mm with TRAC, and rolling on 17-inch wheels, the 182kg CBR600FH delivered more than it promised. Honda promoted the CBR600F through an entertaining one-make production racing series, and this was a machine which

was comfortable, easy to ride, and could do anything. The CBR600's performance was close to many 750s, and *Performance Bikes* achieved 137mph (220km/h).

While the CBR600FJ was unchanged for 1988 except for colours, the CBR400F evolved into the amazing CBR400RR in Japan. This second-generation four now featured a cast twin-spar aluminium frame and triangulated swingarm and was styled like a 250 GP bike. For 1990 it received the GP-style 'Gull Arm' swingarm, and was later (from 1994) styled like the CBR900RR FireBlade. While retaining gear-driven camshafts, the valve adjustment was bucket and shim, and the power 53hp at 12,000rpm. The front fork was a conventional cartridge type, and the wheels were 17-inch front and rear. From 1991 the CBR400RR was joined by the CBR250RR, primarily for the Japanese market, and was almost identical but for the smaller motor. The 48.5 x 33.8mm four included four 20mm carburettors and produced 40hp at 14,500rpm. The engine revved to 18,000rpm, and the 158kg CBR250RR was capable of around 106mph (170km/h).

Also new for 1989 in the USA was the CB-1 (CB400F). Harking back to the classic 1975 CB400F, the naked entry-level CB-1 took the Japanese market CBR400F motor, detuned it slightly, and installed it in a round perimeter-style steel frame with Pro-Link rear suspension, a 41mm fork, and 17-inch wheels. Unfortunately, the high specification CB-1 (the engine redlined at 13,000rpm and still featured gear driven camshafts) was too expensive in America, at $4,498 it costing more than many 600s. Even when the price was reduced by $400 for 1990 it failed to sell, but the 400s remained popular in Japan for many years.

While the 1989 CBR600FK was unchanged apart from colours, there were problems with the fuel pump breather. American Honda recalled 6,294 1989 CBRs to reroute the breather to prevent the fuel pump arcing and igniting the vapours. Increased pressure from other Japanese manufacturers saw the CBR600FL gain 9hp for 1990. The compression ratio went up to 11.3:1, and there were new camshafts, changes to the carburetion, ignition curve, and a freer breathing stainless-steel exhaust. The chassis remained as before, but was becoming outdated so fast such was the rate of change in this class, and already there was a call for a stronger front fork and wider wheel rims. The CBR600F was also no longer the fastest and best-selling in its class, having been overtaken by the Kawasaki ZZ-R600.

One of Honda's most consistently successful models has been the CBR600F. This is the 1993 version, which was very similar to all examples between 1991 and 1994.
*Australian Motorcycle News*

So important was the CBR600F2 (CBR600FM in Europe) that it was Honda's only new model for 1991. Development proceeded on the second-generation CBR600F just after the launch of the original, in August 1986, and included an all-new 599cc engine. There was a wider bore and shorter stroke (65 x 45.2mm), a larger 6.2-litre airbox feeding 34mm semi-flat-slide downdraft carburettors through a shorter and wider (35mm) intake port. The valves were also larger (25.5mm and 22mm) and there was bucket and shim adjustment. Lighter pistons provided a higher, 11.6:1 compression ratio and the chain camshaft drive was moved to the end of the crankshaft. There was a new claw-type (instead of pawl-and-plunger) gear change mechanism, and the upper crankcase and cylinder block were cast in one piece. There was no longer a fuel pump, gravity now feeding the carburettors. The crankcases were 50mm lower and 15mm narrower than before. The result of this development saw an engine which produced 100hp at 12,000rpm, the first production 600 to break the 100hp barrier.

The chassis was evolutionary, retaining a rectangular-section steel beam frame, utilising the engine as a stressed member, and with a steel swingarm. As with the earlier design, Honda's engineers concentrated on mass centralisation. The front fork was a conventional 41mm cartridge style (without TRAC) rather than the new-generation upside down type, and the front discs a relatively small 276mm. The wheels and brakes were deliberately kept as light as possible to centralise the mass. The new six-spoke aluminium wheels also allowed for wider radial tyres, the wheelbase was slightly reduced (1,405mm instead of 1,410mm), and the weight similar at 185kg. The CBR600F2 wasn't a radical motorcycle, but continued Honda's design approach where the engine and chassis were complementary, with the emphasis on creating a balanced machine. *Motorcyclist* magazine summed up the CBR600F2 with: 'It's not only one of the best 600cc bikes on the market but one of the best all-round motorcycles ever built. It covers all bases without resorting to the lowest common denominator.' So good was the CBR600F2 that it remained virtually unchanged in the hottest class for four years. The final F2 (CBR600FR) of 1994 included a cartridge front fork with adjustable damping and a remote reservoir rear shock.

Although the 1995 CBR600F3 (CBR600FS in Europe) looked similar to its predecessor, updates included a more aerodynamic fairing and headlight, higher compression ratio (12:1), larger, 36mm carburettors, straighter and 5mm shorter intakes, and a dual-stage pressurised air-intake system. Chassis upgrades included firmer suspension (with adjustable

Throughout the 1990s the CBR600F received evolutionary updates, and although this 1997 model didn't include the latest state-of-the-art technology it remained one of the best sporting and most reliable middleweights available. *Australian Motorcycle News*

Right: The redesign for the fourth generation CBR600F of 1999 was the most radical of all, with an aluminium beam frame for the first time. *Australian Motorcycle News*

rebound damping on the front fork), a wider (5.0 x 17-inch) rear wheel, and larger diameter (296mm) front disc brakes. There were no changes apart from colours for the 1996 CBR600FT. There was a good reason Honda didn't change the CBR600F too much. In January 1996, production topped 200,000, and it was Honda's best-selling motorcycle over 125cc. While the CBR600F's finish was workmanlike rather than outstanding, as *Bike* magazine said: 'The CBR's quality is where it counts, in the suspension and the unburstable engine. It's the lightest, the best-handling, the truest all-rounder.'

For 1997, the CBR600FV received a deeper oil pan, single valve springs, a new shift drum and freer-flowing muffler which saw the power increased to 105hp. The suspension included an adjustable front fork and rear shock absorber with HMAS, a revised rear suspension linkage, and there was new bodywork. This featured a new air duct in the fairing, and redesigned tailpiece and side panels. Honda claimed more power, improved shifting, and better suspension, for the 1998 CBR600F, and for the USA there was a special commemorative 'Smokin' Joe' edition to celebrate the success in the AMA 600 Supersport series.

Determined to maintain its position as the leading 600, Honda completely redesigned the CBR600F for the fourth-generation CBR600FX (F4 in America) of 1999. The engine was lighter, smaller, and stronger, with a larger bore (67mm), and shorter stroke (42.5mm), and the cylinders featured the aluminium ceramic/graphite sleeves of the CBR900RR and VFR800FI. Inside the cylinder head the included valve angle was reduced yet again, to 24.3°, but the compression ratio was still 12:1. To reduce internal friction, the crankshaft journals were reduced by 3mm to 30mm, and the crankcases also incorporated the swingarm pivot as on the VTR1000F and VFR800. With larger, 36.5mm, flat-slide carburettors and a pressurised 6.5-litre airbox, the power was up to 110hp at 12,500rpm.

Also totally updated for 1999 was the chassis. After running the proven steel twin-spar frame for more than a decade, there was now a CBR900RR-style aluminium frame, with a box-section lower rail and a triple box-section 40 x 90mm aluminium swingarm. The frame was 7kg lighter than before, and the front fork was upgraded to 43mm (from 41mm). The front brakes now included four-piston calipers, and the rear wheel was a wider, 5.50 x 17-inch. One of the most significant changes was a reduction in wheelbase, to 1,395mm, and a reduction in total weight to 170kg. All

## SUPERSPORT RACER

One of the reasons for the sales success of the CBR600F was its racetrack achievements. In the highly competitive world of 600 Supersport racing the CBR600F dominated since 1987. Nowhere has the CBR600 been more dominant than at the Isle of Man, always a Honda favourite. CBR600s won the Production C and 600 Supersport races in 1988 and '89, continuing their dominance in the hands of Steve Hislop, Phillip McCallen and Jim Moodie, in 1991, '92, and '93. When the capacity of the Junior TT was raised to 600cc, the CBR600's reign continued. Iain Duffus won in 1995, McCallen in 1996, Ian Simpson in 1997 Michael Rutter in 1998, and Jim Moodie in 1999. Paul Brown won the British Supersport 600 Championship in 1997, and Rutter the Northwest 200. Stateside too the CBR600 ruled. In 1991, eight of the top ten finishers at the Daytona Supersport race were CBR600F-mounted. Honda went on to win eight AMA Supersport 600 series through until 2000. Miguel Duhamel won his third consecutive Supersport series in 1997, while 18-year-old Nicky Hayden took out the 1999 title, and Kurtis Roberts the 2000 series.

these changes were enough to ensure the CBR600FY remained at the head of Honda's line-up, and would continue virtually unchanged until 2001. *Motorcyclist* had this to say about the F4: 'The CBR600F4 lets more riders go faster, and easier, than any bike we've ridden yet, regardless of how much you're willing to play for it.' Unfortunately for Honda, Yamaha also released the R6 in 1999, rewriting the rules for middleweights.

# THE FIREBLADE: CBR900RR (1992–99)

Few motorcycles have had the impact of the CBR900RR FireBlade. While there was nothing revolutionary about its design, the idea of combining open class horsepower with the weight of a 600 was a recipe for instant success. In one swoop, the FireBlade virtually destroyed the 750 category. Headed by project leader Tadao Baba, the FireBlade initiated the high horsepower, light weight approach that continues today. It has become one of the classic designs of the 1990s, made the opposition seem like fat pigs, and ensured sporting motorcycles were never the same again.

The 16-valve four-cylinder CBR900RR-N engine shared many features with the CBR600F2. Displacing

893cc (70 x 58mm), the one-piece crankcase and cylinder block allowed the transmission to be located close to the crankshaft, and the camshaft drive was on the right. The crank main bearings were 34mm (compared to 33mm on the CBR600 and 40mm on the CBR1000). Big-end journals were up 2mm on the 600, to 36mm. A small one-piece alternator sat on the left end of the crank. The valves were a narrow, 32° included angle, and with an 11:1 compression ratio and four 38mm flat-slide carburettors breathing through a large, 7.2-litre airbox, the power was 122hp at 10,500rpm.

While this power output was unremarkable, when the engine was partially rubber mounted in the twin-spar aluminium frame, with box-section alloy swingarm, the result was spectacular. The suspension included a conventional 45mm front fork, styled to look like an upside down type, and the CBR900RR-N continued Honda's quest for mass centralisation. The wheelbase was an incredibly short 1,410mm, and every component trimmed to save weight. From the tiny 8Ah battery to the small, 296mm brake discs and 16-inch front wheel with specially developed Bridgestone tyre, the emphasis was on keeping the weight down to 185kg. With an intriguing set of holes in the fairing to quicken side-to-side steering transitions, the CBR900RR-N turned the sporting motorcycle world

Providing open class horsepower in a 600 size motorcycle was an instant recipe for success, and the original FireBlade of 1992 took the motorcycle world by storm. *Author*

upside down. It really did provide open class horsepower with 600 class weight, causing *Cycle World* to claim: 'Honda has redefined motorcycle performance, using equal parts of force and finesse. No other bike in the last 20 years has generated as much hype and hoopla as this lightweight flyer, but the CBR900RR lives up to its advance billing. It really is that good.'

While the CBR900RR-P FireBlade was unchanged for 1993, there were minor updates for the 1994 CBR900RR-R (1995 in the USA). The fairing was restyled, and the headlights no longer the distinctive twin round type. Compression damping was added to the front fork, and the transmission included reshaped gears and a gearshift linkage to eliminate the noisy and notchy gearshift on the earlier FireBlade.

More updates were saved for 1996, with the CBR900RR-T receiving a thorough make-over. The engine was bored to 71mm, creating 919cc, with larger, 36.5mm big-end bearings and a new rare earth magnet generator allowing the engine to be narrowed by

9.5mm. A new casting process allowed Honda to insert oversize sleeves into the block while maintaining the same bore centres. The ignition system received a three-dimensional map with a throttle position sensor, and there was a larger, curved radiator to keep things cool. The gearbox ratios were changed, and the power was up to 128hp at 10,500rpm.

The chassis was also redesigned, with higher handlebars and more legroom providing a more comfortable riding position. While the frame looked outwardly similar, in typical Honda fashion the frame tubes were completely different inside, with 1mm wider beams, 2.7mm walls, and two internal ribs instead of three. The reason for the new, less rigid frame, was due to Baba's deduction from the CBR600F frame that stiffer wasn't necessarily better. There was also a less stiff swingarm pivot casting, 5mm higher than before, and a new front fork with internal metering discs instead of shim stacks. Adapted from motocross experience, this HMAS (Honda multi-action system) was also incorporated in the rear shock absorber. There

The FireBlade evolved gradually over the years, but always retained its family likeness. Here is the 1995 version on the left, with the 919cc 1996 example on the right. *Australian Motorcycle News*

was a myriad other changes with the '919', and the overall weight was reduced to 183kg. And when it came to function, the 1996 FireBlade continued where the earlier model had left off. In the words of *Motorcyclist* magazine: 'We assumed the RR was going to be better than before, but we didn't really expect it to be so totally transformed. The RR gives you your cake, slices it for you, and serves it on a silver platter.' Buyers flocked to the new 'Blade, with 2,400 sold in Britain during 1996.

While the FireBlade continued to sell well, by 1997 the opposition was tugging at its heels. Already Suzuki's new GSX-R750 had beaten the FireBlade in some comparison tests, and the time was ripe for a third-generation update. So, for 1998 the CBR900RR-W received its second major update. Maintaining Baba's Bigger Circle Theory, where the goal was an ever-bigger circle encompassing novice riders and expert racers, the new FireBlade still accentuated ease of street use. While the capacity remained at 918.5cc, modification to 80 per cent of the engine internals saw

the power increased to 130hp at 10,500rpm. The cylinder sleeves were the composite metal type pioneered on the RC45, and there was a new digital ignition, more compact clutch, and stainless-steel exhaust. Most changes were to the chassis, with a new frame, revised steering geometry (with much needed increased trail), and a more rigid front fork. The front brake discs were increased to 310mm, with new four opposed-piston Nissin calipers. The weight was down to 180kg, and Tadao Baba's philosophy that 'the bike has to be lighter and more controllable, but still affordable,' continued. *Motorcyclist* noted: 'This is the best CBR900RR Honda's built, refined to a point where it's probably the most highly evolved, sophisticated sportbike in the world.' The biggest criticism of the new CBR900RR was the 16-inch front wheel. *Cycle World* said: 'Why Honda insists on using a 16 is beyond us, and it limits tyre selection.'

Although the CBR900RR was unchanged for 1999, this year, Honda Britain offered the limited-edition EvoBlade. Developed by Russell Savory's RS

For 1998, the FireBlade received its second major update, with more power and less weight. *Australian Motorcycle News*

Right: Introduced in 1997, apart from the adoption of fuel injection, the CBR1100XX Super Blackbird continued largely unchanged for nearly a decade. Although a large motorcycle, the Super Blackbird was surprisingly agile, and extremely fast. *Australian Motorcycle News*

Performance, Savory was determined to maintain Honda's supremacy in the Production TT and British Production Championship. Created in consultation with Baba-san, Savory's EvoBlade featured ram air induction, 41mm Keihin flat-slide carburettors, a close-ratio gearbox, and produced over 150hp. Chassis upgrades included an Öhlins 42mm front fork, Brembo brakes, 17-inch Dymag wheels, and a RAM (Race Application Monaco) single-sided swingarm. The introduction of the Yamaha R1 during 1999 prompted Honda to revise their marketing strategy. The FireBlade had become more powerful and user-friendly over the years, and its incredible record of reliability and value for money saw it a consistent best-seller, especially in Britain. But something new was required, and the new millennium saw an all-new FireBlade.

## THE CBR1100XX SUPER BLACKBIRD (FROM 1997)

Honda had one goal when designing the CBR1100XX: to create the fastest production motorcycle on Earth. To match the Kawasaki ZZ-R1100 the CBR1100XX needed to top 300km/h (186mph), and for this it

needed a lot of power and improved aerodynamics over the venerable CBR1000F. Under the guidance of Project Leader Mr Yamanaka, this wasn't going to be a revolutionary motorcycle, but the result of a carefully executed mission. Powering the Super Blackbird was the evolutionary four-cylinder, 79 x 58mm 1,137cc motor, receiving two harmonic balance shafts, gear-driven in opposite directions at twice engine speed. Inside the cylinder head was a narrower, 30° valve angle, the cam chain was at the end of the crankshaft, and the valve adjustment was bucket and shim like the CBR900RR. The engine block and top of the crankcase were cast in one-piece, and the solidly mounted engine

## RACING THE 'BLADE

Nowhere has the FireBlade been more successful as a racer than at Honda's traditionally favoured racetrack, the Isle of Man. UK Honda boss Bob McMillan encouraged the return of the Production race to the TT programme, and Phil McCallen rewarded Honda with another TT victory. FireBlades filled seven of the top ten places. When Jim Moodie won the 1998 Production TT it marked Honda's 100th victory on the Island.

was 10kg lighter than the CBR1000F. With the cylinders inclined 22° forward, allowing the 42mm Keihin flat-slide carburettors to be downdraft, and an 11:1 compression ratio the power was a staggering 162hp at 10,000rpm.

The chassis was sportbike standard, and like the 1996 CBR900RR, the aluminium chassis incorporated 'engineered flexibility' and the 43mm front fork featured HMAS cartridge dampers. There was nothing startling about the 17-inch wheels, lightweight 310mm front disc brakes, and revised LBS (linked braking system), but aerodynamics were the design focus. The long nose fairing provided a lower drag coefficient with less turbulence, while the 1,490mm wheelbase and weight of 223kg ensured the Super Blackbird would be the best handling open class bike available. The Super Blackbird was certainly a magnificent large-capacity sporting motorcycle, but it failed to deliver the speed it promised. Both *Performance Bikes* and *Cycle World* managed an average two-way top speed of 174mph (280km/h), still shy of the Kawasaki.

In response to the comparatively disappointing top speed, for 1999 Honda updated the CBR1100XX with electronic fuel injection (with 42mm throttle bodies), a new pressurised direct air-intake system feeding a 9.5-litre airbox, and a revised exhaust. The power was now 164hp at 9,500rpm. Also new was the DCBS (dual combined braking system) of the VFR800FI, and the fuel tank was increased to 24 litres (from 22). The CBR1100XX continued with only minor updates over the next few years, receiving a new instrument panel and a 30mm taller screen for 2001. The engine included an air injection system and a three-way HECS3 catalytic converter, and although the claimed power was down to 152hp, in the real world this was barely noticeable. It may have been a large, powerful motorway-style motorcycle, but the Super Blackbird was also amazingly deceptive. Its agility and ease of riding belied its size and weight, and the CBR1100XX was another typical, excellent Honda motorcycle which was beautifully built and easy to live with.

# THE CB600F HORNET, AND CBF600 (FROM 1998)

The naked motorcycle craze saw Honda create the Hornet out of the CBR600F for 1998. Designed specifically for the European market, the Hornet 600 was based on the Japanese market Hornet 250, first

The first 600 Hornet featured a FireBlade 16-inch front wheel and huge rear tyre. *Australian Motorcycle News*

Below: Introduced for 2004, the CBF600 was a softer version of the 600 Hornet. For 2005 there was an ABS option. *Honda*

released in 1996. It was immediately successful, selling more than 20,000 units a year. The 94hp 600cc motor was retuned for mid-range, with smaller, 34mm

carburettors, and there was a FireBlade-style 16-inch front wheel for quick turning. The frame was a basic steel backbone type, the swingarm was steel, and with a huge FireBlade 180-section rear tyre, the 176kg CB600 Hornet was arguably over-tyred. But it was well-suited to its own racing series, the Hornet Cup, initiated for 1999. There was a switch to a wider 17-inch front wheel for 2000, and this year the Hornet was joined by the Hornet-S with a small frame-mounted fairing. All Hornet models retained the earlier 65 x 45.2mm CBR600 motor which now had a new digital ignition and was retuned slightly, with a claimed 1.5hp increase. Offering competent, rather than state-of-the-art equipment, the Hornet and Hornet-S provided an excellent value package. The front fork was a non-adjustable conventional 41mm type, and the rear shock was adjustable for spring pre-load only, but it worked. Arguably the weakest components were the brakes, still with the dual-piston front calipers of the much earlier CBR600.

The Hornet was tweaked slightly for 2003. There

For 2000, a Hornet S with a small fairing joined the Hornet. This year also saw a 17-inch front wheel fitted. *Australian Motorcycle News*

was a new headlight, the tail was redesigned, the front fork received stronger springs and increased damping, the brakes were upgraded, the swingarm pivot reinforced, and the fuel tank was a litre larger. For 2005, the engine features 36mm carburettors, and the power is 98hp at 12,000rpm. But as the Hornet remains one of the most popular motorcycles of its type in Europe there was little reason to change it. As *Performance Bikes* summed up the 600 Hornet: 'They're a lot of fun for the money.' For 2004, the Italian-built 600 Hornet also made it to the USA where it was known as the 599.

A softer version of the 600 Hornet also appeared for 2004, the naked CBF600, and the CBF600S with half fairing. Designed to appeal to more leisurely riders than the Hornet, the Hornet engine was detuned (with softer cams) and a lower, 11.6:1 compression ratio, to produce 78hp at 10,500rpm. To accommodate a wider range of riders the CBF600F featured a three-step height adjustable seat. The weight went up to 191kg (197kg for the S), and there was the option of ABS.

# THE X-11 CB1100SF (1999–03)

Continuing where the CB1 left off, but taking the naked muscle bike to a new level was the X-11. Introduced in 1999, the X-11 was based on the Super Blackbird, the fuel-injected 1,137cc motor detuned to provide 134hp at 9,000rpm and more mid-range. The wide frame was a twin-spar aluminium type, and the running gear included a 43mm front fork and combined braking system with three-piston calipers. Although a very capable machine, the size of the 222kg X-11 was intimidating, and it was quite ugly with its plastic radiator shields obscuring the motor. Not only was the X-11 out-muscled by the comparable Suzuki GSX1400 and Yamaha XJR1300, as a naked bike it was virtually rendered obsolete by the arrival of the CB900 Hornet. The X-11 wasn't one of Honda's success stories, and was quickly forgotten.

With its aggressive styling, and comfortable riding position, the CB900 Hornet replicated some of the classic Hondas of the 1980s. *Motorcycle Trader*

Right: The CB1300 successfully replicated the image of the large classic naked Superbikes of the 1980s. *Motorcycle Trader*

# THE CB900F HORNET (919) (FROM 2002)

In response to the popularity of the CB600 Hornet, a larger version based on the CBR900RR FireBlade appeared for 2002. The design criteria emphasised an all-purpose nature, and a machine equally at home in the city, the inter-city highway, or winding back roads. In many respects the nature of the CB900 Hornet replicated that of the earlier air-cooled CB900F of 1979–83. But this was a much more powerful and compact motorcycle. Continuing the FireBlade concept of shoehorning a 900cc motor into a 600 chassis, the CB900 Hornet was an even more satisfactory marriage.

Like the 600 Hornet, the 900 used an engine from the earlier specification sporting version. In this case it was the 1998 919cc FireBlade motor, tuned for torque rather than outright power, and including fuel injection instead of carburettors. Along with a lower compression ratio (10.8:1), there were different camshafts, and changes to the PGM-FI fuel injection system. These included 36mm throttle bodies with four-hole injectors, and an anti-pollution air induction system feeding air into the exhaust ports. With a unique 4-2-1-2 under-seat exhaust system, the power was 109hp at 9,000rpm. Although this was 20hp shy of the FireBlade, the increase in mid-range power made the Hornet easier to ride.

The matt-black frame was based on that of the 600 Hornet, with the thickness of the steel backbone increased to 2.3mm from 1.6mm. There was additional gusseting around the steering head, and an additional cross-member between the frame's two front engine mounts. The swingarm was FireBlade-style aluminium, and the front fork a 43mm Showa. The rear shock was also adjustable for preload only, and the front brakes were 1996 FireBlade-spec Nissin four-piston caliper 296mm discs. Also ensuring manageability were the compact dimensions. The wheelbase was 1,460mm, and the weight only 194kg. Also released in the USA as the 919, the CB900's only deficiency was that it was a little bland. While other open-class naked bikes were mean and brashly styled, the CB900 was typically Honda. Well built, and conservative, and didn't meet with universal acclaim. *Motorcyclist* magazine said: 'In the end, we're perplexed by the 919's lack of character.'

# THE CB1300 (FROM 1998)

In response to the continuing retro-craze in Japan Honda built the huge CB1300 for 1998. Basically a big-bore CB1000, this was derived from the domestic market X4 'monster cruiser', but it didn't become available in Europe until 2003. Naked machines were the growth area by this time, and Honda believed the CB1300 would appeal to older, more mature riders who still felt nostalgia for the older Superbikes. Under project leader Kunitaka Hara, essentially the CB1300 was a modern version of the 1970s Superbike, the engine dominating the motorcycle, and cradled in a traditional steel frame. When it arrived in Europe the CB1300 engine was still based on the older CB1000, the liquid-cooled 1,284cc (78 x 67.2mm) double overhead camshaft motor featuring a narrower included valve angle to improve breathing. While early CB1300s had four 38mm carburettors, the 2003 CB1300 included PGM-F1 electronic fuel injection with 36mm throttle bodies. With a compression ratio of 9.6:1, the five-speed engine produced a moderate

peak power output of 115hp at 7,500rpm, but provided incredible mid-range power. Like the earlier CB1000, this engine was intentionally styled to complement the brutal image, and included a four into-one exhaust system.

While the Japanese market CB1300 of 1998 featured Pro-Link rising-rate rear suspension, and six-piston front brake calipers, the European CB1300 chassis was remarkably similar to the earlier CB1000. It included a classic double-cradle steel tubular frame, the motor mounted on three points, the rear a rubber mount. The front suspension was a conventional Showa 43mm fork, with the 40 x 90mm box-section aluminium swingarm controlled by twin gas-charged remote-reservoir shock absorbers. The brakes were FireBlade four-piston, gripping 310mm floating rotors, and the wheels were a more up-to-date 17-inch front and rear. For 2005, the CB1300 is available with optional ABS. Despite its imposing size (234.4kg) and dimensions (1,510mm wheelbase), the CB1300 provided a low, 790mm seat height and a very comfortable riding position. Some also had a bikini fairing. Updates for 2005 include narrower sidecovers which help shorter riders to reach the ground more easily.

Doohan carried the Number 1 plate for the first time in 1995, and rewarded Honda with back-to-back world titles. *Author*

# 9 DOOHAN OK:

## TWO-STROKE GRAND PRIX DOMINATION (1992–2001)

After two consecutive losses to Yamaha in the 500cc World Championship, Honda was under some pressure to succeed. Ravenous and desperate for victory, but still committed to the single crankshaft, Honda reassessed the NSR500's development path. By the end of 1991 the riders' status was also changing, with Wayne Gardner at the end of his career, and Mick Doohan becoming Honda's rising hope. Doohan and his crew chief Jerry Burgess wanted the engine characteristics changed so the throttle could be opened earlier, and Honda's engineers responded with the 'Big-Bang' engine for 1992. The new engine revolutionised GP racing, but the idea wasn't new – Suzuki had tried it in the late 1970s, and Cagiva in the mid-1980s. In those days it was a case of bump starting and as this was too difficult with all cylinders firing closely together, the idea was shelved.

## THE 'BIG-BANG' NSR500 (1992–96)

With the 'Big-Bang' engine, the firing interval of the cylinder pairs was reduced to around 66–70°, allowing the tyre to break grip on ignition, but recover with around 290° before the next ignition cycle. This made the power delivery smoother as well as dramatically extending rear tyre life. Drive was from the centre of the crankshaft, and along with the new crank were new cylinders, exhaust and ignition, with a heavier balance shaft to counter the increased vibration. This balance shaft also improved on the chassis balance, but even with around 175hp at 12,500rpm (with 36mm carburettors) Gardner and Doohan felt the bike was slower than before when testing. For 1992 the airflow sensors were mounted in the high air intakes rather than the lower intakes, and there was an improved airbox design. The chassis was basically unchanged from 1991, Gardner retaining a higher engine position than Doohan, but both using a 43mm Showa front fork with carbon inner tubes and steel outers.

In the first GP of the season, a dangerously wet Suzuka, Doohan ran away with an easy victory. Providing less wheelspin, the superiority of the 'Big Bang' engine was immediately evident. Gardner wasn't so fortunate, a crash resulting in a broken leg

The 'Big-Bang' NSR500
revolutionised GP racing, but
Doohan struggled with the 1993
version. *Alan Cathcart Archive*

effectively ending his career. When Doohan took easy wins in Australia and Malaysia the scepticism about the new engine disappeared, and Doohan looked set to take the World Championship easily. That was until everything went awry at Assen. A crash during practice resulted in a badly broken leg, and subsequent complications saw Doohan miss the rest of the season until the final two rounds. Despite severe discomfort, Doohan rode in Brazil and South Africa, but lost the title to Rainey by four points.

For the 1993 season Honda decided to fuel inject the NSR500. They had already raced a fuel-injected NSR250 in the 1990 All-Japan Championship, and for the first 1993 Grand Prix in Australia all three Rothmans NSR500s featured the PGM-F1 injection system. More like an electronic carburettor, a geared fuel pump provided 10kg/cm$^2$ fuel pressure to injectors directly in the inlet trumpets. Flat-slides controlled the airflow. But with Doohan not fit enough to test the new bike over the winter the development was entrusted to

new recruit Daryl Beattie. Without as much experience as Doohan, the bike went back in the direction that Gardner had preferred, and these engine changes affected the chassis.

The debut of the fuel-injected NSR500 was also disappointing. Beattie finished fourth and Doohan retired fearing the bike would spit him off. For the next GP in Malaysia, the NSR500s for Doohan and Beattie had carburettors. In the meantime, Shinichi Itoh continued to test the fuel injection, but it never reached the stage where it provided superior throttle response and was eventually discarded. A more satisfactory development was the adoption of a pressurised airbox, but it took half a season for the NSR500 to get back to the level of 1992. The pressurised airbox improved the throttle response at the expense of top speed, but this suited Doohan's style, and he experimented with 1992 cylinders. Doohan also had the rear brake lever moved to the left handlebar because his leg wasn't strong enough to operate it. Although still not at peak fitness following slow recovery after the 1992 Assen crash, Doohan finally came to terms with the revised NSR500 with a win at Mugello (marred by Wayne Rainey's crash which left him paralysed). At the next GP at Laguna Seca, Doohan crashed at the corkscrew, but his injuries prevented him being able to pull himself up. Having to drag himself off the circuit prompted Doohan to quit the season to concentrate on treatment to improve his badly injured leg. This time he asked Honda to leave the bike exactly the same while he was away. Honda listened, and when Doohan returned for testing prior to the 1994 season he had a machine he was already familiar with.

Although there were small chassis updates, such as a slightly less stiff swingarm, and continual refinement of the pressurised airbox, the NSR500 was virtually unchanged. The engine made less power because of the switch to low-lead 100-octane fuel, although this was around 180hp. After some front suspension updates early in the season Doohan and the NSR500 were an almost unbeatable combination. He won six races in succession, racking up a total of nine victories to totally crush the competition. Considering Doohan could barely walk a year earlier it was an astonishing achievement, and he had the 1994 title sewn up with three GPs to go.

This allowed Honda to test some alternative ideas, and at the European GP at Catalunya Doohan's NSR500 was fitted with a water-injected system designed to cool the exhaust gases and improve the

# SUPREME CHAMPION: MICK DOOHAN

More than any other rider, Mick Doohan displayed the talent, determination, and focus to overcome crippling injury and dominate Grand Prix racing unlike any other. Born in Brisbane, Australia, on 4 June 1965, Doohan came to Honda after an astonishingly quick rise. Although he began dirt racing a Honda MR50 in 1974, the death of his father (who owned a motorcycle shop) saw the young Mick lose interest in motorcycles for a while. With his brothers already racing, Mick took to the track in 1984. Despite this late start, it wasn't long before he was dominating 250cc Production racing in Australia, and soon landed a ride on a factory Yamaha FZR750. When he blitzed the World Superbike field in both legs of the 1988 Australian round, every GP team was interested in him. Doohan chose Honda and went on to become their most successful Grand Prix rider, winning 54 500cc GPs and five consecutive World Championships. Like Jim Redman, all his victories were on a Honda, Doohan steadfastly refusing the lure of other companies, notably Yamaha in 1995.

But there was much more to Mick Doohan than statistics. He towered over the sport for most of a decade, dominating the track and developing the NSR into an unbeatable machine. To overcome serious injury, rise again, and continually improve, indicated more than talent. Doohan displayed a unique combination of strength and drive few humans possess. And as he adapted to his injuries he created a riding style that moved away from the previous tail-sliding style of the American dirt-trackers, to one that accentuated mid-corner speed. Undoubtedly robbed of at least one title (1992), if his

career had not come to a premature end after suffering more serious injuries in a crash at the 1999 Spanish GP, Mick Doohan could surely have won another. Doohan retired as the second most successful 500 rider in history, and of Honda's 61 Grand Prix winners he was the greatest contributor of all. He continues his association with Honda as an advisor for HRC in the development of the RC211V.

The NSR500 was little changed
for 1996, but Mick Doohan
dominated the season. *Honda*

mid-range. But as this system added 7kg, it offered no advantage, and the extra weight in the tank affected the steering, so it was shelved. At the same GP, semi-active electronic suspension was also tested on Alex Criville's machine. Again, this provided no advantage over the existing set-up and the idea abandoned.

By 1995, Doohan had developed the NSR500 to suit his riding style and the Repsol-sponsored Doohan/NSR combination was the most formidable on the grid. Honda was pursuing a path of gradual evolution rather than revolution, and it was paying off. With the 'Big-Bang' engine in its fifth year it was totally reliable, and Honda had an enormous library of data. New carbon brake material was used from mid-season 1994, and cylinder development was aimed at improving bottom and mid-range power. The lower exhaust pipes, as well as the upper, were now titanium, and there was a new hydraulic clutch to ease Doohan's overworked left hand. Although Beattie on the Suzuki provided Doohan with some competition, and Doohan made three

uncharacteristic errors and crashed, mighty Mick came through to win seven GPs and take another World Championship. This year also saw the rise of Spanish riders Alberto Puig and Criville, both winning GPs. Criville realised he had to match Doohan's style, and became a real force on the track.

With Doohan preferring a simple machine, and almost Luddite-like in his rejection of electronic gadgets, everyone else on the grid was clamouring for NSR500s. Following the retirement of Youichi Oguma, Suguru Kanazawa became HRC managing director. 1996 updates were confined mainly to the front suspension, larger (320mm) front discs, and a more aerodynamic fairing. There were minor modifications to the cylinders and airbox, and although the new NSR500 V-twin surprised everyone with its competitiveness at the start of the season, the dominance of the NSR V-four continued. This year Doohan won eight GPs, but was beaten on two occasions by the ever-improving Criville, one in

Czechoslovakia by only 0.002 second. Doohan was enraged at the time, claiming Criville could follow, but not lead, while Criville admitted he was lucky to win.

# THE NSR250 AND RS250R (1992–96)

Luca Cadalora had a completely updated NSR250 for 1992, the engine now a mirror image of the previous version, with the right cylinder vertical and the left cylinder horizontal. The angle between the cylinders was reduced to 75°, allowing the engine to be shorter and provide equal-length intakes. There was now a balance shaft in front of the engine, driven off the right of the crankshaft, and the power was around 90hp at 12,800rpm. The chassis incorporated a single-sided Pro-Arm, and the bike weighed in at 96kg. As the engine was a new design, none of the earlier development was applicable and while Kanemoto managed to get the best out of the NSR250, Cadalora came under increased pressure from the ever-improving Aprilias. Cadalora won seven GPs and the championship, but the future didn't look so secure. The woes also continued for the production RS250. Still based on the previous version, revised porting, exhaust, ignition and power valve gave 81hp. Chassis updates included an upside down front fork, and new bodywork, as in the previous year victories were scarce. This prompted a new RS250 for 1993, based on the 1992 NSR250, but 7kg heavier, at 103kg. With a 38mm carburettor and a strengthened engine incorporating the balance shaft, the power was 85hp. The chassis included a single-sided Pro-Arm swingarm, and Brembo brakes.

There were few updates to the NSR250 for 1993. Development of the airbox and air intake saw ducts through the front of the fairing, and the NSR was still the best 250 racer. This year Capirossi, Max Biaggi and Doriano Romboni headed Hondas' effort, but they were inconsistent. The championship went down to the final race at Jarama, Harada and Capirossi battling until the Honda's tyre failed.

Honda fielded eight riders on leased NSR250s for 1994, although none was an official factory outfit. Changes this year included detonation sensors to cope with the lower octane fuel, and the Hondas were slower than the Aprilias. Headed by Tadayuki Okada and Capirossi, again Honda failed to take the

title. There were also four stock RS250s on the GP grid, all with HRC power-kits. With little development to the NSR250 for 1995, none of the Hondas could really match Biaggi's Aprilia this year. Ralf Waldmann, on his Sepp Schlögl-tuned NSR250, provided Honda with three GP victories, but his third place overall was Honda's worst result in the 250 class since 1984.

Honda thus made significant changes to the NSR250 for 1996. The engine was smaller and a kilogram lighter and was tilted forward to place more weight on the front wheel. With a longer swingarm and revised pivot point, Waldmann struggled with the handling on the new model. After grafting the 1995 suspension, Schlögl eventually settled on the 1996 system with a revised linkage. There were plenty of Hondas on the grid, but although Waldmann won four and Olivier Jacques one GP, Biaggi and the Aprilia again took the rider's title. But for an NSR250 fairing, the customer RS250 was also little changed this year.

# FORGOTTEN CHAMPIONS: DIRK RAUDIES AND HARUCHIKA AOKI

Weighing in at only 8 stone, German Dirk Raudies was another rider tailor-made for the diminutive 125 Honda. Born on 17 June 1964, Raudies trained as a CNC machinist and was unusual in the GP paddock for tuning his own bikes. He began racing the Honda RS125R in 1988, remaining loyal to it until his retirement in 1997. Based in Mittelbiberach, Raudies won 14 GPs between 1992 and 1997, but his most successful season was 1993 when he won the 125cc world title.

The youngest of the three 'Fireball Brothers', who all became leading road racers, Haruchika Aoki was born on 28 March 1976. He began racing in 1991, his GP career beginning in 1993, and he really hit form on the Hans Spaan-prepared RS125R in 1995. After winning back-to-back 125cc World Championships in 1995 and 1996, Aoki moved into the 250cc class on an NSR250 for 1997. By 1999, he was on a private NSR500V, and after a year on World Superbikes headed back to 500s in 2001 and 250s for 2002. Aoki never managed to replicate the form that provided his two 125cc titles.

Intended as a competitive
machine for the privateer, the
NSR500V promised much, but
was disappointing. *Honda*

## THE RS125R (1992–96)

Despite some porting development, there was little new on the RS125 for 1992, and this year it was outclassed by the Aprilia. Fausto Gresini, Ralf Waldmann and Ezio Gianola won most of the GPs but they split their eight wins. RS125R updates for 1993 included new porting and the expansion chamber, new crankcases, and a revised ignition. The power was up to 41hp (from 39hp), while chassis developments saw adjustable compression damping on the front fork and a wider, 2.50 x 17-inch front wheel. The weight was 71kg, and in the hands of Dirk Raudies it provided Honda with their only Grand Prix World Championship, in 1993. Raudies won nine GPs to head the Hondas of Japanese riders Kazuko Sakata and Takeshi Tsujimura. Although there were 18 RS125s entered in the 1994 GPs, the largely unchanged Hondas were swamped by the Aprilia of former Honda rider Sakata.

The failure of 1994, and the re-entry of Yamaha, prompted Honda to build a new RS125R for 1995. The previous design went back to the mid-1980s so it was time for an update. Engine revisions included the addition of a balance shaft above the transmission and a cassette-type gearbox, while the chassis included linkage rising-rate rear suspension. In the hands of Haruchika Aoki, the RS125R dominated the World Championship, with seven GP victories. As the 1995 RS125R was so successful there were few updates for 1996. Now with a thicker crankpin, and producing 43hp, Aoki contested the season without a major sponsor and won the championship through perseverance and consistency. Aoki won two GPs, and Tomomi Manako, one.

## THE NSR500V (1996–2001)

With the NSR500 already well developed and in demand at the end of 1994, Honda decided to create a new-generation production racer that was cheaper for customers, and easier to manufacture. They decided to build a twin, taking advantage of the 100kg minimum weight for twin-cylinder 500s. Retaining Honda's traditional single crankshaft, the 499.7cc (68 x 68.8mm) twin had its cylinders at 100° rather than the 250's 75°. This was to ensure the larger cylinders did not foul each other. A balance shaft sat underneath the crank, and the

reed valves were at the back of the engine. Carburetion was by two 40mm Powerjet Keihins, and the power was quoted as 135hp at 10,250rpm.

The NSR500V chassis was conventional, except for a single-sided Pro-Arm swingarm. The NSR500V was to become generally available for 1997, but during 1996 Okada and Itoh raced a factory version. With magnesium engine castings Okada's bike weighed in at 103kg (the production model was 109kg), and in Malaysia, the first race of the season he surprised everyone by claiming pole position. Okada went on to finish seventh overall, with his best finish of the season, a second place in the Australian GP.

Honda originally envisaged sales of 20 NSR500Vs at $100,000 apiece, but the decision by the FIM to limit grid sizes saw only 11 built for 1997. HRC also continued to develop their factory racer for Takuma Aoki, and this was soon considerably removed from the privateer version. Aoki also had some reasonable success with the twin, culminating in a second in the final GP, in Australia, coming fifth in the championship.

Although always troubled with rear tyre problems, the adoption of unleaded fuel in 1998 was the nail in the coffin for the NSR500V. An accident during winter testing which left Takuma Aoki paralysed saw Sete Gibernau on the factory twin, but the NSR500V suffered piston problems all season. This was even more acute with the privateer models, and as the only bike now with a single-sided swingarm, the handling was also found wanting. Gibernau was back on the NSR500V for 1999, but the twin was shelved during the season and he ended up with an NSR500 four. Privateers continued to race the twin for several seasons, but these did little more than make up the numbers on the grid. Haruchika Aoki rode a TSR-framed special during 2001, and while much was expected, his best result was fifth place in Italy.

## THE NSR500 (1997–2001)

After three consecutive World Championships, Mighty Mick asked Honda to produce an older style pre-'Big-Bang' 180° engine for 1997. The easy-riding nature of the 'Big-Bang' NSR500 was allowing other riders to beat Doohan on occasion, and he believed that a conventional two-stroke 'screamer', emphasising top-end power would be easier to ride, and even out the field. He was right. Only Doohan felt comfortable with the new engine, Criville and Okada reverting to the 'Big-Bang' type, while Doohan won 12 of 15 GPs that year.

Left: Sete Gibernau rode a
factory NSR500V during 1998,
but the machine struggled with
the new unleaded fuel. *Honda*

Right: The 1997 season was Mick
Doohan's most successful, with
12 victories on the little-changed
NSR500. *Honda*

Advances in ignition, cylinder, airbox design and exhaust pipes meant that the 'screamer' wasn't as hard on tyres as the pre-1992 version, but only Doohan possessed the superior throttle control to utilise this to the maximum. The engine featured a split crankshaft, and many of Honda's engineers were sceptical, fearing the 'screamer' wouldn't work. The power was around 195hp but in all other respects the NSR500 continued the evolution that had characterised the previous five years. The suspension was updated with more oil volume in the fork and gas in the rear shock, while the front fork featured steel rather than carbon tubes. Doohan still ejected electronic controls, and found the reduced engine braking of the 180° engine assisted smoother running into corners. Following the success of the 'screamer', Honda also built an engine with a 90° firing pattern, but this engine was less reliable so wasn't used for the 1998 season.

The adoption of 102 (RON) unleaded fuel for 1998 not only blunted the performance of the 180° motor, it reduced the life of many engine components. Crankshaft life was cut by 75 per cent. With a lower compression ratio, and larger carburettor jets, the power was down to 183hp at 12,500rpm. In the first race of the season, Doohan's crankshaft failed, and Honda had to work hard to meet the needs of their five factory-supported and two lease teams. The edge was taken off the extreme power delivery of the 'screamer', and some other riders adopted it. Criville and John Kocinski stayed with the 'Big-Bang' motor, now with a firing interval somewhere between 60° and 90°, while Okada struggled with the 'screamer', and Barros switched to the 'Big-Bang' during the season. The change to unleaded fuel saw a major redesign of all internal engine components (cylinder, head, exhaust, piston and rings), and new Showa suspension (a 47mm fork) was designed to maximise corner speed.

The season didn't start so well for Doohan: 500 newcomer Biaggi (on a leased Kanemoto machine) gave him a hard time early in the year, but Doohan cemented his dominance with four straight victories at the end of the season. With two victories also going to Criville it was the NSR's most successful year ever, filling the top five championship positions.

Knowing the NSR chassis was still little changed since 1991, and realising that Suzuki and Yamaha were improving, Doohan requested a new chassis for 1999. He wanted reduced understeer and higher corner speed, but the new chassis didn't arrive until just before the

first GP in Malaysia. This moved the engine forward and upward, but Doohan raced with an updated 1998 version which was inferior to the earlier bike. Honda's engineers altered the weight distribution slightly by raising the fuel tank to allow for enlarged cooling ducts and a modified airbox. This seemingly minor change was enough to unsettle Mick who had two miserable races before the crash in qualifying in Spain, which ended his career.

This year all riders were equipped with the 'screamer', again with new cylinders and pistons, along with a revised ignition curve and an RC-valve, to produce 188hp at 12,500rpm. A Stage 3 engine was provided mid-season to counter the speed of the Yamaha, but the still largely unchanged NSR500 was no longer the superior and dominant force of before, and was beaten on six occasions.

Without Mick Doohan to guide development, Honda decided the time was right to radically update the NSR500, little changed in nearly a decade. Criville asked for more power, but missed most of the testing due to ill health. Never at a loss to provide more power, Honda's engineers gave the NSR500 more horsepower (increased to 188hp at 12,500rpm), but this proved impossible to get to the ground. Complaints from all the Repsol riders saw HRC bring

Alex Criville took over from Mick Doohan to win the 1999 500cc World Championship, but couldn't repeat it in subsequent years. *Author*

# EMERGING FROM THE SHADOWS: ALEX CRIVILLE

Team-mate to Mick Doohan from 1994, Alex Criville spent the next five years as the sorcerer's apprentice until Doohan was forced to retire early in the 1999 season. Criville then fulfilled his ambition, harboured from childhood, of becoming Spain's first 500cc World Champion. Born in Seva, on 4 March 1970, Criville falsified his age so he could begin racing at 14, and soon made his mark in the smaller classes. After finishing second in the 1988 80cc World Championship on a Derbi, Criville switched to the JJ-Cobas team, winning the 1989 125cc world title. After two years on a 250, Criville got the chance to move into 500s when Sito Pons retired.

As Doohan's team-mate, Criville learned from the master, and was able to match and beat him on occasion. Injury marred his 1998 season, but under the guidance of team manager Gilles Bigot, he came back and won the title in 1999, with six victories. From there it was downhill for the quiet and courteous Criville. Struggling with machine and fitness problems, he managed only one GP victory in 2000, and retired at the end of the 2001 season.

back the 1999 chassis, engines and suspension. At Suzuka the Repsol bikes sported the older shorter, fatter expansion chambers, indicating that development was stagnant.

While the leading Repsol team of Criville, Okada and Gibernau struggled, 250cc World Champion Valentino Rossi impressed, and was the most successful NSR rider. In a satellite team, Rossi inherited Doohan's mechanics, including crew chief Jerry Burgess, and they gelled from the start. Although he began the season with 1999-spec machines, Rossi soon received the 2000 chassis and by June had a prototype chassis with revised weight distribution. It was Rossi who first received the revised chassis, and already he was proving a rider in the Doohan mould who could think outside the square, providing a fresh view. The other satellite team of Sito Pons (Barros and Capirossi) only had 1999 NSRs and they also posted better results than the Repsol riders. For the final GP at Australia, there was an all-new NSR500, with a central air duct and a horizontal belly pan radiator. In his first 500 season Rossi was incredible, winning two GPs and finishing second overall.

Immediately after the final race of 2000, Rossi began testing for 2001. The NSR received different cylinders and slimmer, longer expansion chambers, along with four 36mm dual-body Keihin carburettors with electronic sensors to monitor throttle position. Airflow was improved with a larger main radiator and smaller horizontal belly pan radiator. New crankcases were required so the engine could be located further rearwards, while the swingarm pivot was higher and now adjustable. The raised rear subframe also transferred more of Rossi's weight on to the front wheel. Basically, the engine was still an evolution of the venerable single crank design, retaining the 180° 'screamer' layout, and with the power increased to 195hp at 12,500rpm. The rest of the chassis was much as before, with a 47mm Showa upside down fork, 320mm Mitsubishi carbon brake discs and Brembo four-piston radial calipers. Burgess continued to experiment with chassis stiffness and suspension damping, and there was a new, stiffer, chassis for Assen that was subsequently discarded. The factory NSR500 was supplied to only three riders for 2001: Rossi, Criville and Ukawa. Still in Nastro Azzurro colours, Rossi was unquestionably the number one rider, and at Suzuka, provided Honda with their 500th Grand Prix victory. He went on to totally dominate the season, winning 11 GPs, and the last ever 500cc crown.

The NSR500 in its final, 2001, winning incarnation. This year there was an additional horizontal radiator, but the bloodlines to the earlier NSR500s were still strongly evident. *Alan Cathcart Archive*

Although the premier racing class moved to four-stroke for 2002, a number of teams were denied access to the new and expensive RCV211V, and continued to race the NSR500 two-stroke. With a 15kg weight advantage over the V5 four-stroke, HRC favourite Kato (with the Gresini Fortuna team) tested a variety of frames and swingarms early in the season. The West-sponsored Pons team (Barros and Capirossi) also had NSR500s, updated to Rossi's championship-winning specification, while other NSR satellite teams included Jurgen van der Goorbergh on a Kanemoto bike. The performance of Capirossi and Barros on the West NSRs surprised many, and they were often ahead of all the other four-strokes except the factory RCVs. Barros pushed Rossi hard at Assen, and was a contender for victory in Germany before crashing. By the end of the season, Barros and Kato also had RCVs, and the two-stroke era was over. It had been a magnificent era, dominated by the NSR500. Since debuting in 1984, NSR500s won an incredible 131 of Honda's 156 500cc Grand Prix victories. Although the new RC211V promised much in the new MotoGP class, the NSR500 was going to be a hard act to follow.

## THE NSR250 AND RS250R-W (1997–2004)

Hoping to win the title that had eluded them since 1992, Honda swamped the 250 grid in 1997. The NSR250 was still largely unchanged and although Tohru Ukawa was the favoured rider, with a direct link to HRC, five satellite lease teams received NSRs. Biaggi brought the Number 1 plate to Honda, but struggled with front-wheel chatter. After a mid-season slump the championship went down to the final race in Australia.

For 1998, HRC decided to totally redesign the NSR250. Prompted by the introduction of unleaded fuel, the new NSR was also a radical departure from traditional Honda practice. The engine now had the cylinders spaced at 110° and featured twin contra-rotating crankshafts fore and aft. Initially the bore and stroke were 52 x 58mm, but reverted to the traditional 54 x 54.5mm before the first GP of the season. The new NSR also employed a 'pivotless' frame design like the VTR1000 production four-stroke twin, with the swingarm pivoting on the vertically split crankcases.

195

Valentino Rossi provided Honda with their 500th Grand Prix victory, on the NSR500, during 2001, and went on to win the final 500cc World Championship. *Author*

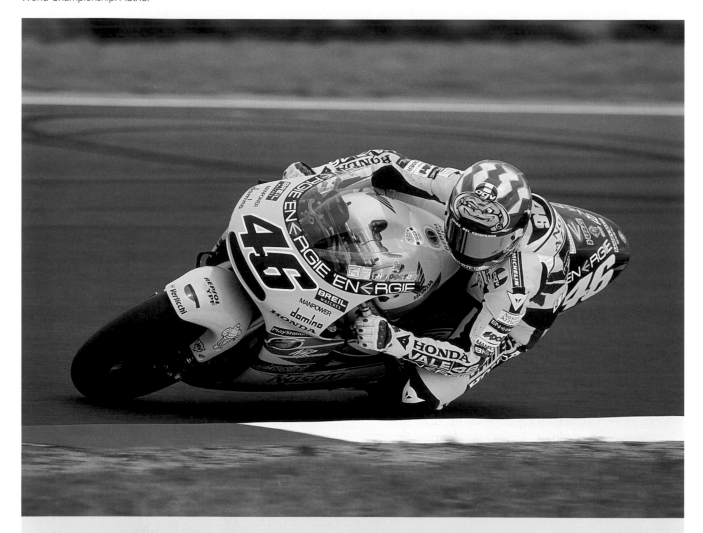

# THE DOCTOR: VALENTINO ROSSI

The son of three-times Grand Prix winner Graziano Rossi, Valentino was born on 16 February 1979 in Urbino, Italy. With motorcycle racing in his genes, the young Valentino accompanied his father to GPs, and began racing karts at three years old, before switching to Mini-moto when he was ten. In 1993, he rode a Cagiva in the Italian 125cc Sport Production Championship, taking this title the following year. Rossi's subsequent rise was meteoric. After winning the 1995 Italian 125cc Championship as an official rider for Aprilia, he moved into the World Championship. With a pattern of learning one year, and dominating the next, Rossi won the 125cc title in 1997 (becoming the youngest ever 125cc World Champion), and moved to 250s in 1998, winning this in 1999

(again the youngest ever 250 champion). He graduated to 500s in 2000, and won in 2001, joining Mike Hailwood and Phil Read as the only other riders to triumph in all three displacement categories. With the introduction of MotoGP, Rossi was just as dominant on the Honda RC211V, winning successive world titles in 2002 and 2003. By the end of 2004 he had amassed a total of 67 GP victories, and he was still only 25 years of age. Of these victories, 33 were on a Honda. But Valentino Rossi is much more than a great motorcycle racer. As a charismatic personality he has made Grand Prix motorcycle racing more exciting and appealing to a wider audience. After amassing the most ever points in a season (357), Rossi stunned everyone by announcing he would ride for Yamaha in 2004. Rossi took his team, including master crew chief Jerry Burgess, and proved he could be possibly the greatest rider ever by winning back-to-back MotoGP titles on different makes.

Induction was still by crankcase reed valves, and the twin forward-facing 39mm Keihin flat-slide carburettors were mounted in a fully sealed airbox. Early examples also featured VTR1000-style side-mounted radiators, but the most disappointing aspect of the new bike was the power. This was initially only 88hp, considerably down on the 100hp of the best factory NSR250s of 1995. During the season the power was up to 95hp at 13,300rpm, but it was still somewhat shy of the best Aprilia. Also new for the 1998 NSR250 was a double-sided swingarm instead of the earlier Pro-Arm, and while the chassis was lighter and presumably stronger, it was underdeveloped and didn't work well. Only new star Japanese rider Daijiro Kato could manage a GP victory, and the regular factory riders (Jacque, Ukawa, Haruchika Aoki and Perugini) were left in the wake of the Aprilias. The 1998 RS250 was still based on the earlier single-crank model, and with 87hp at 12,500rpm (94hp with a factory A-kit) Jeremy McWilliams often showed the 102kg machine to be superior to the works bikes.

The NSR250 was much improved for 1999, particularly with the more traditional twin-spar chassis, and there were only three factory machines. Headed by Ukawa with HRC backing, Capirossi brought the Number 1 plate to Honda after being dumped by Aprilia for knocking off his team-mate. Stefano Perugini received the third NSR. Despite the improvement of the NSR, none of the riders could match Rossi, who completely dominated the season. Ukawa came second overall, with one victory, and Capirossi third, with three GP wins.

The departure of Rossi and Capirossi to 500s for 2000 allowed a space for HRC's rising star Daijiro Kato on a factory NSR250. The other two NSRs went to Ukawa and 18-year-old Australian Anthony West, while four private teams ran production RS250Rs in TSR frames. Honda completely revamped the NSR250 this year. Engine developments saw the power rise to 102hp at 13,300rpm, the first time 100hp was attained on an NSR since the adoption of unleaded fuel. The chassis and swingarm (still pivoting on the engine as well as the frame) were redesigned, and front brakes included Brembo radial calipers. But this year Honda was beaten by the Yamahas of Olivier Jacque and Shinya Nakano. The solace for Honda was the improvement of Kato, who finished third overall with four victories. Honda provided only two works 250s for 2001, to Emilio Alzamora and Kato. With Yamaha

withdrawing their factory support, and Aprilia also entering only two factory machines, Kato was in a class of his own. He virtually ran away with the championship, with 11 victories, breaking Mike Hailwood's 1966 record of 250cc wins in a season. The production RS250R also had success in 2001 with Adrian Coates winning the British Championship.

Honda had only two factory NSR250s for the 2002 season, the final year for the twin crank factory bikes. Amidst a sea of Aprilias, the Gresini Fortuna team consisted of Alzamora and Roberto Rolfo. With only a single-crank production RS envisaged for the future, Honda provided a RS250R-W (Works) developmental machine for Haruchika Aoki. This was a season Honda would prefer to forget: without a single victory, and the RS250R-W particularly disappointing.

After a patchy, and disappointing, history by Honda's standards, the NSR250 was pensioned off in favour of the RS250R-W for 2003. RS250R-Ws were provided to Rolfo (again in the Fortuna team), and Sebastian Porto (riding for Puig in Telefónica MoviStar), with six production RS250s filling out Honda's presence. The basis of the RS250R-W went back to the original NSR250 of 1992, reverting to the single-crankshaft 75° V-twin with balance shaft. Although sharing similar architecture to the production RS250R, the R-W featured larger magnesium-bodied powerjet flat-slide Keihin carburettors, titanium exhausts, RC power valves, and produced 107hp at 12,500rpm. The frame

## THE ROMAN EMPEROR: MAX BIAGGI

After winning three consecutive 250cc World Championships with Aprilia, Max Biaggi switched to the Marlboro Kanemoto Honda for 1997, picking up his fourth championship. He began the season determined to beat the Aprilia, and finished it with a narrow victory over fellow Honda rider Ralf Waldmann. Born in Rome on 26 June 1971, Biaggi first raced the Kanemoto NSR250 in 1993, and his 1997 World Championship allowed him to move up to an NSR500 for 1998. When he won the 1998 500 GP at Suzuka, Biaggi became the first rider in 25 years to win first time out on a 500. He continued to challenge Doohan throughout 1998, but moved to Yamaha for the next four years. The 2003 season saw Biaggi back on a satellite RC211V for the Camel Pramac Pons team.

Loris Capirossi brought the Number 1 plate to Honda for 1999, but couldn't replicate his earlier success on the NSR250. *Author*

Bottom: Daijiro Kato was one of Japan's most promising riders, but his career was tragically cut short in 2003. Kato easily won the 2001 250cc World Championship on the NSR250. *Author*

was a handmade, lighter and stiffer version of the RS250R, and the 43mm Showa front fork included radial Brembo brake calipers. The weight was right on the 100kg minimum. The production RS250R this year produced around 92hp. Although outpaced by the factory Aprilia in 2003, the agile RS250R-W performed much better than in 2002. Rolfo managed two victories, and second in the championship. For 2004, Honda increased the number of RS250R-Ws to four, for two teams. Rolfo remained with Fortuna, joined by Tony

Elias, while 125cc World Champion Dani Pedrosa and Hiroshi Aoyama rode for Puig's Telefónica MoviStar team. Pedrosa made a dream debut on the RS250R-W, winning the first Grand Prix in South Africa, the youngest rider ever to win a 250 GP. The RS250R-W was considerably improved this season, the talented Pedrosa winning six races, and taking the 250cc World Championship. Elias and Rolfo also won a GP each, further cementing the RS250R-W's superiority this season.

# TRAGIC CHAMPION: DAIJIRO KATO

A diminutive, 5ft 4in and weighing only 8 stone, the reticent Daijiro Kato was born 4 July 1976 in Saitama, Japan. He began racing motorcycles at five years old, winning the 1985 Japanese Pocket-Bike Championship when only nine years old. Skipping the 125cc class, Kato concentrated on winning the Japanese 250cc Championship, managing this in 1997 on a Honda, after finishing runner-up twice. When Kato won the 1997 and 1998 Japanese 250 GPs as a wildcard rider it was inevitable he would move into GPs full time. His rise from 2000 was meteoric, and 2002 saw him in MotoGP, initially on an NSR500, but later on the RC211V. HRC's favourite rider, Kato's career was tragically cut short when he died after crashing at the opening 2003 MotoGP at Suzuka.

# THE RS125R (1997–2004)

Noboru Ueda won three GPs in 1997, but finished a distant second in the World Championship, prompting some major updates to the RS125R for 1998. Stronger crankcases, and an improved crankshaft saw it evolve further away from its motocross roots, and with a power-jet carburettor the power of the 71kg RS125R was 43.5hp. The departure of Valentino Rossi to 250s left the field wide open, and Honda filled the grid with 11 machines, mostly A-kitted. This year, Manako's inconsistency robbed him of the title, although he won five GPs. Further improvement to the RS125R for 1999, and with Honda recruiting the best riders, they dominated the 1999 World Championship. Emilio Alzamora, Marco Melandri, and Maseo Azuma fought hard all season, the title going to Alzamora by a solitary point.

Honda provided A-kits to selected riders for the 2000 125cc World Championship, and again it was Alzamora who led the way in Angel Nieto's Telefónica MoviStar team. Although Alzamora won two GPs, and Masao Azuma one, they couldn't match the Aprilia and Derbi this year. Honda again swamped the grid for 2001, headed by Azuma and rising Spanish riders Toni Elias and Daniel Pedrosa. Honda took three victories, but despite the brilliant, but inconsistent riding of Elias, couldn't match the improved Gilera and Derbi. Veteran Japanese riders Azuma and Nobbie Ueda headed Honda's 125cc line-up for 2002, but Pedrosa was the most outstanding Honda rider this year. Taking three victories he ended third in the championship, and was obviously destined for greater things. It was to be Pedrosa's year in 2003, and he had the title won (with four victories) when he crashed in practice at Australia, breaking both legs and ankles. For 2004, the RS125R received new Showa suspension, and a radial-mounted Nissin brake caliper, while Andrea Dovizioso led the Honda charge with an RSW125F. With a 38mm powerjet carburettor the power was 46hp at 14,000rpm. Dovizioso, in his third season, soon led the way in the championship, and although he only won five GPs, his consistency saw him crowned World Champion with two races to go.

# MORE SPANISH AND ITALIAN CHAMPIONS: EMILIO ALZAMORA, DANIEL PEDROSA AND ANDREA DOVIZIOSO

Although Emilio Alzamora didn't win a GP during 1999, his consistency prevailed, and he put his Nieto RS125R ahead of the hard-riding Italian youngster Marco Melandri. Alzamora was born in Lleida, Spain, on 22 May 1973, and was inspired by his father who had ridden in Montjuich 24-hour races. Emilio began racing 80s in 1989, becoming the 80cc champion of Catalonia. By 1994, he was racing in the 125 GPs and won his first Grand Prix in 1995. After unsuccessfully defending his World Championship, Alzamora moved into 250s for 2001 and 2002, before retiring.

Daniel Pedrosa earned his position in Alberto Puig's team after responding to a national advertisement that saw him compete in the Spanish 1999 MoviStar Activa Cup. His subsequent performance elevated him in the World Championships, and he fulfilled all expectations. Born in Sabadell, Spain, on 29 September 1985, Pedrosa's career began when he entered the 1997 Spanish Pocket-Bike Championship. The 11-year-old finished third in his debut season and went on to win the championship a year later. Under Puig's guidance, Pedrosa became the second youngest 125cc World Champion (after Capirossi), and the seventh 125cc Honda winner. For 2004, he moved up to the 250cc class on an RS250R-W, astonishing everyone by winning the title in his first attempt and becoming the youngest ever 250cc World Champion. Now one of Honda's hopes for the future, Pedrosa defended his number one plate in the 250cc class for 2005.

Wearing the racing Number 34, in honour of his hero Kevin Schwantz, another future Honda hope is the young Italian rider Andrea Dovizioso. Dovizioso was born in Forlimpopoli on 23 March 1986, and rode his first mini MX motorcycle at the age of four. Under the guidance of his father, motocross rider Antonio, Andrea raced Mini-moto and Mini-motocross. He made a sensational road racing debut in the 2000 Challenge Aprilia at Misano, winning the opening race and the championship. The 2001 season saw Dovizioso enter the 125cc European and Italian Championships, running away with the European title to guarantee a place on the 125cc GP grid for 2002. He signed for the Pesaro-based Team Scot Honda finishing 16th in his first World Championship season. Gradual improvement saw Dovizioso fifth in 2003, and taking the title in 2004.

Taking over Superbike homologation duties from the RC45 for 2000, the SP-1 was a flawed motorcycle. *Australian Motorcycle News*

# 10 NEW-GENERATION V-TWINS

Two groundbreaking sporting motorcycles shaped the 1990s. One was the Honda CBR900RR FireBlade, and the other was the Ducati 916. Honda had a history of creating supremely successful breakthrough models, so the FireBlade wasn't really a surprise, but the excellence of the Ducati 916 was more unexpected. Until 1993, Ducati was considered a small Italian company which built idiosyncratic motorcycles for eccentric enthusiasts. The 916 changed all that. Certainly, the production numbers were small by Honda's standards, but the 916 took on the best Japan had to offer, and beat them. For the first time a twin could match a four, and the 916 immediately set new standards for handling and aesthetics, and it trounced all comers in Superbike racing. The release of Ducati's 916 changed the nature of sporting motorcycles, and Honda, never wanting to be second, was forced to respond.

What was surprising is that it took so long for Honda to build a Superbike twin. World Superbike regulations initially gave twins a capacity and weight advantage, and only Ducati took advantage of this. After the first two World Superbike Championships went to the Honda RC30, the ever-improving Ducatis became increasingly dominant. The release of the 916 accentuated this dominance, eventually the twin losing its weight advantage, but the 916 kept winning. Although the RC45 won the 1997 World Superbike Championship, Honda needed a twin, and for 1997 they released the VTR1000F FireStorm. The World Superbike homologation special, the SP-1 (RC51) followed for 2000.

## THE VTR1000F FIRESTORM (SUPER HAWK) (FROM 1997)

Aimed at the throat of the 916, the VTR1000F was a full 1,000cc from the outset, and the engine design much more up-to-date than the Ducati. The crankcases were horizontally split, cast with the swingarm pivot, the two integrally cast cylinders were set at a Ducati-like 90°. The two cylinders were identical, and with a bore and stroke of 98 x 66mm, the displacement was 996cc. The basic engine architecture was conventional,

With the release of the VTR1000F FireStorm, Honda finally had a large-capacity sporting V-twin. The FireStorm soon proved an excellent real-world sporting motorcycle and has had a long production run with little change. *Australian Motorcycle News*

with water-cooling, chain-driven double overhead camshafts, four-valves per cylinder, and lightweight 'nutless' con-rods (with the rod bolts threaded into the rods themselves) and skirtless 'slipper' pistons. The intake valves were 38mm, with 34mm exhaust valves, set at an included angle of 26°. With twin Mikuni 48mm flat-slide CV carburettors, the largest yet on a Honda streetbike, and a low, 9.4:1 compression ratio, the power was 110hp at 9,000rpm. There was a six-speed gearbox and a wet multiplate clutch. A pair of side-mounted radiators, drawing air through the bodywork, allowed the frontal area to be reduced.

To keep the wheelbase as short as possible (1,430mm), the V-twin engine was tilted back, and

bolted as a stressed member in a pivotless aluminium twin spar frame that weighed only 8kg. As with the 1996 FireBlade, the frame was designed with tuned lateral flex, and the rigidity of the three engine mounts differed. The bolt closest to the swingarm was hollow, the next less so, and the one closest to the steering head solid. The frame was claimed to be 40 per cent less stiff than even the FireBlade. The welded extruded-section aluminium swingarm was also new, and bolting the Pro-Link rear suspension, sidestand and footpegs to the engine saved weight and simplified the frame structure. The rest of the chassis was predictably conventional with 17-inch wheels, a 41mm fork, four-piston Nissin brake calipers gripping 296mm discs, and an all up weight of 192kg. Unusual for Honda was the rear bias weight distribution of 47/53 per cent front and rear, designed to improve the big twin's corner exit ability.

With its moderate power and three-piece fairing designed for rider protection, the VTR1000F wasn't really targeted at the 916 (more the 900 Supersport). It also wasn't the racing platform everyone expected. This would come later. In the meantime, the VTR1000F proved to be more effective than its modest specification suggested. Continuing the superb all-round nature of the VFR750, *Motorcyclist* magazine named the VTR1000F their joint 'bike of the year' winner for 1997. 'With a more comfortable, upright riding position, lighter steering, and a quick-revving powerplant, the VTR thrives on real-world pavement.' In Australia it was Honda's best-selling streetbike for 1997 and 1998, and an HRC kit was available which included a new ignition, close-ratio gearbox and carburettor kit. This was claimed to give an 8hp increase. The VTR1000F received minor updates for 2001. These included a larger, 19-litre fuel tank, 15mm higher handlebars, a new instrument layout, a revalved front fork, and adjustable rebound damping for the rear shock, continuing until 2005 with minimal updates. It may have been overlooked by the motorcycle press in recent years, but the FireStorm remained one of the most sensible, best balanced, sport-orientated motorcycles on the market.

## THE XL1000V VARADERO (FROM 1999)

As the large-capacity dual-purpose motorcycle continued to be popular in Europe, it was inevitable the

Below: After two years, the FireStorm motor made its way into the adventure cruiser XL1000V Varadero. *Australian Motorcycle News*

Primarily a city bike, the XL125V Varadero was large enough to provide two-up comfort. *Honda*

## BABY VEES

New for 1999 was the learner-legal VT125 Shadow cruiser, with classic American cruiser styling, and powered by a liquid-cooled 90° V-twin. The 125cc (42 x 45mm) twin featured chain-driven single overhead camshafts and four valves per cylinder. With an 11.8:1 compression ratio and a 22mm VP carburettor the power of the five-speed 125 was a modest 15hp at 11,000rpm. Styled like the larger Honda cruisers, with 17 and 15-inch wire-spoked wheels and reasonably large dimensions, the VT125 Shadow was more show than go. The weight was 145kg and the little twin-cylinder engine wasn't able to provide exhilarating performance.

Joining the VT125 Cruiser for 2001 was the XL125V Varadero. The engine was identical, but the 'Adventure Sport' styling replicated the larger Varadero. Aimed for the urban market, the small Varadero was fine around city streets but as it was larger than most similar bikes it also suffered from a lack of power. The running gear included a 35mm front fork, mono-shock swingarm, 18 and 17-inch cast alloy wheels, and a single 276mm front disc brake. The weight was 149kg, and the little Varadero soon earned a reputation as a great two-up city bike.

VTR1000 engine would also be adapted for this purpose. Until the release of the Varadero for 1999, the Africa Twin was the best Honda could offer to counter the success of the BMW R1100GS and Triumph 900 Tiger. For the Varadero, the 1,000cc V-twin was detuned slightly. The compression ratio was dropped to 9:1, and the carburettors downsized to 42mm, but the power was still an impressive 95hp at 8,000rpm. Other engine changes included a smaller sump for increased ground clearance, and a five-speed transmission. The frame continued the pivotless concept of the VTR, but with a box-section steel swingarm. With a non-adjustable conventional 43mm front fork, 19 and 17-inch cast alloy wheels, and the third-generation dual combined braking system, the 220kg Varadero seemed more suited to sealed, rather than unsealed roads.

Several updates occurred for the 2003 Varadero, with a six-speed gearbox, 25-litre fuel tank, three-way adjustable windscreen, and electronic fuel injection (with 42mm throttle bodies). The compression ratio went up to 9.8:1 but the power was still only a moderate 94hp at 8,000rpm. There was new bodywork, an aircraft-style fuel filler cap, optional panniers and top box, while the weight went up to 235kg. For 2004 there was the option of ABS and a redesigned electronic instrument panel.

## THE VTR1000SP-1 (RC51) (2000–01)

Pensioning off the beloved V-four in favour of the twin was not something Honda did lightly, but it was inevitable, and was brought on by Ducati's success in Superbike racing. Appearing for 2000 as the SP-1 (RC51 in the USA), this wasn't a hot VTR1000F. With an all-new engine and chassis, the SP-1 was a pure

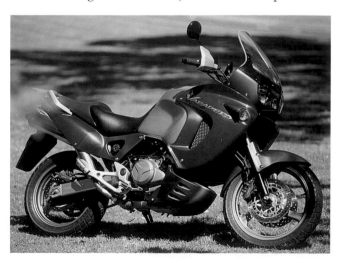

Colin Edwards surprised the pundits by winning the 2000 World Superbike Championship on the SP1-W. *Author*

# FAIRYTALE SUCCESS: RACING THE SP-1

Honda couldn't have asked for a better script in the SP-1's inaugural season of 2000. In a fairytale year, 250cc GP rivals Tohru Ukawa and Daijiro Kato teamed up to win the prestigious Suzuka 8-hour race, while Joey Dunlop won the TT F1 race. After Dunlop complained about being outclassed by the Yamaha R1s in the North West 200, Honda supplied a World Superbike-spec motor. Dunlop proceeded to race away with his eighth and final TT F1 victory at an astonishing 120.99mph (194.67km/h), claiming afterwards 'it's the best bike I've ever ridden.'

More astonishing was its performance in the World Superbike Championship. Provided with factory VTR SP-1W machines, Colin Edwards and Aaron Slight found the SP-1W (W for Works) immediately competitive, Edwards winning the opening races in South Africa. Although undoubtedly aided by the retirement of Carl Fogarty after Round 2, Edwards went on to win the world title easily, with eight victories. Led by Tetsuo Suzuki, HRC engineers created a race-winning machine from scratch. The SP-1W featured PGM-F1 injection, with 62mm throttle bodies, and with a 12.8:1 compression ratio and Akrapovic titanium exhaust, produced 181hp at 12,000rpm. The suspension was Showa, with a 47mm upside down fork. While the frame was the same as the production SP-1, different length swingarms were used depending on the circuit. In the USA, Nicky Hayden also came within an ace of winning the 2000 AMA Superbike Championship on a works-spec RC51. He won five races, but lost by five points. The SP-1W also took out the Le Mans 24-hour race, the first time ever for a twin.

Below: The SP-2 replaced the SP-1 for 2002, and while it was an improvement it was still a heavy motorcycle. *Motorcycle Trader*

homologation special. As with other production racers (the RC30 and RC45), the SP-1's double overhead camshafts were driven by gears, with direct bucket under shim actuation. A wider bore and shorter stroke (100 x 68.3mm) provided 999cc, and the cylinder heads featured 40mm and 34mm valves, set at an included angle of 24°. The cylinder heads bolted to cylinders that featured ceramic and graphite-impregnated aluminium composite cylinders (like the RC45). The cylinders were integrated with the upper half of the horizontally split crankcases for additional strength. A unique ram-air system sucked air through the vent between the headlamps, to a larger (9.4-litre) airbox, and was controlled by an electrically operated valve. The fuel injection system was PGM-F1, with 54mm throttle bodies and twin injectors per cylinder, operating at 50psi. Cooling was by side-mounted radiators, although the racing kit included a central radiator. Completing the high engine specification were nutless con-rods and magnesium engine covers. The power was 126hp at 9,000rpm.

The frame was also different to the pivotless VTR1000F type. Although heavier (at 12kg), the extruded aluminium twin-spar Pro-frame incorporated the swingarm pivot in the crankcase and frame. The frame side plates extended underneath the swingarm, forming a D-shaped swingarm mount to provide a more rigid set-up than the VTR1000F. The front suspension was an inverted Showa 43mm fork, and the 320mm front disc brakes included four-piston calipers. The bodywork was also claimed to be more slippery than even Mick Doohan's NSR500. As the SP-1 was built with Superbike racing in mind, this wasn't a minimalist sporting motorcycle like the new CBR929RR. Superbike regulations required a minimum weight of 162kg so the SP-1 was built with this in mind and weighed 196kg. This didn't detract from its excellence as a sporting motorcycle, and by any standard the SP-1 was an impressive effort. As *Performance Bikes* said: 'Out of the crate the SP-1 gives just enough to make it the new number one V-twin.'

After a slow start to the 2002 World Superbike season, Edwards made an astonishing comeback to win the title. *Author*

# RACING THE SP-2

After the SP-1's incredible debut season, HRC produced an updated works bike for Edwards and Tady Okada in the 2001 World Superbike Championship. Taking a leaf out of rival Ducati's book, Honda homologated a race kit, and dubbed the bike the SP-2 for promotional reasons, although it was still based on the previous SP-1. Reliability was now an issue, and a new, lighter, crankshaft was responsible for some early season failures. During the year a single-pipe exhaust was fitted (after it appeared at the Suzuka 8-hour race). The power was now 186hp at 12,000rpm, but the chassis was essentially the same as before. Although there was still experimentation with different swingarms, only rarely did the man, machine and tyre triangle work satisfactorily. Edwards finished second in the World Superbike Championship, with four victories, but when teamed with Valentino Rossi, he took out the Suzuka 8-hour race.

In the USA, the RC51 finally won the AMA Superbike Championship in 2002, 21-year-old Nicky Hayden fulfilling Honda's expectations with nine race wins, including the important Daytona 200. Edwards and the SP-2W also triumphed in the 2002 World Superbike Championship, one of the most amazing seasons ever in this series. The VTR1000 SP-2W was based on the new production SP-2, but nearly every component was different. The crankcases were a single aluminium casting, while the engine covers were milled from solid magnesium. Homologated through the race kit were 64mm throttle bodies, and there was a much larger airbox this year. The power was 175hp at 12,000rpm at the start of the season, rising to 181hp by Suzuka. The Suzuka-spec motor had a new combustion chamber, new cylinder head porting and saw a return to the 62mm throttle bodies and heavier crankshaft with a twin 50mm exhaust system. A more efficient lubrication system reduced internal friction and this was enough for Edwards and Kato to win the Suzuka 8-hour race, with Makoto Tamada and Okada second. In the World Superbike Championship, Edwards received the Suzuka-spec motor after Oschersleben, and came from a 58-point deficit to win the final nine races in succession, and the championship.

Detail chassis changes this year saw a less stiff frame, with welded front engine mounts as on the production SP-2. The Castrol team also left out an engine bolt to provide even less stiffness, and mid-season the steering head was strengthened. The rear suspension linkage reverted back to the same as the 2000 machine, while brakes remained Nissin with six-piston calipers. Although Honda didn't field the SP-2W in the 2003 World Superbike Championship, the RC51 continued its success elsewhere. Miguel Duhamel won the Daytona 200, and its dominance of the Suzuka 8-hour race continued with a victory by Yukio Nukumi and Manabu Kamada, after the leading VTR1000SPWs crashed out.

Below: Colin Edwards provided Honda with two World Superbike Championships on the VTR1000 V-twin, before moving to MotoGP. *Author*

Following the racing success of the SP-1 during 2000, Honda offered racing versions, the 'Basic Racer' developed by HRC with an Akrapovic exhaust system and simplified wiring without lights. A 'Complete Racer' was also offered, with an HRC race kit. The compression ratio was 12.7:1, and, the claimed power 170hp at 11,000rpm. The weight was 170kg. There were also three HRC Racing upgrade kits available. The SP-1 was unchanged for 2001, although 200 silver examples were available in Britain alongside the red. Honda UK also commissioned RS Performance to build 26 Joey Dunlop SP-1 replicas, commemorating Dunlop's 26 TT wins. All were sold within one month of the sale being announced.

# THE SP-2 (RC51) (FROM 2002)

After only two years the SP-2 replaced the SP-1. Under the leadership of project leader Naoyuki Saito, updates were aimed at curing some of the fuel injection stumbles, and the harsh and uncompromising ride. The SP-2 also incorporated many features from the works racing 2001 SP-2. There were straighter exhaust ports (to accommodate a racing exhaust), and 62mm throttle bodies, with 12-hole injectors (instead of four-hole), and the power was increased to 133hp at 10,000rpm. Chassis updates included a 700gm lighter, 10mm longer swingarm, lighter wheels, and slightly revised Showa suspension. The aluminium twin-spar frame now included larger-diameter steering head bearings and new, press-forged engine hangers like the HRC racers. Revised bodywork featured a 30mm taller screen, but the SP-2 was still not featherweight, at 194kg. A limited-edition race replica of Edward's 'Stars and Stripes' SP-2 seen at Laguna Seca was soon available, and the 2004 US RC51 included racing decals and a Nicky Hayden signature on the fuel tank.

Somehow, Honda still didn't get it right with the SP-2. Although technically impressive, superbly engineered, and an improvement over the flawed SP-1, other sportsbikes were now leaner and meaner. The SP-2 remained heavy, and it felt it. This was still a bike of an earlier generation, but although sales were modest it remained in the line-up. The 2005 model included a black frame and swingarm with silver-coloured wheels, but by any logical test the SP-2 was outclassed by its cheaper brother, the CBR1000RR.

# THE TEXAS TORNADO: COLIN EDWARDS

Unlike some World Champions, Colin Edwards II had to wait, and work hard for his success. Born to an Australian father and an American mother on 27 February 1974, in Houston, Texas, Edwards followed his father into motocross, and was racing at four years old. His road racing career began in 1991, Edwards winning the AMA 250cc Championship in 1992. He signed for Yamaha to race Superbikes in the USA in 1993 and 1994, before moving into World Superbike for 1995. The next few years were inauspicious, and apart from a win in the 1996 Suzuka 8-hour race his results were marred by injury. Even when he landed a ride in the Castrol Honda Team RC45 for 1998, Edwards struggled, until he managed to win two races in the third round. From then on Colin Edwards matured, taking the World Superbike title in 2000 and 2002, and along with Troy Bayliss, was then the class act of World Superbike. Strangely, Edwards was passed over by Honda for an RC211V in 2003, accepting a ride with Aprilia, but 2004 saw him back with Honda on the Telefónica MoviStar RC211V as a team-mate to Sete Gibernau. His performance this year was more representative of his ability, and he finished fifth in the 2004 MotoGP standings, ahead of many more experienced riders.

The FireBlade grew to 929cc for
2000, and was more powerful
and lighter, than before.
*Motorcycle Trader*

# 11 PERFORMANCE FIRST

By 1999, Honda motorcycles were in decline, beaten on the race track and in the marketplace. Apart from Mick Doohan's dominance of the 500cc Grand Prix category, there was little for Honda to cheer about in racing. The smaller GP classes, World Superbike Racing, and even their usual playground, the Isle of Man, had become the domain of Yamaha, Ducati, and Aprilia. Although still a market leader courtesy of massive sales of scooters and small-capacity motorcycles, Honda was losing their hard-earned image and prestige. Even their staple diet CBR600 was getting hammered by the new Yamaha R6, with sales falling by 30 per cent during 1999, and the Gold Wing was unseated by the BMW K1200LT in the luxury cruiser stakes. By 2000, Honda remained the only manufacturer without a big-bore V-twin cruiser, and there was no market segment where Honda led the world. It was time to take charge again, and this Honda did with a vengeance under a new mantra, 'Performance First'.

## THE CBR900RR (CBR929RR) (2000–01)

FireBlade creator Baba-san was quiet, but remained busy during the late 1990s, and for 2000 provided an all-new CBR900RR-Y FireBlade (CBR929RR in the USA). Continuing a two-year evolution cycle of previous FireBlades, the new version again strove to find the balance between power, weight and ease of use that appealed to a wider range of riders. Not only was the look new, with new bodywork, but the entire motorcycle was redesigned.

Now displacing 929cc, the short-stroke (71 x 58mm) motor featured shorter crankcases which brought the crankshaft and swingarm pivot 20mm closer together. This was so the engine could be moved more forward in the chassis, and the swingarm pivot closer to the countershaft sprocket. The compression ratio went up to 11.3:1, and the included valve angle was reduced to 25°. The camshafts were now hollow and 20 per cent lighter. With fuel injection already installed on the VFR800 and CBR1100XX Super Blackbird, it was no surprise to find it on the new FireBlade. The Keihin-built PGM-F1 injection had

Below: A new 'King of the Cruisers',
the imposing VTX1800 set new
standards of cruiser performance.
*Australian Motorcycle News*

# MARYSVILLE MISSILES: THE VTX1800 AND VTX1300

Alongside the new Gold Wing for 2001 was the VTX1800 high-performance cruiser. Built in Marysville, the inspiration for the VTX came from the Zodia, Honda's 1995 concept cruiser displayed at the Tokyo Motor Show. As the final Japanese manufacturer to produce a large-displacement V-twin cruiser, Honda wanted to make a statement with this bike, providing it with a new 1,795cc (101 x 112mm) 52° liquid-cooled, single overhead camshaft V-twin. These were the largest cylinders ever for a Honda motorcycle, and the con-rods were also the longest. The 15.5kg forged steel crankshaft included bolted counterweights, reducing crankcase width by nearly 50mm and crankshaft weight by 3.3kg. As usual for many Honda V-twins, the VTX also featured a 72° offset dual-pin crankshaft for perfect primary balance, but also included two gear-driven primary shaft balance weights to reduce secondary and crankshaft offset vibration. To minimise engine height, lubrication was dry sump, with the oil reservoir inside the gearbox case. The cylinder head featured three valves, and there were two spark plugs per cylinder. With PGM-F1 electronic fuel injection, including 42mm throttle bodies and 12-hole injectors, the VTX1800 engine produced 103hp at only 5,000rpm. This motorcycle was all about roll on power, and that it had in spades. Transmission was through a five-speed gearbox and shaft final drive.

A tubular steel frame supported this massive engine with rubber mounts, while suspension included a 45mm upside down fork and dual shock absorbers. The 18 and 16-inch wheels were a flashy cast aluminium style, and it was equipped with Honda's combined braking system (CBS) with three-piston front brake calipers. Setting the VTX1800 off was street-rod styling, and a low, 693mm dragster-style seat, with extensive chrome plating on many engine components. As a high-end cruiser, there was a large range of optional equipment for the VTX1800, and no attempt was made to conceal its size and weight. Rolling on a 1,715mm wheelbase, the VTX1800 weighed in at a hefty 320kg. The weight

was irrelevant though because the engine had no equal in its class. In the words of *Cycle World:* 'So, if you're wondering whether the VTX1800 is a great leap forward in the huge-bore performance cruiser realm, just twist the throttle and you'll know. Immediately.'

For 2002 there were two further variations of the VTX1800, the retro R with cast wheels and radial tyres, and the VTX1800S with wire-spoked wheels and bias-ply tyres. Both featured valanced mudguards, footboards and pullback handlebars. Drawing its styling cues from the neo side of the neo/retro cruiser was the radial-tyred N-model for 2004. A closely related smaller VTX1300S, and lighter VTX1300C, were also available for 2003. The 52° motor was new, displacing 1,312cc (89.5 x 104.3mm), with a lighter single-pin crankshaft and dual counterbalancers. Fed by a single 38mm CV carburettor instead of fuel injection, the power was 74hp at 5,000rpm. Although downsized in every respect (a shorter 1,670mm wheelbase and a weight of 299kg), the styling was similar to the VTX1800S. The suspension included a conventional 41mm fork, and there was only a single 336mm front disc brake. With considerably smaller tyres, the VTX1300S was also a much more agile cruiser than the gargantuan 1800. As *Cycle World* said: 'The 1300 strikes a balance. It's a cruiser of subtle pleasures and no extremes. And it may be the best cruiser Honda has yet built.'

40mm throttle bodies and a single injector per cylinder, while the pressurised airbox included an H-VIX (variable intake and exhaust control system) to vary the amount of air for the injection system. Inside the exhaust collector was an H-TEV (Honda titanium exhaust valve) to boost mid-range power. The result

was an engine that produced considerably more power than the 919, with 151hp at 11,000rpm.

Also new was the chassis. The semi-pivotless frame, with the swingarm supported in the crankcases, was narrower in the seat area to keep the fuel load closer to the centre of mass. The quadruple box-section

The successful CBR600 evolved into the more sporting fuel-injected CBR600FS for 2001. *Motorcycle Trader*

aluminium frame rails were claimed to be 30 per cent stronger, while the 21mm longer swingarm allowed more progressive suspension operation. Despite the longer swingarm, the wheelbase was 5mm shorter, at 1,400mm. But the big news on the chassis front was the adoption of an upside down fork and a 17-inch front wheel for the first time on a FireBlade. The fork was a 43mm Showa and Nissin four-piston calipers gripped larger, 330mm discs. And to crown off the new Blade, the weight was reduced by 10kg to 170kg.

How successful was Baba-san with his new 'Blade? Almost everyone raved about the new CBR929RR and in a comparison test between the Yamaha YZF-R1 and Kawasaki ZX-9R *Cycle World* had this to say: 'Overall, the CBR929RR has an uncanny balance. Comfortable enough to ride slowly, and easier for everyone to ride fast. It turns like a 600, torques off corners like a Twin and leaves its litre-class brethren behind. The imbalance of power has shifted: the CBR929RR is performance

defined.' This was ably demonstrated by Kurtis Roberts, who won his second US Formula Xtreme series on the Erion Racing CBR929RR, prompting the release of a limited edition Erion Racing version in America for 2001. While there were no updates to the CBR900RR for 2001, the competition moved up a notch with the release of the Suzuki GSX-R1000. No longer at the top of the class, after two years it was time for another displacement boost.

## THE CBR600F, CBR600FS (F4i) (FROM 2001)

With the CBR600 almost an institution, and one of Honda's most successful models with sales totalling 320,000 over 14 years, Honda was taken by surprise by the success of the Yamaha R6. Under project leader Hiroyuki Ito, the new CBR600 followed the R6 direction, becoming sportier and more suited to racing. Thus it evolved into two versions for 2001, both the CBR600F and FS receiving PGM-F1 fuel injection, with the CBR600FS (CBR600F4i in America and Australia) designed for Supersport racing. (America and Australia only received the F4i Sport version.) The basic engine architecture remained unchanged from before, with the FS having double-valve springs, a lighter flywheel and a beefed up clutch. The PGM-F1 injection system was based on that of the FireBlade, with 38mm throttle bodies, and with a 12:1 compression ratio the power of

the FS was 109hp at 12,500rpm. The frame was similar to before, but stiffened by a claimed 5.9 per cent, and was painted black for the FS. The aluminium swingarm now pivoted in three bearings and there were 929-spec four-piston Nissin front brakes, and wheels. The FS also had a 4mm shorter wheelbase than the F (1,386mm), tipping the scales at 169kg. Setting the new CBR600F apart were styling cues from the CBR900RR, maintaining a family likeness. More importantly though, the CBR600F continued to provide a supreme balance between usability,

# NEW-GENERATION V-FOUR: THE VFR800 (FROM 2002)

In the wake of the increasing sporting emphasis with the in-line fours, the updated VFR800 for 2002 was refocused. Over a 15-year period the VFR had seduced nearly 200,000 buyers worldwide, and Honda wanted to maintain its position as the leading all-rounder available. Along with more aggressive styling, the engine incorporated developments aimed at boosting the VFR's appeal to a wider audience.

The new VFR800 engine featured Honda's VTEC, designed to offer the high-rev power of a 16-valve motor and the low-rev advantage of two valves per cylinder. Already a feature on many Honda cars, and used on the Japanese market CB400 for the past five years, below 7,000rpm VTEC prevented one inlet and one exhaust valve opening. Above 7,000rpm hydraulic lifters operated all valves. While the 781cc V-four was largely unchanged apart from the VTEC, the traditional gear drive for the double overhead camshafts was ditched in favour of a cheaper chain set-up. Images of the first VF750F returned, but Honda claimed the new camshaft drive was lighter (by 2.8kg) and quieter. It also allowed the included valve angle to be reduced by 1.5°. A revised fuel injection system featured 12-hole injectors (first seen on the VTX1800) rather than single hole as before. With a new under-seat exhaust system the power was 107hp at 10,500rpm. Battery charging problems saw all 2002 models recalled to have a higher-output alternator installed.

Apart from a reinforced steering head, the pivotless frame, with single-sided swingarm, was essentially unchanged. The brakes were a new DCBS linked system, and ABS was an option. The new VFR800 retained a conventional fork (beefed up to 43mm) with a

rebound adjustable shock absorber as before. In some respects the VFR800 was a disappointment. The suspension was unremarkable, and the weight was increased to 213kg. But as a real-world motorcycle the VFR800 remained supreme, *Performance Bikes* saying: 'There is no way to describe the VFR800 other than perfect. In 16 years everything about the bike has changed, but at the same time nothing has changed at all; the VFR is still the best sports-tourer.'

Although faster and sharper focused, the 954cc FireBlade of 2002 couldn't quite match the improved competition. *Australian Motorcycle News*

performance, style and comfort, and regained its class leadership. The CBR600FS was also good enough to provide Honda with their elusive, first victory in the Supersport World Championship, Fabien Foret winning on the Ten Kate machine.

# THE CBR900RR (CBR954RR) (2002–03)

To meet the challenge of the Suzuki GSX-R1000, the FireBlade was updated for 2002. Tadao Baba's goal was to retain the FireBlade's concept of 'Total Control', maintaining a balance between road and track use. A 1mm bore increase to 75mm saw the displacement rise to 954cc, although the pistons were 10gm lighter due to shorter skirts. The pistons were now cooled by oil jets under the skirts, and the compression ratio went up slightly, to 11.5:1. The fuel injection throttle bodies went up to 42mm, and the Honda variable intake/exhaust control system (H-VIX) continued to maintain optimal performance throughout the rev range by modulating the volume of air flowing into the air cleaner. A new titanium exhaust still included the H-TEV, and the power went up to 154hp at 11,200rpm.

Most updates were confined to the chassis, with the frame's steering head and swingarm pivot redesigned for added rigidity. The rear shock absorber top mount included a ride height adjuster, and the curved swingarm replicated HRC racing machines. Mass centralisation also saw a shorter, 10mm lower fuel tank, and while the brakes were unchanged, the wheels were 300gm lighter. The total weight was reduced to 168kg. With a narrower, more aggressive look, the resulting 954 FireBlade still provided a fine balance between power and handling, but the lighter handling came at the expense of stability. Now sharper focused, some of the friendliness of the earlier 'Blades seemed to have disappeared. The only changes to the FireBlade for 2003 were a revised bottom steering yoke and bearings, and the usual colour variations. But it was still overshadowed by the improved Suzuki and Yamaha.

Below: Valentino Rossi
dominated MotoGP on the
RC211V during 2002 and 2003.
*Author*

# MOTOGP MAGNIFICENCE: THE RC211V

The reign of the two-stroke ended in 2002 with the introduction of 990cc MotoGP four-strokes. With two-strokes struggling with emissions, and development stagnant, the FIM sought to enliven the premier class by opening it to four-strokes. And just as they did in the 500cc class, Honda continued to lead the way in MotoGP. 'Performance First' was the slogan of the next millennium, and nothing epitomised this more than the astounding RC211V (211 for the 21st century's first factory machine), one of the most efficient and effective racing motorcycles ever created. From a blank sheet of paper, Honda produced a motorcycle able to lap circuits faster than the previous 500s. It wasn't difficult for a company with Honda's resources to create horsepower, but to build a manageable package was a supreme accomplishment.

The project began as soon as the FIM announced the new regulations in April 2000. With the minimum weight for four and five-cylinder machines set at 145kg, and six cylinders and over at 155kg, a six-cylinder engine was initially considered. Project leader Tomoo Shiozaki recalled the prototype FXX 60° V-six built in 1988, and although this never made it into production it outperformed the RC30 and provided the inspiration for the RC211V. With the minimum weight an important consideration, in September 2000 it was decided to build a V5, and by the end of the year the first prototype motor was running. Under new project leader Heijiro Yoshimura, the engine layout included three front cylinders, and two rear cylinders set at 75.5°, with the PGM-F1 injection system between the vee. This featured five throttle bodies, twin multi-holed injectors running in sequence, one for low speed and the other for full throttle. The forward-spinning crankshaft included four main bearings, and with the outer cylinder pairs running on common big-end crankpins there was no need for a balance shaft. The three-ring pistons ran on titanium con-rods. The bore and stroke were not disclosed (possibly 76 x 43.7mm), and the double overhead camshafts were driven by gears. The cylinder head included four valves per cylinder (controlled by valve springs), and the lubrication system was semi-dry sump, with the oil contained in a reservoir behind the gearbox (like the VTX1800 cruiser). Extremely compact and robust, the 220hp at 14,700rpm RCV engine was said to have 3,000km service intervals.

While retaining the usual twin-spar aluminium beam frame, the 'Unit Pro-Link' rear suspension was different to other designs. The frame was designed to provide 17 per cent less lateral stiffness than the NSR500, and 23 per cent torsional rigidity, while the rear suspension set-up provided space under the seat to lower the fuel tank and improve mass centralisation. The wheelbase was also longer than usual, at 1,440mm, and the front suspension a 45mm Showa inverted fork. Early testing was by Shinichi Itoh, the first test in April 2001. By the start of the 2002 MotoGP season the RCV was well developed, and met expectations. Rossi won its debut race at Suzuka, with the RCV winning 14 of 16 races during 2002. After starting the season with two bikes, for Rossi and Tohru Ukawa, Kato and Barros also had RCVs by the end of the season. With the RCV, Honda found that elusive balance between power and usability. Beautifully conceived and executed, it was devastatingly effective.

Under new project leader Shogu Kanaumi, there were several detail updates to the RC211V for 2003. In response to Ducati's increasing competitiveness, during the season there was a new, noisier, exhaust system. This gave the central front cylinder its own pipe, and Rossi had the choice of new cams and injection mapping for higher revs and more top-end power. With a refined ram air induction system, the power was up to 240hp, but service intervals were increased to 4,000km. There was also an improved electronic slipper clutch, and a slightly different frame design. Chassis changes included a revised swingarm pivot (3mm higher), and a revised rear suspension linkage providing improved stability under braking. Along with a new compact rotary steering damper, the fairing was redesigned for improved ram pressure. The weight was 148kg, 3kg over the minimum, and there were seven RC211Vs on the grid for 2003. But they weren't all the same, and the Repsol

Rossi's 2003 RC211V unclothed.
One of the finest racing
motorcycles ever created. *Alan
Cathcart Archive*

bikes of Rossi and Nicky Hayden included a superior slipper clutch with turbine air scoops for cooling. Again, Rossi and the RCV triumphed, Rossi winning nine races and the championship, and RCVs 15 of 16 MotoGP races. Sete Gibernau and Max Biaggi filled out second and third in the championship.

There were six RC211Vs on the grid for 2004, with again the Repsol team receiving priority. Project leader Shogu Kanaumi announced the engine rev ceiling was increased by 3 per cent, to around 15,000rpm. Evolutionary changes included vents in the bodywork behind the front wheel, there was a new slipper clutch and a new chassis with double-squeeze rear suspension, with the main mechanism at the top rather than underneath. Along with a new swingarm this offered improved traction, tyre life, and weight distribution. With Michelin's move to 16.5-inch tyres (previously a 17-inch front), the RCV required a different chassis and damping set-up.

Rumours circulated of a shorter stroke engine, and there was a new exhaust system for Barros at Sachsenring. The two-into-one pipe now linked the two left front cylinders, with the right cylinder receiving its own pipe. Improving torque and throttle response, this soon made it to Hayden, Biaggi, and Gibernau, and contributed to a 5 per cent power increase and improvement in fuel economy. The new exhaust system allowed for a narrower rear seat, and there was a new fairing nose to improve high-speed aerodynamics. At Montegi, wild card rider Ukawa also rode a 2005 prototype RC211V with a 22-litre fuel tank, in anticipation of upcoming fuel tank capacity regulations. Honda also revealed they had an electronic 'Honda intelligent throttle control system', to prevent wheelspin in the lower gears. Already well developed, and presenting Honda some difficulty in increasing horsepower while maintaining feel and usability, newly appointed HRC managing director, Satoru Horike, indicated mid-season that the RC211V had one or two more years life left. Beaten by Rossi and the Yamaha during 2004, the RC211V was still a consistent performer winning seven MotoGP races, but they were spread between Gibernau, Tamada and Biaggi.

Taking its styling cues from the RC211V, the CBR600RR was the most race track-orientated CBR600 ever. For 2005, it received an inverted fork and radial-mounted brake calipers. *Honda*

# THE CBR600RR (FROM 2003)

With the pace of 600 Supersport development increasing, Honda released the incredible, even more track-orientated, CBR600RR for 2003. Under the direction of Hiroyuki Ito, and a guiding development theme of 'Innovative Wonder', the CBR600RR was modelled on the RC211V. The styling, under-seat exhaust and rear suspension linkage set-up were all similar to the all-conquering racer. While retaining the bore and stroke (67 x 42.5mm) of the previous CBR600FS, everything from the sump pan up was new. The crankshaft starter gear was moved from the left, to the right allowing the alternator to be moved inward

and the engine narrower. Inside the engine the mainshaft was moved 48.4mm higher, allowing the countershaft and crankshaft to be placed closer together, and the motor was 30mm shorter. Lighter pistons (by 15gm), stronger nutless con-rods, and dual-nested valve springs allowed a 15,000rpm redline, while the dual-stage fuel-injection system included two sets of injectors, one for high rpm and one for lower revs. The throttle bodies were increased to 40mm, and the exhaust ports were angled downwards by 30 per cent. The power was 117hp at 13,000rpm.

The alloy frame was now fine die-cast and welded in nine sections, while the rear suspension included a longer swingarm, with the remote Showa shock absorber mounted to linkage bars rather than the frame (as on the RCV). Apart from the anchoring lower arms,

With the CBR1000RR Fireblade the performance emphasis moved towards the racetrack, and the 2005 Repsol replica looked a clone of the MotoGP RC211V. *Honda*

the rear suspension was totally self-contained within the swingarm. Honda's 'mass centralisation' continued with a dummy fuel tank over the six-litre airbox, with two thirds of the fuel in a tank behind the motor. The adjustable front fork was a conventional 45mm Showa, the largest standard cartridge-type fork on a production Honda since the 1991 NR750. Upgraded front brakes included larger, 310mm discs, with Nissin four-piston calipers. The rider's weight was moved forward 70mm, and the wheelbase was a short, 1,390mm. The weight of this amazing motorcycle was 169kg, and in the hands of Chris Vermeulen provided Ten Kate Honda with the 2003 World Supersport Championship. With an HRC race kit, and the power up to around 135hp, the Ten Kate CBR600RR was supreme, winning seven of eleven rounds. The

CBR600RR also won the 2003 British Supersport Championship, in the hands of Karl Harris. Ten Kate's World Supersport dominance continued for 2004, this time with Karl Muggeridge triumphant.

After only two years, the CBR600RR was again updated for 2005. In the quest to provide the ultimate Supersport track tool, Honda aimed at improving the power-to-weight ratio. Resisting the urge to increase peak horsepower, Honda's engineers focused on intake and exhaust development that would enhance mid-range torque. While the fuel injection system was fundamentally unchanged, the intake ports were narrowed to accentuate the venturi effect.

Most of the chassis updates were designed to reduce weight and optimise mass centralisation. The frame now had variable section walls, and the frame weight was reduced by 1.5kg. The bolt-together die-cast seat rails were also lighter. Not only was the power-to-weight ratio improved, the weight was more concentrated around the rolling axes. Revised styling extended to an RCV-style nose and seat, while one of the most significant changes was a new front fork. This was now a 41mm inverted type, with radial-mounted brake calipers. Considering other middleweight sporting bikes had had inverted forks for nearly 15 years, it was surprising it had taken so long to arrive on the CBR600.

The swingarm was also revised. While retaining the Unit Pro-Link design, isolating the frame from the shock absorber, the composite aluminium swingarm now featured an integrated upper damper mount, replacing the bolt-in unit. This allowed a lighter and more compact design. The total weight was reduced by 5kg to 163kg, and HRC could supply an optional racing kit on request. This included engine, chassis, suspension and body components, combining to provide more power, lighter weight, improved handling and better aerodynamics.

# THE CBR1000RR (FROM 2004)

Acknowledging the change in World Superbike regulations (allowing homologated 1,000cc fours), and the increasing popularity of 1,000cc production-based racing around the world, Honda produced a new-generation CBR1000RR Fireblade (without the capital B) for 2004. Following the retirement of the FireBlade creator, Tadao Baba, the new Fireblade also shifted in design parameters, away from the street and to the track. The new project leader, Kunitake Hara, started with a clean sheet of paper, and like the CBR600RR, the CBR1000RR drew heavily on the RC211V.

While the bore remained at 75mm, changes in World Superbike rules relating to maximum revs to the bore/stroke ratio saw the stroke lengthened to 56.5mm. The displacement increased to 998cc. The arrangement of the engine's crankshaft, mainshaft, and countershaft was completely revised, with the countershaft positioned under the mainshaft, shortening the motor, and allowing a longer swingarm. There was a balance shaft and repositioned starter motor and larger, hydraulically operated (140mm) clutch, while considerable attention was

paid to reducing internal friction. The cylinders were only inclined slightly, moving the engine as far forward as possible. Inside the cylinder head the intake ports were raised for a straighter path, and the included valve angle reduced to 23°30'. The valve sizes remained at 29mm and 24mm, but the valve stems were reduced from 4.5mm to 4mm. Similar to the CBR600RR, the sequential PGM-DSFI injection system included 44mm throttle bodies and a 32-bit (up from 16-bit) ECU processor. New fuel injectors featured 12 radial holes, while the six-speed gearbox was now a cassette type. Moving the oil filter from the front to the right side of the engine allowed the exhaust to tuck tightly under the engine. There was also a redesigned cooling system, with coolant entering the cylinder block from the sides rather than from behind. With a compression ratio of 11.9:1 the power was 172hp at 11,250rpm.

Wanting to link the CBR1000RR with the all-conquering RC211V MotoGP racer, the frame consisted of large gravity die-cast aluminium sections, reaching around the engine-mounted swingarm pivot. The quadruped steering head design was also derived from the RC211V, linking not with the cylinder head, but with the engine cases. The 43mm Showa inverted fork was as before, but with less fork offset, and the front brakes included Tokico (rather than the customary Nissin) radial-mount calipers, gripping smaller (310mm) discs. The Pro-Link rear suspension system was similar to the RC211V and CBR600RR, but with a different damper position, and a longer (by 33mm) swingarm. New for the CBR1000RR was a Kayaba electronic steering damper on the top triple clamp. This automatically compensated for speed and acceleration. Also like the CBR600RR was the forward-positioned airbox, and the locating of the fuel tank in the centre of the chassis for improved mass centralisation. Rolling on a slightly longer, 1,410mm, the weight was also higher (at 179kg), and while all the other Japanese manufacturers had updated litre-class sportsbike for 2004, Honda continued to provide the most mechanically refined package. There were no technical updates for 2005, although the Fireblade was also available in Repsol colours.

HRC also offered a race kit for the CBR1000RR, boosting output to 206hp, and transforming the Fireblade into an astounding Superbike. The Ten Kate CBR1000RR was the surprise package of the 2004 World Superbike series, Chris Vermeulen staying in

contention for the championship right through until the final round. In the Suzuka 8-hour race the new Fireblades totally dominated, filling 14 of the top 20 places, with Tohru Ukawa and Hitoyasu Izutsu taking Honda's eighth consecutive victory, and their 19th overall. Their CBR1000RRW Fireblade also broke the reign of the VTR1000SPW in this event.

By 2004, 'Performance First' was working for Honda. Motorcycle sales in the first quarter of 2004 were at an all time high, at 2,582,000 worldwide (up 29 per cent over the previous year). With the largest and most active R&D department of any motorcycle company, technology from machines like the RC211V was filtering through to the production line. Concept motorcycles which seemed almost surreal only a few years earlier were becoming a reality. Honda was firmly back in control, and it looked like it would stay that way. Soichiro Honda's dream was alive and well.

Dominated by the dual exhaust system, the FMX650 was Honda's first attempt at a Super Motard-style motorcycle. *Honda*

# THE FMX650

With the increasing popularity of 'Super Motard' bikes in Europe, Honda produced the 2005 FMX650 for this niche market. Super Motard bikes are generally customised off-road machines adapted for pavement, providing a combination of the responsiveness of off-road machines and street bike equipment. Distinguished by fat, low-profile tyres, the European-developed FMX650 was the first Honda designed exclusively for Super Motard.

Powering the FMX650 was the venerable air-cooled 644cc (100 x 82mm) RFVC single overhead camshaft single-cylinder engine, last seen in the NX650 Dominator. It retained a single counterbalancer to quell vibration and dry sump lubrication. With an 8.3:1 compression ratio, and 40mm VE-type carburettor, the power was 37hp at 5,750rpm. There was a five-speed gearbox, and electric start was integrated with an automatic decompression system. The exhaust system was a high-rise dual-muffler stainless-steel type.

The single-cradle steel Mono-Backbone frame was similar in design to the Hornet, consisting of large diameter, thin-wall, rectangular-section steel tubing. The frame backbone was also the oil reservoir, and the swingarm was rectangular section steel. Emphasising the performance aspect of the FMX was a 45mm inverted fork, and a Delta-Link Pro-Link rear suspension system. The wheels were 17-inch wire spoked, while the brakes were disc, front and rear. The single front 296mm disc was gripped by a dual-piston caliper, while agile handling was assured by the 1,490mm wheelbase. The dry weight was 163kg. While the FMX650's specification was unremarkable, the styling set it apart. The small, 11-litre fuel tank was enshrouded by the bodywork, with a rectangular headlight incorporated in the beak-like upper front fender. The Super Motard style may not appeal to everyone, but there would be few motorcycles which could touch a well-ridden FMX650 in an urban environment, or on tight mountain roads.

# INDEX